Risk Management for Video Game Professionals

Game development is a high-stakes, high-pressure world where failure often feels inevitable, and success relies on navigating uncertainty. This book gives developers, producers and leaders the tools to manage risk proactively – before it becomes a crisis.

Grounded in 30 years of cross-industry experience and enriched by real-world case studies, this book offers a comprehensive, practical framework for identifying, analysing and mitigating risk across all stages of development: from indie prototyping to AAA multi-studio pipelines. It covers operational, creative, technical and strategic risks and maps them to game lifecycle stages with clarity and precision.

The book is built for the realities of production, and each chapter is paired with actionable templates, toolkits and conversational techniques designed to help teams spot early warning signs, make better decisions and build more resilient cultures.

Whether you are leading a team through a liveops crunch, juggling dependencies across time zones or simply trying to avoid the traps that derail so many good games, this book will help you ask better questions, have the right conversations and treat risk as a creative ally. Become a Risk Management Champion!

Liam Wickham is an experienced leader, teacher and game development executive with over 30 years of cross-industry expertise. He has held senior roles at Sony PlayStation, Sumo Digital, Wargaming and beyond. Passionate about mentoring, he founded Game Production Academy and created the top-rated Udemy course Risk Management for Video Game Professionals. He holds multiple accreditations in Agile, Kanban and programme management and continues to champion learning through podcasts, videos and writing.

Risk Management for Video Game Professionals

Navigating Uncertainty in Game Development

Liam Wickham

CRC Press
Taylor & Francis Group
Boca Raton London New York

CRC Press is an imprint of the
Taylor & Francis Group, an **informa** business

Designed cover image: Shutterstock

First edition published 2026
by CRC Press
2385 NW Executive Center Drive, Suite 320, Boca Raton FL 33431

and by CRC Press
4 Park Square, Milton Park, Abingdon, Oxon, OX14 4RN
CRC Press is an imprint of Taylor & Francis Group, LLC

© 2026 Liam Wickham

ISBN: 978-1-041-08580-5 (hbk)
ISBN: 978-1-041-08579-9 (pbk)
ISBN: 978-1-003-64608-2 (ebk)

DOI: 10.1201/9781003646082

Typeset in Alon
by Deanta Global Publishing Services, Chennai, India

Contents

PART III ▪ GAME DEVELOPMENT RISKS

PART IV ■ MAJOR RISKS IN THE COMMON STAGES OF GAME DEVELOPMENT

Preface

HOW THIS BOOK IS ORGANISED

This book is designed to be both a practical guide and a strategic resource. It is structured in six distinct parts to support you at different stages of your journey, whether you are new to risk management or looking to deepen your understanding.

Part I: Foundations of Risk in Game Development

We begin by exploring what risk looks like in real-world game development – not in theory, but in the practical choices, trade-offs and patterns that shape success or failure. We then introduce core risk management concepts and terminology, before surveying the major trends reshaping our industry in 2025. This part sets the stage for everything that follows.

Here we cover:

- What Risk Looks Like in Game Development

- Foundations of Risk Management

- 2025 Risk Landscape: Trends Reshaping the Games Industry

Part II: Implementing Risk Management – Step-by-Step

This part delivers a clear, six-step model for managing risk in any environment and at any scale. Each chapter walks through a core step: From identifying and assessing risks to mitigation, tracking, communication and review. We also go deeper into practical tools like risk registers, cultural factors, crisis management and how to manage risk across project, program and portfolio levels.

This is the first part where, from now on, we include a Toolkit for every chapter where appropriate. You can find these exclusively online. All templates, risk trackers and examples are downloadable at: https://www.game-production.com/riskbook

Here we cover:

- Overview of the Six Steps
  - Step 1: Identify Risks
  - Step 2: Analyse and Assess Risks
  - Step 3: Develop Risk Mitigation Strategies
  - Step 4: Implement and Track Mitigation Actions
  - Step 5: Monitor and Review Risks
  - Step 6: Communicate and Report Risks
- Risk Registers in Practice
- Fostering a Proactive Risk Culture
- Implementing Crisis Management Strategies
- Managing Risk at Project, Program and Portfolio Levels

Part III: Risk Categories in Game Development

Risks come in many forms: Technical, financial, operational and more. This part of the book explores the major risk categories encountered across game development. Each chapter provides practical triggers to look out for, mitigation strategies and real-world case studies. It also covers emerging approaches such as Kanban, Lean and Agile methods applied through a risk lens.

Here we cover:

- Introduction to Risk Categories
- Technical Risks
- Design and Art Risks
- Operational Risks
- Financial, Legal and Compliance Risks
- Market, Platform and External Risks
- Strategic Risks
- Reputational, Marketing and Audience Risks
- Collaboration and Partnership Risks
- Communication Gaps Risks
- Staffing Risks

- Governance Risks

- Agile, Lean and Kanban Risk Management

Part IV: Risk Across the Game Lifecycle

Game development is not linear, but it does follow an evolving lifecycle: Often from concept through post-release and live game support. This part maps key risks to each stage of the development lifecycle, showing how challenges shift over time.

Here we cover:

- Major Risks by Development Stage

  - Concept

  - Pre-Production

  - Production

  - Alpha

  - Beta

  - Release

  - Post-Release

Part V: Special Topics and Emerging Risk Frontiers

Here we turn to critical frontier topics: From mobile game risk profiles and product management as a mitigation discipline, to the challenges posed by AI tools, security vulnerabilities and volatile online communities. We also examine how risks vary across different studio models, from solo indies to multi-studio giants. It also addresses specific risks tied to LiveOps and content pipelines, where the pace and pressure intensify.

Here we cover:

- LiveOps and Content Pipeline Risks

- Mobile Game Risk Profiles

- Product Management as Risk Control

- User Testing and Feedback Loops

- Community and Social Media Risks

- Security and Data Privacy in Games

- Risk Realities Across Studio Models

Part VI: Tools and Resources

The final part provides plug-and-play tools, frameworks and worksheets that can be adapted to your own studio or team. Whether you are running a premortem, managing technical debt or planning a crisis simulation, these resources are designed to turn ideas into action.

- Evidence-Based Tools for Risk Management

  - Premortem Workshop Kit

  - Anti-Pattern Deck

  - Kill-Gate Funnel

  - LiveOps Exit Tree

  - Technical Debt Tracker

- Worksheets/Toolkits for almost every chapter (website only) at https://www.game-production.com/riskbook

Final Word

Wrapping Up the Risk Management Journey.

CHAPTER 1

Overview

WHY WRITE THIS BOOK?

As I write this, I have spent the last week putting together a list of risks, issues, assumptions and dependencies for a project with a hard deadline and not enough time to complete everything we would like to. We need to understand fast what Minimum Viable Product (MVP) we can provide, when all our stakeholders are busy and under pressure. Sound familiar? Under that pressure, the first thing we did was understand the scope and the plan, then translate every risk, issue and the rest into actions or information requests. Everything has been tied back to deliverables or milestones, with dependencies clearly documented. Every day, the team is aware of what they need to do and where they need the most help with unblocking and gathering more information to unlock their work. I am able to approach stakeholders and express exactly what I need from them, when and why. We all understand the priorities together.

This is the power of risk management – it ties together the often chaotic world of what we want to do with how to actually do it, while presenting a transparent explanation of where we are or where we are likely to come across our major problems and opportunities. By understanding risk management, you unlock the often missing link between the vision, the plan and the conversations that need to keep happening. You give yourself and the team the chance to better control chaos and to better express what you need from others, in a prioritised manner.

If that sounds useful and powerful, keep reading.

I have been in the games industry for well over a decade now, but before that, I worked in consulting, e-learning, knowledge management and even running my own website company (very badly as it turned out). I have worked across private and public companies, including local education, defence, pharmaceuticals, telecoms and even the Foreign Office. That outside experience exposed me to structured approaches to project, program and portfolio management – areas that many who enter the game industry never encounter;

DOI: 10.1201/9781003646082-1

often they do not realise they exist. But those principles have been invaluable in helping me and the teams I have worked with navigate the unpredictable nature of game development.

This lack of foundational knowledge in structured approaches is one of the reasons our industry struggles with game planning and completion. If you listen to other game production and leadership professionals, you will often hear the statistic that only five per cent of games are completed on time and within scope. While I am sceptical of that exact number, there is no denying that we, as an industry, have a reputation for poor planning. Deadlines slip, budgets balloon and teams crunch to hit milestones that were never realistically planned in the first place. These are not just project management failures; they are risk management failures.

I am so passionate about the lack of foundational knowledge and training that I created the game-production.com website, filling it with free resources, including YouTube teaching videos, articles and blog posts.

Risk management is a critical component of game development, but one that most game development professionals are unaware of, or perform sporadically. This book aims to introduce the fundamental principles of risk management and equip you with the tools necessary to identify, assess and mitigate risks and issues at every stage of game development. By understanding risk and implementing proactive strategies, game developers, producers and executives alike can make informed decisions that reduce uncertainty and increase project success.

Risk management as it is taught in other industries does not translate directly to our own, as what we do is unique; it is difficult to find any other business that mixes creative arts with computer engineering science, psychological behavioural insights with marketing, live event planning with season passes, coupled with apparently crazy business plans. Where else does a business plan rely on a single product launch and risk closing down if it is not successful, yet seems to attract major investment on the "off-chance" of a hit?

I wanted to write a book that directly confronts the complexity, insanity, complications and nuances that combine when making games and when running game companies. By talking about risks, you can build a culture within your teams and studios that will then continue to discuss and spot them, enabling everyone to plan for them and decide how to treat them. Rather than crashing into each disaster or problem as if it were an inevitably, I am hoping that this book will assist you in seeing that you can talk about, visualise and grasp risks firmly and use them as opportunities for reducing the chaos, noise and being ready for what comes next.

SIDEBAR: WHAT WE MEAN WHEN WE SAY "RISK"

In game development, the word *risk* can sound abstract or formal. We all already encounter risk, but we just do not call it that. Here are some of the ways risk shows up in everyday game dev conversations:

- "Something feels wrong about that".
- "I have a bad feeling about it".
- "We assumed it would work, but it hasn't".

- "Nobody flagged that early enough".
- "That could come back to bite us".
- "This is a ticking time bomb".
- "It broke…as I kept telling people it would".

In this book, we will talk about risks, but I am rolling in issues too. **Issues are simply risks that ended up materialising.**

Risk is not just about big failures. It is about patterns you notice, assumptions that go unchallenged, and problems that creep up when no one is looking.

This book aims to help you *spot those moments sooner* and give you the language, tools and confidence to do something about it and start those conversations. The final section of the book is filled with templates, examples, toolsets and the rest to back up each chapter. This is not a purely academic book; the content will teach but also empower you to stand up and become a Risk Champion.

Conversations are the real secret of risk management: By being able to talk about risks, we realise that risks are simply the list of fears and concerns that our team has. They will bring them up to us and we can help them describe them along with what we could do about them. They will then feel empowered and hopeful. More risks and issues will emerge as we continue these conversations, and we will learn how to map those and create action-able tasks to deal with them, if that is what is required.

More than a forum for expressing and exploring fears and concerns, you can use the framework presented in this book to capture them and do something about them. You can also choose to take no actions except be aware.

Over time this process will create a history of risks and issues that form a safety net around future games you are involved in. There is no longer a blank page or a need to rein-vent the wheel and make the same mistakes all over again. You have already come up with the responses in advance and you are ready. Yes, new risks and opportunities will arise, but you and your team are ready to respond and trust in the process defined in this book.

Make it your own and share what you learn. Spread the word, please!

The Pressure of Game Development

Making games is chaotic. If you have worked in development, you already know that. The day-to-day job of making a game – whether as a designer, engineer, business manager, marketing guru, artist, QA expert, producer or any of the other countless roles required – is an endless cycle of problem-solving. Something will always break. Features will need reworking. Tools will not work the way they should. Teams are forced to make tough deci-sions daily, balancing limited resources, time and shifting priorities. Everyone, at every level, is constantly weighing trade-offs. We are always facing the truth of sacrifice: What will you give up today with the finite number of people and amount of time available and what will you prioritise? Has anyone ever taught you how to prioritise? Or is it always the loudest person in the room or the most senior director?

Producers are asked to make schedules work despite shifting deadlines and scope creep. Designers push for creative vision while balancing technical limitations. Programmers are tasked with building systems that not only function but are scalable, performant and future-proof. QA teams juggle ever-growing lists of bugs and testing requirements while being pressured to hit key deadlines. It is relentless. Somehow, we lose track of budgets and how much we are spending in the middle of all this, as most often it is only the top leadership who control that. Without the visibility of budget, how do producers make decisions? How do we know that our game, our studio, will succeed when we do not have all the information? These are all potential risks or issues.

And then there is the pressure from outside forces: Publishers demanding updates, investors seeking return on investment and players with high expectations. At larger companies, these pressures compound as multiple stakeholders, each with their own priorities, push and pull development in different directions. At smaller studios, the challenge is just as intense, as small teams scramble to do everything themselves with limited resources and often higher pressure to perform and never miss those critical demo deadlines.

Risk management provides a framework to navigate these pressures. It is not about stopping unexpected problems from occurring (because they always will), but about being prepared for them when they do. It allows teams to make informed decisions about where to focus effort, how to allocate resources and what trade-offs make the most sense for the long-term health of the project.

I think that risk management brings everyone together around a framework that is understandable and empowering. I think that even if you try, even if you take small steps, champions will emerge and you will find a positive culture emerging where risks and issues are not dreaded but are handled positively within an effective system. It may sound dull, as bringing order from chaos is not always exciting, but it may just save your game or even your company. It will certainly save your sanity. It will also strengthen your plans, empower you to prioritise effectively and drive far more powerful conversations.

Risks Are Rarely Isolated

Risk in game development exists at multiple levels. There is the team level, where individuals are making decisions that affect their immediate work. Then there is the program level, where the combined efforts of multiple teams contribute to the delivery of a single game. Above that, we have portfolio-level risks, which affect multiple initiatives within the same organisation – such as a company developing multiple titles or working across different studios. Portfolio risks also include company-wide strategic risks that come into play, including business decisions, funding priorities and long-term sustainability. Initiatives may not be about the games but about the workflows, processes or transformations.

A common mistake teams make is focusing only on risks at their immediate level without considering how they cascade upwards or downwards. For instance, a technical risk in one team's feature implementation could snowball into a major production bottleneck at the program level, impacting deadlines and investor confidence at the portfolio level. Understanding these layers and how they interconnect is fundamental to effective risk management. It is human nature to focus on your own work when under pressure, perhaps raising your head long enough to notify your immediate team of an incoming problem, but without a positive risk culture and established processes, there is nowhere else for it to go. Usually, we rely on producers or team leads to escalate and far too often we are used to nothing happening as a result, through no fault of theirs.

What becomes clear with experience is that risk is rarely isolated. The decision not to address a small UI bug today might ripple into schedule, testing and marketing misalignment later. A dependency not flagged during planning may unravel five other teams' efforts just weeks before a milestone.

Skill Development

Throughout this book, you will develop key skills that are essential for managing risk effectively in game development. These include:

- **Identifying Risks**: Understanding and recognising potential threats that could impact development, such as technical failures, budget constraints or shifting player expectations.

- **Mitigating Risks**: Learning techniques such as risk matrices to prioritise risks based on their probability and impact and implementing strategies to reduce potential negative outcomes.

- **Communicating Risks**: Enhancing the ability to effectively report and discuss risks with stakeholders, ensuring alignment and proactive decision-making.

Identifying risks requires experience, insight and a structured approach. One of the biggest misconceptions about risk management is that it is just about writing things down in a spreadsheet. The most effective risk management is conversational and dynamic. It requires teams to openly discuss potential challenges, recognise warning signs early and establish a culture where risk awareness is valued rather than dismissed as pessimism.

Some good news is that, since the current state of risk management within the games industry is so poor, even taking the smallest steps to improve that without your own area will do a world of good for you, your team and the wider community. If you were to search the internet for real-world examples of risk registers and risk techniques within the games industry currently, you would find only my own resources (at time of writing).

Examples and Case Studies

Risk management is not just a theoretical concept; it is applied in real-world scenarios across the game industry. This book will explore various case studies to illustrate how risk is managed in different development environments, including:

- **AAA Game Development**: Large-scale projects should have detailed and structured risk plans from the outset. We will examine how major studios would benefit from approaching risk assessment and management to keep multi-million-dollar games on track.

- **Indie Game Development**: Smaller teams often take a more iterative and agile approach to risk management. We will explore how indie developers navigate uncertainty and adapt their strategies dynamically to maximise efficiency and creativity.

- **Real-World Examples**: Practical insights from past and present game development projects, highlighting successful risk management approaches and lessons learnt from projects that encountered significant challenges.

If you have ever worked in a large AAA studio, you have possibly seen risk handled in a more structured way: formal risk registers, mitigation plans and project managers dedicated to tracking potential issues. But indie studios often handle risk differently, with fewer resources and tighter timelines, risk management can become a more fluid, adaptive process, where risks are assessed and mitigated on the fly. Both approaches have their merits and this book will explore how to apply risk management strategies regardless of your studio's size or structure.

This book will also cover how different types of companies handle risk at different levels. A large studio might treat risk as a formal process, but that does not mean smaller teams can afford to ignore it. Risk management does not have to mean rigid processes, as it can be adapted to fit your environment, whether you are working on a AAA blockbuster or a passion project in your spare time.

Whether you are a producer trying to balance schedules, a designer advocating for a risky but innovative feature, or an executive making high-level business decisions, risk management will help you make smarter choices and deliver better games.

Risk Management Empowers Us

Risk management might sound simple: Identify risks, talk about them and do something about them. But it is much more than that. Game development operates within a complex system involving workflows, tools, teams, hierarchies, business pressures and unpredictable creative processes. Within this dynamic environment, effective risk management empowers us in many ways. I have highlighted the improvements in planning and stakeholder communication, but here are some more:

- **Anticipate and Make Change**: Identifying potential risks allows teams to act before issues arise, rather than reacting after they've caused disruption.

- **Improve Decision-Making**: Without visibility into risks, teams make decisions blindly. Risk management ensures that discussions around challenges are happening openly, leading to better-informed choices.

- **Lower the Cost to Prevent Than to React**: Everyone who has worked in game development knows that firefighting a crisis costs far more than preventing it in the first place. When a feature is delayed, it has a ripple effect, disrupting other teams and leading to wasted effort.

- **Increase Chances to Realise Opportunities**: Risks are not always negative. Recognising opportunities is just as critical – whether it is a new technology, a change in market demand, or a feature that could dramatically increase engagement if implemented well.

- **Increase Awareness of Uncertainty**: The games industry is full of unknowns, and leaders at all levels need to build a clear picture of potential risks. Visibility leads to smarter planning and stronger execution.

- **Be Aware of Industry Transformations**: The games industry evolves rapidly. Think about how AI is reshaping workflows today or how Agile methodologies disrupted development norms a decade ago. Understanding long-term shifts in technology, consumer behaviour and platform policies is vital for studios to stay competitive.

- **Support Agility and Resilience**: True agility is not just about "doing Agile", it is about adapting quickly. Risk-aware teams are better prepared to shift direction without descending into chaos.

I am excited to have you come on this journey and hope you will find it empowering and revealing.

Online Risk Management Support

All templates, risk trackers, and examples are downloadable at:
https://www.game-production.com/riskbook

What's there:

- Risk register and RAID templates

- Retrospective and anti-pattern decks

- All accompanying chapter toolkits

They are free to use, adapt or quietly ignore.
Our Discord server is ready to welcome you: https://discord.gg/69nAY46A47.

Special Thanks

Many thanks to all those who agreed to read through the book as it was being developed. Also, thank you to the Udemy course students, who gave me essential feedback that helped shape this book. A big hug to everyone who sent in risk management examples I could use in the book through the Game Production Academy community.

Special contributors who made a big difference to specific chapters:

- Patrick O'Luanaigh, Non-exec Chairman and co-founder of nDreams

- Tamsin O'Luanaigh, Founder, Wise Cat Strategy

- Michael Gallegos, Indie Founder and Marketing Guru
- Vijay Dwarakanath, Director of Infrastructure
- Purva Garg, Senior Producer
- Chris Keeling, CEO, Mars Games
- Those who wished to remain anonymous

PART I

Foundations of Risk in Game Development

CHAPTER 2

What Risk Looks Like in Game Development

REAL-WORLD EXAMPLES OF RISK IN GAME DEVELOPMENT

Risk is not just an abstract concept; it is something that manifests differently depending on the type of game you are making and your role in the process. Here are a few real-world scenarios where risk management plays a key role:

- **User-Generated Content (UGC) and Season Pass Content**: If you are working on a game that relies heavily on user-generated content (UGC) or ongoing season pass updates, risks include balancing community engagement with moderation, ensuring timely content drops and avoiding player fatigue. Poor planning can lead to delays in seasonal content that drives players away.

- **Outsourcing and External Dependencies**: If you work with outsourcing studios, you must manage risks related to delivery schedules, art pipeline dependencies and client-studio communication breakdowns. A missed delivery from an external team could delay the entire production pipeline. If you are not ready when the engagement commences, you risk garbage in, garbage out.

- **Multiplayer and Live Service Games**: Developing a multiplayer game without prior experience is a huge risk. You might realise too late that you lack the expertise to handle server stability, matchmaking algorithms or anti-cheat systems. Risk-aware teams hire specialists or consult experienced teams to mitigate these issues early.

- **Emerging Technologies and Industry Changes**: Consider the rise of AI-assisted development and how it is reshaping workflows. Studios that do not assess the risks of relying on AI tools – such as content authenticity concerns, legal implications or over-reliance on automation – may find themselves at a disadvantage.

DOI: 10.1201/9781003646082-3

RISK VS VALUE

Risk is not inherently negative – it emerges from what we do and is an unavoidable part of making creative, innovative products. The key is balancing risk with the value it can create.

- **Balancing Risk Exposure with Value Creation**: The right level of risk-taking can lead to breakthrough innovations, while unchecked risk can cause projects to collapse.

- **Encouraging a Culture of Risk Awareness**: A team or whole studio that actively identifies risks is more prepared to deal with them. This is one of the most vital value goals for me in writing this book, so thank you for reading it.

- **Harnessing Positive Change**: Some risks open the door for opportunities that might otherwise be missed.

- **Reducing Complexity Through Clarity**: Risk management helps teams refine objectives, define requirements and streamline scope to reduce unnecessary complications.

- **Optimising Everything We Do**: Managing risk effectively allows game developers to maximise the value they deliver while maintaining sustainable workflows.

IGNORE AT YOUR PERIL

The consequences of poor risk management are staggering. Game studios and their IPs have collapsed simply because risk wasn't addressed early enough.

- **Unprecedented Job Losses Across the Industry**: The industry has seen massive layoffs over recent years, largely due to poor financial planning, failed games or mismanaged expectations (usually a combination of those). Indie studios are struggling to find sufficient funding to reach important milestones and are forced to shut down or keep skeleton teams.

- **Seismic Shifts in Technology and Game Success**: Advances in AI, procedural generation and cloud gaming are reshaping development and studios that fail to adapt are struggling.

- **A History of Poor Project Execution**: The industry has a long track record of missed deadlines, exceeded budgets and failing to deliver promised features. There is an almost complete lack of training in planning, roadmapping and program management.

- **Shareholder Demands and Financial Pressure**: Investors and stakeholders expect returns on their investments, which creates immense pressure on leadership teams. This pressure cascades down to developers, artists and producers, forcing decisions that may not align with the original creative vision. A studio that is not prepared to balance investor expectations with development realities is at significant risk. With so many previously independent game companies now owned by investors, this will only worsen.

- **Gambling vs Data-Driven Decisions**: Many studios bet on risky creative ideas without properly analysing data, leading to costly failures. I have worked in some studios (as have many of my friends) where greenlighting a game is handled by the company owner alone or the executive leadership team, without any data to back them up. The classic "I like this sort of game and I own the company" gamble.

- **Vision vs Reality**: Every project starts with ambitious creative visions, but many of them collapse under technical, financial or scheduling realities. Removing whole pillars of a game can often render it unrecognisable from the original greenlit proposal. Often, the new game being delivered has not been tested against market conditions or the original target audience.

WHY TRADITIONAL RISK MANAGEMENT DOESN'T WORK

Game development is not just about applying traditional risk frameworks. Many of these methodologies assume predictability and repeatability, whereas game development is an iterative and uncertain process.

Consider a AAA studio working on a new movement mechanic, such as Call of Duty's *omni-movement system*, which allows players to slide and fire from new angles. Before implementation, it was an unproven concept and developers had to gamble on whether the risk of failure was worth the potential competitive advantage and market differentiation. This is very different from traditional software risks, which typically involve system failures, not questions of whether an experience will even be enjoyable.

UNDERSTANDING THE THREE LEVELS OF RISK

Risk in game development exists at multiple levels, each with its own unique challenges and impact on projects. Understanding these levels helps teams and leaders anticipate, mitigate and manage risks effectively. The three primary levels of risk are portfolio, program and project risks. Each of these levels determines the type of risks being discussed and the nature of the conversations that need to happen to address them. Regardless of your personal position, role and interests, it is important to understand how the levels interrelate and influence each other, if you are to make use of them effectively.

When I first realised that these levels existed, it was quite a revelation, as I suddenly understood why I had been unable to win over certain senior stakeholders or gain traction in unblocking certain risks or issues. I had not understood the need to alter the conversation to fit the lens through which each level presents. While we cover these in greater detail later in the book, I believe you would benefit from a quick starter earlier on.

PORTFOLIO-LEVEL RISKS

Portfolio risks exist at the highest level of the organisation. These are structural risks that impact multiple initiatives, games, the business strategy and the overall sustainability of a studio or publisher.

- **Broad Exposure and Interrelated Risks**: Risks at this level do not exist in isolation. If one decision is made, it could ripple across multiple products, teams or business units. A funding decision for one game may impact resource allocation for another.

- **Risk Balancing Across the Business**: Portfolio-level decisions often involve managing risk exposure across multiple initiatives to ensure sustainability.

- **Strategic Decision-Making**: A strong business model and corporate strategy determine how risks are handled at this level. These could be decisions about acquisitions, new projects or whether to cancel a game in development.

- **Multiple Games and Initiatives**: Managing risks at this level includes overseeing multiple studios, balancing priorities between live-service games, new IPs and ongoing development.

- **Governance and Compliance Risks**: This includes equality, diversity and inclusion (EDI), corporate audits, external funding negotiations and legal compliance across different global markets.

A key example of portfolio-level risk is deciding whether to shut down an entire game project. It might not just be about that one title – other teams, technologies or business dependencies may be affected. For instance, if a studio is working on multiple projects and one gets cut, it can trigger layoffs, resource reallocations and damaged reputation.

Program-Level Risks

Program risks focus on a single game or large initiative, encompassing multiple teams or departments that contribute to a unified goal. These risks sit between high-level corporate strategy and ground-level execution, often involving people in roles such as executive producers, production directors, creative directors, development directors and lead producers.

- **Game or Department-Level Focus**: These risks impact entire game franchises, large internal teams or multi-studio collaborations.

- **Operational Risks and Bottlenecks**: Unlike portfolio risks, these are more immediate risks, such as key technology dependencies, milestone delays or cross-team conflicts.

- **Alignment with Strategic Goals**: This level ensures that game development aligns with corporate expectations while remaining realistic within its constraints.

- **Budget, Scope and Timeline Management**: Key discussions here involve which features are essential for launch, which can be delayed for post-launch updates and which should be cut altogether. One of the biggest risks that often occurs here is a lack of clarity and understanding of the budget that would then enable economic decision-making.

- **Workflow and Process Risks**: Teams at this level also focus on improving production pipelines. A game may fail not because it lacks creative vision, but because its processes were broken – team workflows, inefficient toolchains or ineffective coordination between departments are all very common and a common source of discontent.

An example of a program-level risk is the misalignment of different departments. What if an art department is creating assets that do not match the game engine's requirements? What if animation teams and Enemy AI programmers aren't working together efficiently? These bottlenecks can derail entire stages of development.

Project-Level Risks

Project risks exist at the team or feature level, where day-to-day execution and dependencies play a significant role. This is the level where most developers, artists and designers operate, dealing with tangible, day-to-day challenges.

- **Feature or Team-Specific Risks**: These risks directly impact a feature team, product team or outsourcing project.

- **Highly Influenced by Ground-Level Operations**: A project's success depends on how well different teams interact. Are back-end teams available to support multiplayer infrastructure? Is the data team too overloaded to provide analytics? Is the animation team waiting for input from design and art before it can commence work, causing a chain of events leading to costly delays?

- **Resource and Dependency Issues**: Effective project risk management ensures that necessary tools, people and assets are in place to support development without causing delays. Often though, efforts to reduce dependencies fail, or tracking and visualising them falters. A smooth development path can then become strewn with unexpected blockers.

- **Last-Minute Feature Cuts or Changes**: Teams at this level frequently face scope changes based on high-level decisions. Imagine working on a major feature for six months, only to hear that it has been cut due to budget constraints or a swing in the game vision. Many of us do not need to imagine, for it has happened to us.

A significant risk at this level is being blocked by other teams. For example, an engineering team working on multiplayer features might be completely dependent on a backend team that is already stretched too thin. If that backend team fails to deliver on time, the entire multiplayer experience could be compromised. Information sharing can multiply the impact, where apparently small and subtle changes at the design end were not communicated to engineers, resulting in being faced with rework or worse. This is why risk management at project level is just as critical as at the portfolio and program levels.

The Reality of Risk Across All Levels

Many studios operate in a single-game environment, where everything hinges on the success of that one project. If the game flops, the studio could shut down. This creates a single point of failure, which is a huge risk. The challenge for us in this book is that many traditional risk management approaches come from industries with multiple revenue streams and diversified portfolios – not an industry where everything depends on one hit game.

Risk discussions are often misaligned between levels. At the portfolio level, leadership may be focused on strategic goals like "How do we ensure funding sustainability?" Meanwhile, at the project level, developers are struggling with more immediate concerns like "We've run out of time to make this feature fun". The gap between those perspectives can lead to poor communication, bad decisions and missed risks.

Understanding the Lifecycle of Video Game Projects

Game development follows a structured lifecycle, with each phase presenting unique risks that must be managed to ensure a smooth and successful release. The traditional development cycle tends to flow from Concept, Pre-Production, Production, Post-production and Live Operations. There may be Alpha and Beta thrown in. Live Operations may be missing in games that are not hosting a community expecting more content. Differing business models, funding structures and platforms influence how these phases play out.

For example, mobile games may move through these phases much faster, prioritising speed to market, while AAA console titles often have multi-year cycles with rigid milestones that are often broken. Similarly, Games as a Service (GaaS) titles like *Fortnite* continuously evolve beyond traditional post-production, creating unique long-term risks that require ongoing mitigation strategies.

Similarly, across all games, the emerging requirements for tying game development with community building and marketing can greatly affect milestones and the importance of meeting certain deadlines – particularly if high-quality demos are required for player events and gamedev conferences.

Understanding how risk manifests at different stages of development allows teams to proactively address challenges before they escalate into major issues.

CHAPTER 3

Foundations of Risk Management

UNDERSTANDING THE LIFECYCLE OF RISK MANAGEMENT

Risk management is not a one-time activity but an ongoing process that evolves throughout the lifecycle of a game project. Whether dealing with financial uncertainties, technical challenges or production delays, teams must continuously identify, assess, mitigate and monitor risks. The risk management lifecycle ensures that studios remain agile and proactive rather than reactive to problems.

Here is a brief overview. Part II of the book is dedicated to working through this lifecycle.

The risk management process can be broken down into six core stages, each of which plays a critical role in handling risks effectively.

Identifying the Risk

Once objectives are clear, the next step is to figure out what could go wrong. Identifying risks (and issues that are already present) requires a strong risk culture that ensures that teams feel comfortable raising concerns early, before small issues spiral into major crises. As with the other chapters, a toolkit is provided to assist you with the first steps towards identifying risks and building this culture.

Assessing the Risk

Once risks are identified, we need to evaluate them based on:

- **Likelihood**: How probable is it that this risk will occur?

- **Impact**: If this risk materialises, how severe will the consequences be?

- **Urgency**: Does this need immediate attention, or can it be monitored over time?

One common tool for this is a Risk matrix, where risks are categorised based on likelihood and impact. This structured approach ensures that teams prioritise the right risks rather than focusing on minor issues while major problems remain unresolved.

Mitigating the Risk

Once we understand which risks are most critical, we move into mitigation strategies: Figuring out what actions we can take to reduce, control or eliminate risks.

For example, if a team identifies that outsourcing animation could create bottlenecks, they might mitigate the risk by building internal capacity or setting up clear contractual milestones to ensure deliveries stay on track.

Carrying Out the Actions

A risk management plan is only effective if actions are implemented correctly. This means:

- **Assigning Ownership**: Who is responsible for tracking and mitigating each risk?

- **Embedding Mitigation into Workflows**: Risk management should not be a separate process, but part of regular production meetings, stand-ups and retrospectives.

- **Ensuring Accountability**: Risks do not just disappear; they require continuous attention to ensure mitigation efforts are followed through.

Monitoring the Risk

Risk management does not end when mitigation strategies are in place – it requires continuous monitoring to ensure controls are effective and to identify new risks as they arise.

I think it is important to realise that this is not extra work for you; it is simply an empowering and exciting opportunity to assist you in ordering the chaos you were already attempting to control.

Key monitoring questions include:

- Have mitigation measures worked, or do they need adjustment?

- Have new risks emerged that we did not anticipate?

- Is the risk still relevant, or has it changed in nature?

For example, a team that launches a live-service game must continually monitor risks related to player engagement, monetisation trends and server health. If an unexpected surge of players causes login failures, the team must immediately reassess whether additional server resources are needed. If a new feature unbalances gameplay, what is the fallback plan?

Communicate and Report Risks

The final step in the core risk cycle is often overlooked: Sharing what you have learnt. Good communication makes risk management effective and builds that culture.

In this chapter, we look at:

- How to tailor risk messages for different audiences (execs, producers and developers)

- Ways to embed risk conversations into regular meetings and updates

- Using dashboards, summaries and visual tools to keep risks visible

- Encouraging ownership and escalation in a safe, structured way

- Avoiding communication failure patterns seen in high-profile case studies

Many studios could benefit from conducting postmortems on risks – analysing what went right and wrong in a game's or initiative's risk management approach. This feedback loop ensures that future projects benefit from past experiences, refining the risk management process over time.

TERMINOLOGY IN RISK MANAGEMENT

Below is a breakdown of key risk management terms.

Risk

An uncertain event or condition that, if it occurs, may have a positive or negative impact on project objectives.

- **Example**: A new animation system could either revolutionise the production pipeline or cause integration issues with the existing engine, delaying milestones.

Risks, then, can be either Threats or Opportunities:

Threats

Negative risks that could destroy value or hinder progress.

- **Example**: A major bug in the core gameplay loop discovered late in production threatens the game's launch timeline.

Opportunities

Positive risks that, if realised, could enhance value or provide competitive advantages.

- **Example**: A viral marketing campaign unexpectedly drives massive interest in an early-access title, creating a surge in potential revenue.

Benefits

Opportunities that may or have actually occurred and led to a positive outcome.

- **Example**: The decision to invest in procedural content generation could or did reduce development time and allow for a richer game world.

Issues

Risks that have already materialised and must now be addressed. These may simply have appeared, already exist or may have been known risks.

- **Example**: A key middleware provider shutting down mid-project forces the team to find an alternative solution, delaying production. There was no warning.

Ambiguity

The level of uncertainty caused by incomplete or unclear information.

- **Example**: Developing a game for a next-gen console before final hardware specs are available introduces ambiguity in performance optimisation.

Uncertainty

The probability of an event occurring, which directly influences the likelihood of risk.

- **Example**: Uncertain player reactions to monetisation models can affect revenue projections for a live-service game.

Effect and Impact

The consequences of a risk materialising.

- **Example**: A failed certification process on PlayStation results in a two-month delay, impacting planned marketing campaigns.

Risk Assessment

Evaluating the probability and impact of potential risks to prioritise mitigation efforts.

- **Example**: A studio assesses the risk of a server outage on launch day and decides to invest in redundancy measures.

Risk Attitude

An organisation's stance towards risk, ranging from risk-averse (avoiding uncertainty) to risk-seeking (embracing risk for potential high rewards).

- **Example**: A major AAA publisher may be risk-averse and focus on sequels, while an indie studio may embrace innovative mechanics despite financial uncertainty.

Risk Appetite

The level of uncertainty a team or company is willing to accept in pursuit of its goals.

- **Example**: A studio developing an ambitious new IP may have a higher risk appetite than a company working on a sequel to a successful franchise.

Risk Threshold

The level of exposure to risk before an escalation or intervention is required. This is rarely utilised and difficult to implement, but an important goal for maturing teams and studios.

- **Example**: A project team may accept a 5% delay to meet quality standards but escalate concerns if delays exceed 10%.

Mitigation

Actions taken to reduce the probability or impact of a risk.

- **Example**: To mitigate the risk of missing a deadline, a team schedules mid-project reviews to course-correct before it is too late.

COMMON RISK ARTEFACTS

Risk management is not just about theory: It depends on practical tools that help teams identify, track, discuss and respond to risks. These artefacts are simple but effective ways to make risks visible and maintain shared understanding. Not every team will use all of them, but even one or two used consistently can make a tangible difference.

- **Risk Register**: A central record of known risks, including descriptions, impact ratings, mitigation actions, ownership and status. It often includes issues that have already materialised. The format varies, but what matters is that it is actively maintained and easy to use within your context.

- **Risk Heat Map**: A visual grid mapping risks by likelihood and impact. Helps highlight which risks are most urgent and where attention should be focused. Often colour-coded for clarity.

- **Risk Radar**: A radial diagram used to cluster and display risks thematically (e.g. technical, design, delivery). Particularly helpful for programs or portfolios trying to spot patterns across projects.

- **Mitigation Plan**: A brief summary of agreed actions for key risks – what will be done, by whom and when. Sometimes part of the risk register, sometimes maintained as a separate list for clarity.

- **Escalation Pathway**: A simple flow or table defining when risks need to be raised, and to whom. Often includes criteria for escalation (e.g. impact level, cross-team effect) and links directly to RACI matrices to ensure roles are clear. Prevents the "I thought someone else was handling it" problem.

- **RACI Matrix**: A chart that clarifies who is Responsible, Accountable, Consulted and Informed for risk management tasks. Especially useful when risk ownership spans disciplines or project levels. Helps avoid confusion and ensures no task is left unmanaged.

- **Weekly Risk Summary**: A one-page update for leads or stakeholders, showing the top open risks, recent changes in status and current mitigation progress. Supports rhythm and avoids the need for long meetings. Needs to take into account which level lens the report is directed at.

- **RAID Log**: A combined log for **Risks, Assumptions, Issues and Dependencies**. Popular in program-level oversight and complex projects. Offers a broader view than a pure risk register.

- **Postmortem or Risk Retrospective**: A short review at the end of a milestone or release. Highlights which risks were managed well, which escalated and what can be improved. Encourages continuous learning and cross-team insight.

- **Crisis Management Toolkit**: Templates, checklists and communication plans used when a major risk has materialised. The toolkit may include holding statements (a short, prepared message used in the early moments of a crisis), internal response roles, contact lists and predefined workflows. Ideally prepared in advance and stored somewhere easy to access under pressure.

CHAPTER 4

Risk Landscape

Trends Reshaping the Games Industry

THIS CHAPTER FOCUSES PURELY on trends and can safely be returned to later, should you wish to move on to **Part II: Implementing Risk Management**.

INTRODUCTION: WHY TRENDS MATTER FOR RISK PLANNING

The games industry does not operate in a vacuum. Strategic and operational risks at the studio level are often shaped by broader trends, such as economic, technological and cultural factors. These trends may emerge gradually or shift rapidly, but in either case, they can redefine what risks are likely, what mitigations are viable and what expectations investors or platform holders bring to the table. By understanding the prevailing landscape, game developers can position themselves more effectively and calibrate their risk management practices to reflect the realities of the market.

This chapter outlines the most relevant industry-wide developments currently shaping game development, funding, publishing and distribution. These are not isolated observations; they interlink with the themes that recur throughout this book, such as financial risk, publisher dependency, live service planning and market volatility.

MACRO-ECONOMIC PRESSURES

See also Chapter 18: *"Financial, Regulatory, Legal and Compliance Risks"*

The Cost of Borrowing Has Risen

One of the clearest shifts in the post-pandemic economy has been the rise in interest rates, driven by central banks seeking to curb inflation. This change has made capital more expensive to access, which is particularly impactful in an industry where development timelines are long and upfront investment is required.

DOI: 10.1201/9781003646082-5

In practical terms, this means:

- Fewer new studios are able to secure loans or private equity.

- Publishers and investors are more selective, often requiring projects to be closer to completion.

- Many large organisations are slowing their acquisition pace or offloading assets, rather than expanding.

GameSpot (2024) reported that gaming investments fell from $14.6 billion in 2022 to just $4.1 billion in 2023, with a near standstill across 2024. Investors have turned towards safer asset classes such as Treasury bills. As a result, many developers who might have relied on funding during pre-production have found themselves needing to self-fund or pivot entirely.

Industry-Wide Layoffs and Retrenchment

The knock-on effect of reduced capital access is evident in the widespread layoffs across the games sector. Over 10,000 industry jobs were lost in 2023, with an additional 14,600 cuts in 2024 (Wikipedia contributors, 2025). These layoffs were not limited to small companies. Large players like Microsoft Gaming, Unity Technologies and Amazon Games also reduced headcount (GameSpot, 2024).

However, reduced capital is one of three key reasons for these job losses. The other two are:

- Compensating for significant over-hiring after the Covid sales bubble

- Too many games underperforming (also as a result of the post-Covid boom in development), meaning that publishers reduce the number of titles they make, falling back to safer sequels and more predictable launches (Game Developers Conference, 2025)

While layoffs are often presented as isolated restructurings, the scale and consistency across companies point to an industry-wide recalibration. Studios are trimming scope, reducing experimentation and placing stronger emphasis on sustainable revenue models. This background sets the tone for risk appetite and operational conservatism throughout the development lifecycle.

PLATFORM AND MARKET SHIFTS

See also Chapter 18: "Market, Platform and External Risks"

The Rise of PC Parity

In prior generations, console-first development was dominant. As of 2025, PC is no longer treated as a secondary platform by many publishers (Polygon, 2025). Companies are increasingly targeting simultaneous releases across console and PC, and in some cases, prioritising PC entirely. Contributing factors include:

- The success of hybrid devices like the Steam Deck
- Digital storefront maturity (Steam, Epic Games Store, GOG)
- More flexible update pipelines for PC-based builds

This shift requires studios to invest earlier in compatibility and scalability. It also raises expectations for live patching, mod support and player configuration flexibility. From a risk perspective, multiplatform planning has become a requirement rather than a stretch goal for many.

Subscription Models Under Pressure

The early optimism around services like Xbox Game Pass is being tempered by questions of sustainability (Polygon, 2025). While subscriptions offer players value and publishers discoverability, the economics of these models have not proven universally successful.

Studios now face the challenge of evaluating whether to launch into subscription eco-systems, balancing immediate exposure with potential long-term revenue loss. The risks include:

- Unclear revenue-sharing models
- Difficulties tracking attribution and player behaviour
- Loss of control over pricing and promotional strategy
- Platforms such as Xbox Live and Epic spending less money on content and giving smaller amounts on average to game developers

This uncertainty adds a new layer to business model risk and complicates forecasting for investor pitches.

Regional Volatility and Platform Policy

Chinese regulation continues to reshape global strategy. In addition to licensing slowdowns and restrictions on content, macroeconomic changes such as the RMB:USD exchange rate drop (4% as of early 2025) are affecting international revenue projections.

Global publishers with exposure to the Chinese market have had to adjust roadmaps, reconfigure publishing partnerships or delay launches. Studios seeking entry into the Chinese market now face longer timelines and higher due diligence thresholds.

PUBLISHER AND INVESTMENT REALIGNMENTS

See also Chapter 19*: "Strategic Risks"*

Embracer's Retrenchment

Embracer Group became a prominent acquirer of mid-sized studios between 2020 and 2022. However, a failed $2 billion funding deal in 2023 triggered a substantial restructuring. The group closed or divested 44 studios, cancelled 80 projects and laid off nearly 8,000 employees.

This has not only affected the teams directly, but has also had a chilling effect on other developers hoping for publisher acquisition or long-term partnership. It is a clear reminder that publisher stability is not guaranteed, even when part of a large corporate group.

Tencent and NetEase Recalibration

Tencent and NetEase, both headquartered in China, have made significant investments in Western game development (VentureBeat, 2020). However, recent moves suggest a shift towards strategic re-evaluation:

- Tencent increased its stake in Ubisoft's franchises (e.g. Assassin's Creed), but largely to stabilise debt structures (Polygon, 2023).

- NetEase continues to expand live service operations, but with greater focus on operational efficiency and data-driven cost control.

These adjustments reflect broader caution from Eastern investors in response to both regulatory constraints and the cooling of the global games market.

Square Enix and the Retreat from the West

Square Enix's decision to sell its Western studios to Embracer was not simply a financial divestment (GameSpot, 2022). It represents a strategic re-focusing on core Japanese IP and emerging technologies. Their roadmap now highlights AI, cloud-native development and blockchain experimentation. For risk professionals, this shift signals that publisher alignment must account for broader geographic and cultural priorities.

MONETISATION PRESSURES

Related topics also appear in Chapters 17, 19 and 36

Live Service Game Viability

Live service remains a highly sought-after model due to its potential for recurring revenue. However, it is increasingly clear that many such projects fail to reach sustainability. High-profile examples like *MultiVersus*, *The Finals* and *Splitgate* illustrate the challenge of retaining audiences and maintaining profitability.

These games often launch with substantial fanfare but struggle with:

- Player churn

- Content droughts

- Monetisation backlash

Even when gameplay is solid, service delivery (matchmaking, updates, live events) can falter. The lesson is that infrastructure and operations must be in place long before launch, and the studio must plan resourcing across multiple years and not just pre-launch. This model is high-risk and not suitable for all teams.

Key Risk Moments:

- **PSN Account Backlash**: In May 2024, Sony attempted to retroactively require all *Helldivers II* players on Steam to link a PlayStation Network (PSN) account (The Verge, 2024). This sparked a massive backlash:

  - Over 200,000 negative Steam reviews in two days.

  - The game was delisted from 177 countries where PSN accounts are unavailable (PC Gamer, 2024).

  - Sony reversed the policy following public outcry and developer pressure.

- **LiveOps Overload**: Arrowhead Game Studios acknowledged the internal strain. CEO Johan Pilestedt noted they were "not prepared for this level of success", citing the need to stabilise servers, respond to feedback and keep up with content expectations without burning out the team (Massively Overpowered, 2024).

- **Patch Cadence Missteps**: Community frustration grew over rapid-fire balance updates that lacked sufficient testing. Arrowhead responded by deliberately slowing patch releases to preserve quality and avoid disruption (GamesRadar, 2024).

Helldivers II exemplifies the double-edged sword of live service popularity. Massive engagement creates equally massive expectations for uptime, responsiveness and content delivery. Even successful games can become risk-intensive if infrastructure, policy alignment and live operations are not scalable from day one.

Cost Inflation

Across both indie and AAA development, production costs have continued to rise. Inflationary pressures affect salaries, software licences, hardware and marketing. Combined with lower funding availability, this creates a scenario where fewer games are greenlit and each must prove its worth earlier in the cycle.

The implication is that vertical slice development, clear monetisation plans and community engagement metrics are increasingly required even at pitch stage. Risk champions should advise teams to prepare early for questions about ROI, retention and scalability.

Many people predict an anti-inflationary effect over the next few years due to the increasing use of AI in many parts of the development process.

DISCOVERY AND AUDIENCE BEHAVIOUR

Expanded treatment in Chapter 20: "Reputational, Marketing and Audience Risks"

Streaming and Discovery Trends

Discord data cited in the Gaming 2025 report shows that 28% of players launch a game within one hour of watching it streamed (EA & Industry Analysts, 2025). A further 1.4 million users per month try a new title after seeing it on a stream. This demonstrates that discoverability is now deeply intertwined with streamer activity.

This changes the nature of launch risk. A well-timed influencer stream can dramatically boost uptake, while a lack of coverage may result in missed momentum. For indies and AA teams especially, marketing risk now includes:

- Managing influencer expectations
- Coordinating embargoes and first-look content
- Tracking real-time feedback loops post-stream

Platform-Centric Engagement

Consumer attention varies by platform. For example, users of TikTok, Discord and mobile platforms exhibit shorter attention spans but higher re-engagement potential (Activision Blizzard Media, 2025). Meanwhile, console players tend to favour deep gameplay systems but are slower to discover new IPs.

Studios must therefore understand the typical behaviour patterns for their primary platform and adjust their pacing, communication and post-launch planning accordingly.

MOBILE GAMING IN 2025: INDUSTRY OVERVIEW

See also Chapter 35: "Unique Risks in Mobile Game Development"

Market Growth and Revenue

The global mobile gaming market is projected to reach over $126 billion in revenue by the end of 2025, marking a significant recovery and growth trajectory. In-app purchase (IAP) revenue has increased by 4% year-on-year, with time spent in mobile games up by 7.9% and session counts rising by 12% (EA & Industry Analysts, 2025).

Regional Variation Is Strong: North America has led in growth, driven by casual gaming trends, while Asia has experienced a dip in IAP revenue, indicating regional divergence in player behaviour and spending habits.

Monetisation and Business Models

Developers are adopting hybrid monetisation strategies, combining IAPs with in-app advertising (IAA). This model provides diversified revenue and supports broader user acquisition strategies. There is also renewed focus on live operations (LiveOps), with studios investing more heavily in ongoing events and content to extend player lifetime value (Activision Blizzard Media, 2025).

Technological Innovations

Artificial Intelligence (AI) is being used to accelerate development and content creation. For example, King now uses AI to generate and balance thousands of new levels per week in *Candy Crush Saga*. Cloud gaming has also continued to grow, with Tencent and NetEase pushing cloud-first initiatives that reduce friction for new players and support more demanding titles on mobile hardware.

Some companies are using AI to track behaviour and predict which players are likely to churn in the near future, allowing the opportunity to take action to prevent this.

Strategic Shifts and Demographics

A growing number of publishers, including Tencent, are shifting away from licensed foreign IPs in favour of internally developed games. At the same time, mobile player demographics have expanded to include more female gamers and older audiences, which is reshaping design and marketing strategies (TechJury, 2025).

These developments all affect risk planning. Mobile-focused studios must now account for infrastructure scalability, shifting monetisation mechanics and diversified audience needs. As the industry continues to mature, so too must the frameworks used to assess market timing, operational readiness and lifecycle viability.

THE HUMAN COST

Further explored in Chapter 23: "Staffing Risks"

Studio Developers: Navigating Layoffs and Instability

Between 2023 and 2024, the video game industry experienced significant workforce reductions, with over 25,000 jobs lost globally (Wikipedia contributors, 2025). These layoffs affected major companies such as Embracer Group, Unity Technologies, Microsoft Gaming, Electronic Arts, Sony Interactive Entertainment, Epic Games, Take-Two Interactive, Ubisoft, Sega and Riot Games. The repercussions included project cancellations, studio closures and a pervasive sense of uncertainty among developers.

A 2025 survey by the Game Developers Conference revealed that 41% of developers reported being directly impacted by layoffs, with 29% witnessing their colleagues being let go (Game Developers Conference, 2025). The psychological toll has been considerable, leading to decreased morale, burnout and a re-evaluation of career paths within the industry.

Unionisation: A Collective Response

In response to these challenges, there has been a notable increase in unionisation efforts within the gaming industry. Notably, nearly 200 developers from Blizzard Entertainment's Overwatch 2 team formed the Overwatch Gamemakers Guild (PC Gamer, 2025) under the

Communications Workers of America (CWA) in May 2025. This movement followed similar initiatives, such as the World of Warcraft team's unionisation in 2024 (The Verge, 2025).

Furthermore, the launch of the United Videogame Workers-CWA in March 2025 (Communications Workers of America, 2025) marked the establishment of an industry-wide union, aiming to provide a unified voice for game developers across North America. These unions advocate for improved job security, fair compensation and better working conditions, reflecting a growing movement towards collective bargaining in the gaming sector.

Aspiring Developers: Facing a Challenging Entry

The current industry climate has also impacted aspiring game developers. The availability of junior positions has significantly declined, with only 2.9% of game development jobs in the UK being entry-level in 2023, down from 9.4% in 2022 (IGDA, 2023). This scarcity has led to intense competition, with some positions receiving thousands of applications.

Additionally, programs like Grads in Games have been put on hiatus due to the lack of entry-level hiring, further limiting opportunities for newcomers. This situation not only hampers the influx of fresh talent but also raises concerns about the long-term sustainability and diversity of the industry.

LEADERSHIP GAPS AND THE TRAINING DEFICIT

Intersects with themes in Chapters 17*: Operational Risks, 25: Agile, Lean and Kanban Risk Management and the Governance material in Chapter 26.*

A Disparity in Training Resources

While the gaming industry boasts a plethora of training programmes and educational resources for roles in art, design and engineering, there is a noticeable scarcity of structured training for leadership positions such as producers, project managers, team leads and executives. This imbalance leaves many in leadership roles to rely on self-directed learning, mentorship or trial-and-error approaches to develop the necessary skills for effective project and team management (Weststar & Legault, 2022).

The absence of formal training pathways in many companies for these critical roles poses significant risks to project outcomes (IGDA, 2023). Leaders are often expected to manage complex projects, coordinate cross-functional teams and make high-stakes decisions without the benefit of comprehensive training in project management methodologies, leadership principles or organisational behaviour.

The Consequences of Inadequate Leadership Training

The lack of proper training for leadership roles can lead to several adverse outcomes:

- **Project Delays and Budget Overruns**: Without a solid foundation in project management, leaders may struggle with planning, resource allocation and risk management, leading to projects that exceed timelines and budgets.

- **Team Dysfunction**: Ineffective leadership can result in poor communication, low morale and high turnover rates within teams, undermining productivity and cohesion.

- **Strategic Misalignment**: Leaders without adequate training may lack the skills to align project goals with broader organisational strategies, resulting in products that miss market needs or company objectives.

Overlooked Disciplines: Risk, Change and Programme Management

Of particular concern is the near absence of robust training in:

- **Risk Management**: Studios rarely train producers or leads in formal risk identification, mitigation planning or escalation processes.

- **Change Management**: Few leaders are taught how to guide teams through evolving scope, strategic pivots or stakeholder realignment.

- **Project and Programme Management**: While Agile and Scrum certifications exist, they are often superficial and lack grounding in broader programme-level coordination, value delivery and dependency management across titles.

The effect is that even highly experienced game producers may find themselves unprepared for executive-level responsibilities or complex multi-studio coordination.

The Need for Structured Leadership Development

Addressing this training deficit requires a concerted effort from industry stakeholders to develop and implement structured leadership development programmes. Such programmes should encompass:

- **Project Management Education**: Training in methodologies like Stage-Gate development, Agile, Scrum and Kanban to equip leaders with tools for effective project execution.

- **Leadership and Communication Skills**: Workshops and courses focused on developing soft skills essential for team management and stakeholder engagement.

- **Mentorship and Coaching**: Establishing mentorship programmes that pair emerging leaders with experienced executives to facilitate knowledge transfer and professional growth.

By investing in the development of leadership capabilities, the gaming industry can enhance project success rates, improve team dynamics and ensure that those entrusted with guiding projects are well-equipped to meet the challenges of their roles.

THE CHANGING PLAYER LANDSCAPE

Connects with Chapter 15, *"Design and Art Risks"*, and Chapter 20, *"Reputational, Marketing and Audience Risks"*

Evolving Demographics

As of 2025, the global gaming community has expanded to approximately 3.5 billion active players (Exploding Topics, 2025) . Notably, the United Kingdom and Japan have the highest video game user penetration rates, each at 58%, with the UK projected to reach 70% by 2027. The age distribution of gamers has also shifted: In the United States, 38% of players are aged 18–34, and 26% are 34–54, signalling that gaming is no longer dominated by younger age groups (TechJury, 2025).

Cross-Platform Engagement

Players are increasingly active across multiple platforms. While 79% engage with mobile games, 42% also play on PC or laptop and 55% also play on consoles (Activision Blizzard Media, 2025). This overlap in behaviour makes it more critical than ever to deliver consistent experiences and game economies across devices.

Diverse Motivations and Preferences

Beyond competitiveness and challenge, many players are now drawn to games that offer relaxation, routine or gentle creativity. The rise of "cozy games" like *Stardew Valley* and *Animal Crossing* underscores a growing desire for low-pressure experiences (My Journal Courier, 2025). Simultaneously, social connection and personalisation have become more central, with many games integrating chat systems, emergent multiplayer dynamics or AI-driven narrative branching (80.lv, 2025).

Why It Matters for Risk Management

Understanding the modern player is vital for managing creative, design and market risks. Assumptions based on outdated player profiles can lead to feature decisions, tone, monetisation plans or platform strategies that miss the mark. Game success or failure often hinges not only on production execution but on whether the product resonates with a fragmented and evolving audience. Misreading that audience can result in wasted investment, brand damage or systemic underperformance, especially if such misalignment is not surfaced early.

> "So many games fail because they are designed for the developers and there is no market research or really any thought about whether there is a gap in the market and whether the idea will resonate with the latest demographics of players on the platform(s) you're targeting". Patrick O'Luanaigh, Non-exec Chairman and co-founder of nDreams.

TECHNICAL AND ENGINEERING TRENDS

Directly linked to Chapter 14, *"Technical Risks", and partially to Chapter 26, "LiveOps and Content Pipeline Risks"*

AI in Production Pipelines

Artificial Intelligence is no longer an experimental edge case – it is increasingly embedded in everyday workflows. Studios now use AI to automate animation clean-up, generate dialogue options, balance game economies and accelerate QA. While this offers efficiency gains, it introduces new risks:

- Overreliance on third-party AI tools with unclear licensing

- Undetected bias or imbalance in procedurally generated content

- Team disruption due to poorly integrated automation

Leadership must understand where AI augments rather than replaces and build internal literacy around evaluating, supervising and retraining AI models where needed.

It is important to explain why/how AI is being used to the team, in order to bring them along on the journey. Google is working with a big publisher to introduce AI, but being smart about it – starting on the rock, ground and dirt textures and all the things the artists do not like doing, and giving them more time to make hero characters and amazing environments. It needs to be used as a way to let the developers do more (and do more fun stuff) and not as a way to lower dev costs or reduce the team size.

Cloud Infrastructure and Virtualisation

Cloud-native development environments are gaining traction, especially for multi-studio collaborations. Developers can now access shared codebases, test builds and art assets from anywhere, using containerised services or virtual machines. This shift reduces onboarding time and increases scalability but also introduces:

- Dependency on specific cloud vendors

- Greater attack surface for security breaches

- Downtime risks during provider outages

Risk planning should include fallback infrastructure, vendor diversification and rehearsed continuity protocols.

Backend Complexity and Automation

Live service and multiplayer games demand scalable, high-availability backend systems. Studios are increasingly turning to managed backend platforms or middleware such as

PlayFab, Nakama or Firebase. They also automate deployment pipelines through CI/CD (continuous integration and delivery). These changes can:

- Reduce latency and human error

- Increase release frequency

- Shorten time to patch critical issues

However, technical debt can accumulate if underlying systems are not revisited, documented and owned with sufficient clarity.

Middleware and Engine Evolution

The battle between Unity and Unreal continues, but so does investment in proprietary and niche engines. Middleware ecosystems now include analytics, telemetry, monetisation, content delivery and even compliance solutions. This ecosystem can be a boon – but it also creates:

- Upgrade dependency risk

- Vendor lock-in

- Integration complexity across builds

Studios must map and maintain a current view of their tech stack dependencies, assigning clear risk ownership for each external tool or library.

Web3 and Decentralised Infrastructure

While the hype around blockchain gaming has cooled, some studios continue to experiment with digital ownership and decentralised economies. These models introduce speculative design risk, legal ambiguity and heightened scrutiny from platforms. Any engagement with blockchain must be grounded in clear legal advice and robust risk-benefit analysis.

Engineering Resource Risk

All of the above trends place increasing pressure on engineering teams. Studio-wide transformations in infrastructure, AI adoption or backend scaling often require deep expertise – and many teams are under-resourced or fragmented. Skill shortages in build engineering, security, backend infrastructure and DevOps now present a systemic delivery risk.

ENGAGEMENT SATURATION AND PROFITABILITY RISK

The past three years have shown that visibility and initial traction are no guarantee of long-term success. Even well-funded, well-received multiplayer and live service games can quickly become unsustainable.

Risk of Content Fatigue

Players now face a saturated content environment. With live service models pushing seasonal updates, event cycles and FOMO mechanics, there is limited space for long-term commitment. Player burnout, attrition and churn are rising.

Misleading Metrics

Metrics like peak concurrent players or launch week downloads may no longer predict long-term viability. Investor pressure to chase these KPIs without a deeper sustainability model can lead to overcommitment and early collapse.

Strategic Response

Studios must re-centre evaluation criteria around retention, monetisation health and cost-of-service. Product teams should examine whether the value proposition can support year-two engagement – not just a spike at launch.

See also Chapters 19 ("Strategic Risks") and the Chapter 36 ("Product Management").

STRATEGIC CONSOLIDATION AND TOOLING ECOSYSTEMS

Major publishers are increasingly building vertically integrated development platforms – internal engines, shared services, common toolchains. While this improves visibility and coordination, it introduces systemic risk.

Toolchain Dependency Risk

If a proprietary engine or workflow platform fails to scale or evolve with hardware, dozens of dependent projects are at risk. Examples include shared animation or lighting systems, unified build infrastructure or dependency on central CI/CD.

Platform Imposition

Studios acquired by larger groups may face requirements to move onto shared systems – causing productivity loss, morale impact or knowledge gaps.

Governance Questions

Who maintains these platforms? How are bugs prioritised? Who sets roadmap scope? Shared infrastructure raises complex governance and risk ownership issues.

Risk managers should assess not just the tools in use, but the stability, autonomy and upgrade pathways of any centralised systems.

See also Chapters 15 ("Technical Risks"), 17 ("Operational Risks"), 34 ("LiveOps") and 26 ("Governance").

STRATEGIC IMPLICATIONS

The trends described above make one point very clear: Static approaches to risk management are increasingly inadequate. Studios must build adaptive systems that reflect the realities of 2025:

- Funding is harder to secure and subject to sudden shifts.

- Platform priorities are changing, especially as PC continues to grow in influence.

- Publisher relationships carry greater political and structural risk.

- Monetisation models need to account for post-launch viability.

Rather than treating risk as a check-box exercise, teams must embed risk thinking into pitch design, production planning, go-to-market strategy and live operations.

These structural and human-level issues – ranging from layoffs and burnout to the lack of formal training in leadership and risk – cannot be separated from broader project outcomes. Effective risk management must now account not only for features and milestones, but for the capacity and resilience of the people building them.

The rest of this book explores exactly how to do that, using real-world tools, examples and frameworks.

REFERENCES

80.lv. (2025). *2015 vs 2025: What people played then and now.* Retrieved from: https://80.lv/articles/2015-vs-2025-what-people-played-then-and-now/

Activision Blizzard Media. (2025). *Gaming in 2025: Advertising trends and platform behaviours.* Retrieved from: https://www.activisionblizzardmedia.com/blog/gaming-industry/gaming-in-2025-advertising-trends

Communications Workers of America. (2025, March). *Video game workers launch industry-wide union with Communications Workers of America.* Retrieved from: https://cwa-union.org/news/releases/video-game-workers-launch-industry-wide-union-communications-workers-america

EA & Industry Analysts. (2025, January). *State of the video game industry 2025.* Retrieved from: https://tinyurl.com/StateofVideoGaming2025-EA

Exploding Topics. (2025). *How many gamers are there?* Retrieved from: https://explodingtopics.com/blog/number-of-gamers

Game Developers Conference. (2025, February). *GDC 2025 State of the Industry: Devs weigh in on layoffs, AI and more.* Retrieved from: https://gdconf.com/news/gdc-2025-state-game-industry-devs-weigh-layoffs-ai-and-more

GameSpot. (2022, May). *Why Square Enix sold its Western studios.* Retrieved from: https://www.gamespot.com/articles/why-square-enix-sold-its-western-studios/1100-6503122

GameSpot. (2024, February). *Video game industry layoffs are worse than ever - How did we get here?* Retrieved from: https://www.gamespot.com/articles/video-game-industry-layoffs-are-worse-than-ever-how-did-we-get-here/1100-6521799

GamesRadar. (2024, May). *Helldivers 2 will "slow down patch cadence" to maintain quality and stability.* Retrieved from: https://www.gamesradar.com/games/third-person-shooter/helldivers-2-is-slowing-down-the-release-of-new-patches-to-maintain-the-quality-standard-we-want-and-you-deserve

IGDA. (2023). *Developer satisfaction survey: Training, education and career growth.* International Game Developers Association. Retrieved from: https://igda.org/resources/research-reports/

Massively Overpowered. (2024, April). *Helldivers 2 CEO talks live service pressure and leadership under fire.* Retrieved from: https://massivelyop.com/2025/04/07/helldivers-2-ceo-talks-live-service-sudden-popularity-and-business-leaders-who-have-taken-stupid-risks

My Journal Courier. (2025, March). *'Cozy games' redefine relaxation for a new generation*. Retrieved from: https://www.myjournalcourier.com/features/article/cozy-games-redefine-relaxation-new-generation-20265467.php

PC Gamer. (2024, May). *Helldivers 2 delisted in 177 countries as PSN login policy sours community*. Retrieved from: https://www.pcgamer.com/games/third-person-shooter/with-over-84-thousand-negative-helldivers-2-steam-reviews-in-two-days-developer-arrowhead-seems-to-be-grappling-with-sony-over-its-controversial-psn-sign-in-requirement

PC Gamer. (2025, May). *Nearly 200 Overwatch developers at Blizzard form a new union: The Overwatch Gamemakers Guild*. Retrieved from: https://www.pcgamer.com/gaming-industry/nearly-200-overwatch-developers-at-blizzard-form-a-new-union-the-overwatch-gamemakers-guild

Polygon. (2023, September). *Tencent increases investment in Ubisoft's key franchises*. Retrieved from: https://www.polygon.com/news/548281/ubisoft-tencent-investment-assassins-creed-far-cry-rainbow-six

Polygon. (2025, January). *PC gaming has gone mainstream - Here's what that means for consoles*. Retrieved from: https://www.polygon.com/gaming/500266/pc-gaming-mainstream-console-comparison-2025

Polygon. (2025, January). *The video game industry's 2025 turning point*. Retrieved from: https://www.polygon.com/gaming/512115/2025-video-games-big-events-releases

TechJury. (2025). *Video game demographics: The latest industry stats*. Retrieved from: https://techjury.net/industry-analysis/video-game-demographics/

The Verge. (2024, May). *Sony reverses controversial Helldivers 2 PSN login requirement after massive backlash*. Retrieved from: https://www.theverge.com/24150327/sony-helldivers-2-review-bombing-psn-login

The Verge. (2025, May). *Nearly 200 Overwatch developers form a new union at Blizzard*. Retrieved from: https://www.theverge.com/news/664873/overwatch-union-microsoft-activision-blizzard

VentureBeat. (2020, January). *Tencent makes $148 million offer to acquire Funcom*. Retrieved from: https://venturebeat.com/business/tencent-makes-148-million-offer-to-acquire-all-shares-of-dune-developer-funcom

Weststar, J., & Legault, M.-J. (2022). Video game developers' experiences of project management training and team leadership. *Game Studies, 22*(3). Retrieved from: https://gamestudies.org/2203/articles/weststar_legault_training

Wikipedia Contributors. (2025, March). *2022–2025 video game industry layoffs*. Wikipedia. Retrieved from: https://en.wikipedia.org/wiki/2022%E2%80%932025_video_game_industry_layoffs

PART II

The Six Stages of Implementing Risk Management

OVERVIEW

Risk management is not just a theoretical exercise – it is an active, ongoing process that helps game developers anticipate, mitigate and respond to challenges before chaos reigns supreme. By following the Six Stages, game studios can embed risk awareness into their development culture, reducing surprises and improving overall efficiency.

This chapter briefly walks through the six key stages of implementing risk management. While we do go into some detail, subsequent chapters will delve much deeper into each of these steps so that you are empowered and enabled to commence your own Risk management practice.

Further chapters in Part II also include the Risk Register, how to foster a proactive culture, crisis management strategies and the Project/Program/Portfolio Lenses. It is my hope that Part II gives you the foundational tools, while Part III onwards looks at game development specific risks and mitigation techniques.

These six stages were introduced in the previous chapter to give you the full picture of what risk management involves. Here, we quickly revisit each one before unpacking them in detail across the next six chapters.

Step 1. Identify Risks

Recognise what might go wrong before it happens. This includes structured brainstorming, past project analysis and tapping into team knowledge. Different roles spot different risks.

Step 2. Analyse and Assess Risks

Once identified, assess the likelihood and impact of each risk. This helps prioritise which ones to act on and guides where mitigation effort should go.

DOI: 10.1201/9781003646082-6

Step 3. Develop Risk Mitigation Strategies

For key risks, decide on an appropriate strategy, such as avoid, reduce, accept or transfer. The goal is to reduce the chance or severity of the problem.

Step 4. Implement and Track Mitigation Actions

Translate strategies into concrete tasks. Assign owners, integrate into team workflows and ensure mitigation does not get lost among other delivery priorities.

Step 5. Monitor and Review Risks

Risk management is not static. Regularly revisit risks, track what has changed and ensure mitigation remains relevant.

Step 6. Communicate and Report Risks

Good risk management only works if people know what is happening. Use clear, timely updates and match the message to the audience – whether a producer, lead or exec.

Each of these steps is covered in detail in the chapters that follow. You will find examples, toolkits and real-world insights that show how studios apply them in practice.

Together, they form the heart of your risk management system.

CHAPTER 5

Step One

Identify Risks

R ISK IDENTIFICATION IS THE first and most crucial step in implementing risk management. This stage sets the foundation for the entire process, ensuring that teams proactively anticipate potential challenges rather than reactively dealing with crises. Without the space to think, crises tie up our attention and focus, and we become less and less able to plan and respond. To counter this, we need to commit to understanding what could go wrong before it does – which means taking a structured approach and ensuring the right people are involved from the start.

Remember the importance of properly identifying the objectives before you commence this stage: What are your goals, what are you interested in and what is too far out of your remit? Feel free to keep a record of the outliers so that you can pass them on to appropriate risk management champions, but for these first sessions it is important to decide on focus points and the lens through which you wish to collaborate.

As an example, if you are a development team working on a set of features, you may raise queries around budget and strategic risks that can be taken to appropriate people afterwards. However, during these sessions, you choose to focus on developmental and operational issues that could affect your team and potentially disrupt your feature work (or raise new opportunities).

SIDEBAR: RISK BEFORE ANYTHING ELSE

Risk should be the first thing you really learn about – even before you start building the game. It helps you decide whether the game is worth starting at all, what needs scoping, and where to focus discovery efforts first. If you skip this, you are gambling with time and money. Remember my example in the opening chapter of the book. It is so important to start right to give yourself a chance when the real noise and chaos descends!

DOI: 10.1201/9781003646082-7

UNDERSTANDING OUR OBJECTIVES – AND OUR RED FLAGS

Before we can manage risk, we need to agree on more than just what we're trying to achieve – we must also understand our boundaries. What *must* go right? What *cannot* be allowed to fail? And what are the early warning signs that we are drifting off track?

It is tempting to define objectives in vague or creative terms, such as "make a great game", "hit our milestone", "keep the team happy", but effective risk management depends on defining:

- **Core delivery goals** (e.g. "launch on PlayStation and Xbox in Q4")

- **Critical constraints** (e.g. budget cap of £3 million, headcount freeze)

- **Unacceptable outcomes** (e.g. crunch conditions, reputational damage, security breach)

- **Tripwires**: Predefined thresholds or events that trigger action (e.g. "If level design falls more than 2 weeks behind, escalate to production leadership")

For example, if your game must support online multiplayer from day one, then any slippage in backend development or QA becomes a critical risk. If your funding round depends on a vertical slice demo, that becomes a fixed point around which all other risk tolerance must bend.

Equally, defining what is *not* a concern can reduce noise. You might choose not to worry about potential staff churn in a non-critical team during pre-production, or avoid over-planning for extremely low-probability events ("zombie apocalypse" style scenarios). In my experience, most game developers are already prepared for the zombie apocalypse.

When evaluating objectives, producers should also ask: *What would make this project fail?* Scoping risk is as important as scoping opportunity. This includes staffing gaps, platform uncertainty, and feasibility doubts. Even in the concept stage, I have seen games stall because a key hire was delayed or the core idea changed mid-way. Those are risks, not bad luck – they can be predicted.

In practice, this can be formalised through a short workshop or even a team conversation. Ask:

- What does failure look like for us?

- What do we *need* to protect?

- Where are we least willing to take risks?

- What would trigger a pivot, pause or escalation?

These are your real objectives from a risk perspective. Everything else is planning.

I have included a worksheet in the accompanying **Part VI Tools and Resources** to help you get started. From now on, **be sure to check out the Toolkits that are in Part VI for nearly every chapter in the book**. There is also more general assistance in the next section.

BRAINSTORMING AND TEAM WORKSHOPS

The next step in identifying risks is getting the right people in the room. Who you involve depends entirely on the nature of the risks you are trying to uncover.

- If you are an Executive Producer or Development Director, you may want to look at risks across the entire game: Interdependencies, operational risks, budget constraints and marketing factors

- If you are a Producer or Discipline Lead, you might focus on a specific team's risks – such as an Art Producer gathering art leads to discuss potential bottlenecks

- If you are embedded in a development team, you could hold informal conversations with smaller groups before expanding the discussion further

Make sure that you adapt the format of the session to the group. In remote teams, visual tools are especially useful. Shared editable documents can become brainstorming boards. In hybrid or physical spaces, post-it walls, whiteboards and breakout clusters can work well.

Try to move beyond "what could go wrong" and begin framing scenarios. Start with stories: "Imagine if the outsource partner misses their drop by 2 weeks. What would that mean for the level build?" or "What if the animation system does not integrate by the time the trailer needs to be locked?". Risk thinking is often easier when linked to milestones, media beats or known bottlenecks.

SIDEBAR: HOW CAN WE USEFULLY FRAME RISKS DURING IDENTIFICATION?

Try to jog memories of past risks that everyone has experienced of, so that it "clicks" with them what we are looking for this time and why:

- "Was there a moment you saw a problem coming but it was ignored?"
- "What was a sign something might break down?"
- "Did you ever spot something that looked off early?"
- "What is a kind of problem you wish teams noticed sooner?"
- "What have you learned the hard way about catching issues early?"

USING MIND MAPPING AND VIRTUAL WHITEBOARDS TO CAPTURE IDEAS

Mind mapping and whiteboarding can be an effective way to structure brainstorming sessions – especially in remote teams. Tools like **Miro** allow teams to:

- Visually organise risks by letting team members add ideas to a shared board.

- Cluster risks into themes to reveal larger patterns.

- Encourage discussion as people react to each other's ideas, surfacing risks that might not have been considered.

One of the biggest benefits of a visual brainstorming tool is that it maps the system of how the company works. As people contribute, connections between departments, processes and dependencies start emerging – giving a broader picture of risks across the organisation.

Mind mapping can also help you detect structural fragility. For example, if many different risks all connect to a single tool or individual, that is a sign of systemic dependency. These insights often emerge visually before they are consciously acknowledged.

Involving Stakeholders to Broaden Risk Visibility

A single brainstorming session won't catch everything. As discussions unfold, you may realise key perspectives are missing. When that happens:

- Identify who else needs to be involved.

- Hold follow-up meetings to expand the risk picture.

- Map out who influences what – this naturally builds a RACI matrix (Responsible, Accountable, Consulted, Informed), helping clarify ownership over different aspects of risk.

If your team lacks a formalised risk process, this exercise is also a great way to start building one. Understanding who needs to be involved in risk management is just as important as identifying the risks themselves.

This also prevents risk management from becoming isolated. If only production owns the risks, you miss the nuance of discipline-specific concerns. Make it everyone's job.

SIDEBAR: YOU SEE IT, YOU OWN IT

The problems you perceive are the problems for which you are accountable
– JIM MCCARTHY'S 23 1/2 RULES OF THUMB

It perfectly captures what risk management means to me; if you see a risk – even one that doesn't directly impact your team – you're accountable for raising it... If you notice another team struggling and understand why, it's not enough to stand on the sidelines. Step in. Share your perspective. Help them. It's not about blame, it's about ownership.
– SHAUN BOND, SENIOR PRODUCER/PROJECT LEAD

ANALYSE PAST PROJECTS

One of the best ways to identify risks is to learn from past mistakes. But let us be honest – most teams are not motivated to take the time to meet together to produce postmortem reports. If you do, fantastic! If not, you are probably jumping from project to crisis to project, never capturing what went wrong.

How to Leverage Past Experience for Risk Identification

- Review postmortem reports (if available) to identify recurring issues.
- Look for patterns – have the same bottlenecks occurred multiple times?
- Ask key questions:
  - What caused major delays in previous projects?
  - Were certain risks underestimated or overlooked?
  - Did communication breakdowns lead to avoidable crises?

Many studios fail to build a knowledge base of previous risks, meaning that lessons are lost as soon as a project ends. But risks tend to repeat themselves – so keeping track of what's gone wrong before helps prevent history from repeating itself.

Even if you only gather anecdotal recollections from key team leads, try to create a short shared document, such as "5 things we never want to go wrong again". It can be more effective than a dry report.

You may find that you are able to build substantial Crisis Plans as a result of this formal soul-searching. More on Crisis Management in a later chapter.

Spotting Recurring Patterns

Sometimes, risks are not caused by individuals but by systemic issues. For example:

- A bottleneck always forms around a key stakeholder who has too many responsibilities.
- Teams consistently fail to escalate risks early enough, leading to crunch periods.
- Outsourcing delays repeatedly stem from misaligned expectations, not vendor incompetence.

Recognising patterns allows teams to implement proactive solutions rather than putting out the same fires repeatedly. We cover Key Risk Patterns in detail in Part III onwards.

Useful Tip: QA Teams are Very Good at Identifying Risks

You may benefit from running a risk workshop with your QA team to uncover pain points that development teams overlook. They might flag risks such as lack of automation coverage, last-minute crunch to test levels or unrealistic expectations around regression testing – all of which are foreseeable risks that could be mitigated with earlier planning. Your QA team or department often contains an enormous wealth of knowledge about your game and other teams – use it wisely.

Try asking QA to identify the ten most disruptive patterns they saw on the last three projects. The insights you get back may be uncomfortable – but that is exactly why they matter.

Use Risk Categories

Once risks are identified, the next step is organising them. If you have just run a brainstorming session, you might now be staring at a massive, chaotic list of risks. How do you make sense of it? A simple solution: Use risk categories. These help structure risks and ensure no major area is overlooked.

We have chapters dedicated to Risk Categories in Part III, along with potential mitigation strategies, which you can use as a foundation if you wish. You can of course create your own, if it fits your own circumstances better.

Risk categories also help identify imbalance. For example, if 80% of all risks raised come from technical areas, it could signal either an overemphasis or a genuine production fragility.

Assigning Owners to Risk Categories

Depending on the size of your team, you might:

- Assign one person per risk category, ensuring specialised attention.

- Have smaller groups tackle different areas, promoting shared responsibility.

- Treat risk ownership as a collective responsibility, ensuring everyone has input.

- Break down risks into their project, program and portfolio level (covered in a later chapter).

A structured approach to risk categories also makes risk reporting easier – stakeholders can immediately see which areas are at the highest risk and make informed decisions accordingly.

As an example, I have utilised this method to demonstrate on a Miro board how most problems we were facing were due to Operational Risks, through visual clustering of cards. Once the team were brought along on the journey to identify risks, they were then much happier to discuss this frankly, as they experienced sharing the ownership. If I had simply told them what I already knew, they would not have responded with that same level of emotional binding.

There is a well-known piece of Change Management advice: Bring people on the journey, rather than attempting to inform them of the problems and solutions.

My final advice for you here is to start small. Simply by identifying a few risks and commencing your part through the Six Steps, you will come to build a comprehensive list of risks and issues and be given the tools to manage them.

If you are struggling to understand how you might log all this information, that is what the chapter on the Risk Register is for – keep reading!

CHAPTER 6

Step Two

Analyse and Assess Risks

R ISK ANALYSIS AND ASSESSMENT are critical steps in the risk management process. This stage ensures that teams not only assess the likelihood of risks occurring but also understand their potential impact (also known as severity) and prioritise them effectively.

Without proper analysis, mitigation strategies may be misguided, wasting time and resources on low-priority risks while ignoring the ones that could derail the project. Anybody (but particularly producers) reading this will understand the importance of gaining such powerful tools to help us properly prioritise.

UNDERSTANDING LIKELIHOOD AND IMPACT

Understanding and evaluating Impact (or Severity) and Likelihood is crucial for effective risk management in game development. **Impact** measures the potential impact a risk could have on the project, while **Likelihood** assesses how probable it is that the risk will occur. By systematically analysing both factors, teams can prioritise risks appropriately, ensuring that the most critical threats receive immediate attention.

The key takeaway is that we are evaluating how bad something could be and how likely it is to happen.

Evaluating Likelihood

One of the easiest ways to assess risk likelihood is by using a probability scale. This could be as simple as a 1–5 rating or a set of descriptive terms (e.g. rare, unlikely, possible, likely, almost certain). The key is to ensure consistency in evaluation, so that risks can be compared effectively.

Who Should Be Involved?

- **Subject Matter Experts (SMEs)**: Engineers, designers, or producers with technical knowledge can estimate the likelihood of specific risks better than anyone else.

DOI: 10.1201/9781003646082-8

- **Cross-discipline Representation**: Risks often have knock-on effects across multiple departments, so it is essential to involve not just the team at risk, but those who will feel its impact.

For example, if assessing the risk of a server infrastructure failure, you will need:

- Network engineers to discuss likelihood based on system resilience.
- Producers and QA leads to discuss impact in terms of game downtime and player retention.

Estimating Impact

Once likelihood is evaluated, the next step is understanding how bad it would be if the risk materialised.

- Rate the potential impact on key project areas like budget, timeline, or quality.
- Quantify impacts where possible (e.g. "this risk could cause a six-week delay" rather than simply "high impact").
- Consider cascading effects – some risks might seem minor in isolation but can snow-ball into major crises if not addressed.
- When a risk is given a "high" label, ask *why*. What will be lost or delayed? Encourage teams to quantify in terms of:
  - Weeks of slippage
  - Projected cost increases (if known)
  - External consequences (missed partner deadlines, PR fallout)

Example prompt: *"If this tech debt is not addressed, how much delay might it create once we hit feature freeze?"*

Adding SMART Impact Estimation:

- When building a risk register (covered later in this Part), consider adding a column for measurable impacts (e.g. additional costs, timeline extensions, expected player churn if a live-service feature is delayed).
- Think in terms of SMART goals – instead of labelling a risk "high impact", clarify why with quantifiable data.
- You might want to leave this until you have established risk management and are comfortable with the idea of adding more detail.

PRIORITISE RISKS

Once likelihood and impact are assessed, the next step is to prioritise risks effectively.

- Combine likelihood and impact into a risk matrix (covered below) to visualise risk severity.

- Focus first on high-likelihood, high-impact risks, as these have the greatest potential to disrupt the project.

- Reassess prioritisation frequently – what seems like a low-priority risk today may escalate as development progresses.

EXAMPLE: HOW PRIORITISATION HELPS AVOID A MAJOR CRISIS

A hypothetical studio working on an open-world RPG initially categorised performance issues as a medium-priority risk. However, after developers provided deeper insights into potential CPU bottlenecks, the risk was escalated to high priority. Because the issue was addressed early, optimisations were made before full-scale content integration, avoiding a major performance crisis late in development.

SIDEBAR: ROOTING OUT THE REAL RISKS

We were consistently missing milestones and there was growing frustration... The assumed solution was to keep adding more people, but this only made things worse... Everyone had a theory without any supporting structure or evidence. I introduced a Root Cause Analysis process... The ensuing discussion was eye-opening... The result was a more targeted, effective set of actions. Sometimes, the most impactful thing you can do is slow down, create space for conversation and give people the tools to find answers together.

– SHAUN BOND, SENIOR PRODUCER/PROJECT LEAD

SCORING SYSTEMS

To effectively categorise and prioritise risks, you can use a scoring system. Frequently, people use five scores for each, but here is a really simple example using just three:

- **Impact (Severity)**:

  - **Low**: Minimal impact on development or player experience (e.g. a minor UI bug that is unlikely to frustrate players).

  - **Medium**: Noticeable disruption that could delay features or increase workload (e.g. art assets needing rework due to mismatched styles between teams).

  - **High**: Major disruption that threatens milestones, performance, or the project's overall success (e.g. severe game-breaking bugs late in production).

- **Likelihood (Probability):**

  - **Rare:** Very unlikely but still possible (e.g. a sudden policy change from a platform holder like PlayStation or Steam).

  - **Likely:** There is a strong chance the risk could happen (e.g. team members leaving mid-project due to crunch-related burnout).

  - **Certain:** This risk will happen without intervention (e.g. known server instability for an upcoming multiplayer launch).

THE RISK MATRIX APPROACH

A common method for assessing risk severity and likelihood is a **Risk Matrix**, where risks are mapped based on their impact and probability.

Likelihood	Rare	Likely	Certain
High Impact	Monitor	Urgent Attention	Critical Mitigation Required
Medium Impact	Low Priority	Manage and Mitigate	Requires Strong Monitoring
Low Impact	Acceptable Risk	Low Effort Fix	Manage as Needed

This visual representation helps teams focus on the right risks, rather than becoming overwhelmed by minor issues while critical threats go unaddressed.

Please refer to the accompanying online material for examples of the Risk Matrix.

CASE STUDY: CYBERPUNK 2077 – A HIGH-SEVERITY, HIGH-LIKELIHOOD RISK IN ACTION

One of the most widely known risk management incidents in game development occurred with *Cyberpunk 2077*. The project faced high-severity risks tied to cross-platform performance, as the game needed to run on both high-end PCs and older console hardware (Schreier, 2021).

- **Impact:** The technical gap between PC and last-gen consoles was enormous, leading to game-breaking performance issues on older hardware.

- **Likelihood:** The risk of poor performance was highly probable, as optimisation challenges were well-documented during development.

- **Consequence:** Despite warnings, the rushed timeline resulted in unplayable versions on certain platforms, leading to refunds, lawsuits and a damaged reputation.

This example illustrates how risks can be both high-impact and highly probable, making them critical to address early. The failure to properly mitigate these known risks ultimately led to long-term financial and reputational damage.

This case demonstrates the danger of deferring known high-severity risks. CDPR had evidence, internal feedback, and time to escalate – but delivery pressure overrode sound analysis.

This example reinforces my belief that **risk analysis is not just technical – it is also cultural**. Risk registers without authority and trust behind them do not prevent disaster.

VISUALIZING RISK WITH A HEAT MAP

Another common visualisation tool is a heat map, where risks are colour-coded based on their severity and likelihood. The most critical risks appear in deep red, while lower risks are green.

Consider a Scenario:

- A game-breaking bug has been identified, but is extremely unlikely to occur at launch. This would be categorised as low likelihood, high impact, meaning it should be monitored but is not an immediate priority.

- Cross-platform performance issues are almost certain to happen and will significantly affect the player experience. This is a high-likelihood, high-severity risk, requiring urgent mitigation efforts.

A heat map enables teams to visually align on which risks need immediate attention and where resources should be allocated.

Please refer to the accompanying online material for the fictional example referenced here:

Heat Map Examples:

- Game-Breaking Bug (Low Likelihood, High Impact)
  - A critical bug that, while severe, was considered unlikely to occur frequently.
  - Despite its potential to significantly harm player experience, it was not prioritised as a top concern.
- Combat Imbalance (Moderate Likelihood, Moderate Impact)
  - Balancing issues in combat mechanics were expected to arise but were not seen as game-breaking.
  - These could lead to player dissatisfaction and negative reviews but were not considered critical to the game's functionality.
- Rushed Timeline (High Likelihood, Moderate Impact)
  - The aggressive release schedule introduced development bottlenecks and crunch, making it a high-likelihood risk.

- While this would cause inefficiencies and quality concerns, the immediate impact was expected to be manageable.

- Cross-Platform Performance (High Likelihood, High Impact)

  - The most severe and certain risk was optimising the game for older console hardware, which was a known challenge.

  - This ultimately led to severe performance issues, mass refunds and long-term reputational damage.

As you can see, the matrix is a useful visual representation, but the details are kept elsewhere – such as in the Risk register that we will explore in detail in a later chapter.

These tend to be very useful for identifying issues and tracking some of them in a visual manner that works best when in workshops or group sessions you are facilitating. They are also a very useful tool for reporting.

A NOTE ABOUT ISSUES

While we are discussing risks in these chapters – and indeed we are covering a **Risk Management** framework – please remember that you will find yourself often listing out **Issues**.

A risk becomes an issue the moment it materialises. At that point:

- Remove the Probability column entry as it has happened!

- Add a new field: **Status/Impact Realised**

- Track actions and ownership as you would a live blocker

This is also a useful time to look back. Did your implementation of the risk management process help you spot this earlier? If not, why?

An issue used to be a risk, but it happened! Now it is an actual issue. You will see how an issue also appears in the risk register when we cover that, but for now, do keep a record of known issues, particularly those brought up during workshops. After all, you are not commencing from a blank page and there will always be plenty of ongoing issues.

The impact of an issue can still be measured when analysing and assessing risks, but of course the probability is irrelevant as it has happened already.

Risk Management and hence this book includes advice on how to deal with risks once/ if they become an issue.

REFERENCE

Schreier, J. (2021, January 16). Inside Cyberpunk 2077's disastrous rollout. *Bloomberg News.* Retrieved from: https://www.bloomberg.com/news/articles/2021-01-16/cyberpunk-2077 -what-caused-the-video-game-s-disastrous-rollout

CHAPTER 7

Step Three

Mitigation Strategies

INTRODUCTION TO MITIGATION

Once risks have been identified and assessed, the next step is mitigation: Deciding what to do about them. Effective mitigation involves taking tangible, strategic action to reduce the chance of failure and protect value.

It is important to note that during workshops and risk assessment sessions, you may find that you cover this stage at the point of identification, rather than following each step one at a time – this is perfectly acceptable. Sometimes it can become a little overwhelming to dive into detail for every risk (or issue), so be sure to facilitate and control (time management is key!).

PRIMARY MITIGATION STRATEGIES

In the standard Risk Management frameworks available, there are some common mitigation strategies. Reduction is the most common (often referred to as "mitigating the risk"), but we also include other useful ones here.

1. Avoidance

Avoidance means removing the risk entirely by changing your plan or even eliminating a risky feature.

Example: When *Star Wars 1313* was cancelled, part of the justification was the cost and risk of developing an ambitious new IP amid LucasArts' uncertain future (IGN, 2013). Rather than pursue a high-risk project, the publisher opted to shut it down.

DOI: 10.1201/9781003646082-9

When to use:

- The risk has a high potential impact.

- There is a safer alternative that still aligns with your game's goals.

- The cost of pursuing the original path outweighs the benefit.

2. Reduction

Reduction focuses on lowering either the likelihood or the impact of a risk. This is what most people mean when they say "what are we doing to mitigate the risk?". However, do not fall into the trap of always thinking you must reduce every risk – remember that you have the other options available to you. Always think in terms of cost vs reward: How much will it cost to reduce this risk to an acceptable level vs what is the best we can expect.

Example: CD Projekt Red might have reduced the fallout from *Cyberpunk 2077*'s technical problems by expanding QA resources earlier. Postmortems suggest that automated testing, more internal transparency and honest milestone tracking were missing during key phases (Schreier, 2021).

When to use:

- The risk cannot be eliminated, but its effects can be minimised.

- Historical data or postmortems show this type of risk recurring.

- Preventive steps are affordable and feasible.

3. Transference

Transference shifts risk to a third party that is better equipped to handle it – such as outsourcing, insurance, legal contracting or platform partnerships.

Example: Bungie transferred hosting and server infrastructure risks for *Destiny 2* to Google Cloud to ensure reliability at scale during seasonal content launches.

When to use:

- External vendors can take on the risk more efficiently.

- Internal capabilities are limited.

- Financial, legal or operational risk is too high to absorb internally.

4. Acceptance

Acceptance means acknowledging the risk without taking immediate mitigating action – either because it is minor, or because mitigation is not worth the cost. Remember what we said about Reduction – sometimes it is simply too expensive (in terms of effort, people, etc.) vs the value of the expected outcome.

Example: Hello Games launched *No Man's Sky* knowing that some features were not fully realised. They accepted the reputational risk and committed to post-launch updates, which eventually turned the game's perception around.

When to use:

- The risk is low-impact or low-likelihood.

- The team has confidence in its ability to respond reactively.

- Budget or timeline constraints prevent deeper mitigation.

Facilitation Prompt:

During risk workshops, ask the group: *"Would this risk be better eliminated, managed, or transferred?"*. Encourage teams to role-play each option briefly, especially for large or systemic risks. Document pros/cons directly in the risk register or Miro board.

ADDITIONAL MITIGATION APPROACHES

While the top four tend to be the most popular, they are not the only ones available. Here are some other approaches that are well known. In particular, you will note Escalation below – this is the formal Risk Management response, rather than the daily escalations that occur across game development and production.

5. Contingency Planning

Create a fallback plan in case the risk materialises.

Example: Blizzard maintains redundant server infrastructure to cope with player surges during *World of Warcraft* expansions.

Quick Exercise:

Ask the team: *"If this risk turns into a real issue during the milestone, what do we need in place to recover?"*. Have everyone write one action on a sticky note. This can build a lightweight contingency map in ten minutes.

6. Diversification

Spread dependencies or revenue sources to avoid single points of failure.

Example: *Genshin Impact* uses a mix of gacha, cosmetic and event monetisation to reduce reliance on any one system.

7. Risk Sharing

Collaborate with partners who share the risks and rewards.

Example: The *Call of Duty* franchise regularly splits development across multiple studios (e.g. Infinity Ward, Treyarch, Sledgehammer), sharing technical and timeline risks.

Use Case Prompt:
"When should we seek co-dev, not just outsource support?" Risk sharing applies best when partners gain from mutual success – not just when you pay them.

8. Escalation

Raise risks to higher authority when they exceed your scope or resources. Clearly, this is quite an appealing solution to many risks, so use sparingly – there is a difference between engaging higher authorities to assist and officially escalating a risk away from you to someone else.

Example: In *Destiny's* early development, Bungie producers escalated technical risks related to their custom engine, prompting a full rework of world-building tools (D'Angelo, 2015).

Facilitation Prompt:
Run a "red card" drill – ask leads to flag 1–2 risks per team that *must* be escalated. This pre-primes escalation awareness early. It can also help build a RACI (covered in Crisis Management).

SIDEBAR: CHOOSING MITIGATION APPROACHES WISELY

While these options may seem obvious, game teams often struggle to apply them with discipline. Use these strategic questions as a framing lens:

- Can this be eliminated completely?
- Can we reduce its chance or scale meaningfully?
- Can someone else manage it better than us?
- If it happens, are we OK with that?
- If not, what is Plan B?

APPLYING MITIGATION IN PRACTICE

Here is some advice on how to make the theory come to life.

1. Select the Right Strategy

Align mitigation strategies with risk priority, team capacity and those boundaries and goals you set at the beginning. You need to be realistic at this point: By all means attempt to 'do the right thing', but if you cannot afford to approve the apparent best solution, work the problem until you reach a solution that is doable. I have often seen engineering teams, for example, being asked to develop fallback features into the backend systems, when the backend team comprises one person. Be realistic! Sometimes that means hiring more people, but not often. Once you have a clear view of your risks and issues, you will be in a much better position to prioritise with the limited resources and time available.

2. Break It Down into Actions

Large risks should be decomposed into actionable tasks (e.g. "build a fallback server" or "implement scope change review process"). Each of those tasks can then be added to your project management system (more on this in subsequent chapters).

Workshop Tip

Use a shared board (e.g. Miro or Trello) where each risk is assigned a mitigation card. Have participants draft the mitigation on a sticky and assign owner/responsible timeline right there. Convert cards into a "ticket" later.

3. Assign Ownership

Each mitigation task should have a named owner with authority and a timeline. Otherwise, follow-through is unlikely. This cannot be overstated in its importance – if nobody owns it, it will be moved swiftly down the prioritisation order and disappear.

4. Track Progress

Mitigations should appear in your risk register and be reviewed regularly – ideally during sprint planning or milestone reviews.

REFERENCES

D'Angelo, W. (2015). Bungie discusses destiny's engine and development tools. *VGChartz*. Retrieved from: https://www.vgchartz.com/article/260465/bungie-discusses-destinys-engine-and-development-tools/

IGN. (2013). *Star Wars 1313 was cancelled due to Disney acquisition*. Retrieved from: https://www.ign.com/articles/2013/05/08/star-wars-1313-cancelled

Schreier, J. (2021). Inside Cyberpunk 2077's disastrous rollout. *Bloomberg*. Retrieved from: https://www.bloomberg.com/news/articles/2021-01-16/the-inside-story-of-cyberpunk-2077-s-disastrous-rollout

CHAPTER 8

Step Four

Implement and Track Actions

W HEN IT COMES TO risk management, it is easy to stop at identifying risks and assigning them a category. Maybe you've even discussed the best approach – avoid, mitigate, etc. However, none of that creates a meaningful positive change unless you successfully implement risk mitigation actions within the project, program or portfolio workflow.

Without proper implementation and tracking, risks can linger in a risk register without ever being addressed. This section focuses on how to turn risk mitigation strategies into action and ensure they remain visible and effective throughout the development cycle.

BREAKING DOWN MITIGATION ACTIONS

Once a risk has been identified and assessed, the next step is breaking down the mitigation actions into clear, specific, actionable tasks. This is often where teams struggle. It is common to see people enthusiastically listing out risks and saying, "Oh, we should definitely fix that!" only for it to go nowhere because it was not properly embedded into the development workflow.

How Do You Make Sure Risk Mitigation Does Not Just Become Another Ignored To-Do List?

- **Make Mitigation Tasks Specific and Measurable**: Instead of vague directives like "improve performance", break tasks into quantifiable actions such as "optimise rendering pipeline for Level X by 15%". This becomes much easier if you collect success/acceptance criteria when you are creating the tasks.

Example:

Break down "reduce server costs":

Vague: "Review server costs"

DOI: 10.1201/9781003646082-10

Better: "Audit AWS usage and propose 2 optimisations by end of Sprint 14 (target £500/ month saving)".

- **Make it Actionable**: Each mitigation action should be written as a clear task that someone can execute. It should have an owner, a deadline and a defined success criterion based on your quantifiable action above.

- **Embed Risk Actions into Existing Workflows**: Risk mitigation should not be treated as a separate task list; it should be integrated into sprint backlogs, milestones and roadmaps. The risk is simply the justifying force for the tasks and therefore helps to set the priority – and keep it a priority.

- **Use Project Management Tools**: Jira, Monday, Kanbanize and other tools help integrate risk actions into team workflows.

- **Link it to Ongoing Work**: Repeating for emphasis – risks that exist in isolation get ignored. Connect them to existing epics, user stories, or features. **Example**: If a game's physics engine is prone to instability at high frame rates, the mitigation action should be part of the engineering backlog, not an isolated risk task.

- **However! Prioritise Based on Impact**: Just because a risk has been identified doesn't mean it should disrupt everything else. Determine where it fits within team priorities. We cover this below.

- **Motivate and Reward**: At Sumo Digital, I ran a leadership team meeting where we reviewed a live risk and issue log. Leads had to talk through the risks they owned. It was not a punishment – it was a chance to show progress, own the outcome and share solutions.

The Challenge of Risk Actions in Agile Workflows

If your team is using Scrum, Kanban, or a hybrid model, interrupting the backlog to address risks can be tricky. The question you'll often face is: "What's the value to the game if we stop what we're doing and fix this risk or issue?"

Project Lead Prompt

Use this facilitation question: *"If we do not fix this risk, what will it block later?"*

Push teams to trace the cost of inaction into future delivery pressure or quality impact. This helps non-technical stakeholders reprioritise more rationally.

From a product perspective, there needs to be a compelling reason to integrate risk mitigation actions into the backlog. Here's how to tackle that challenge:

- Teams often struggle to prioritise risk tasks alongside feature development. The key is to **frame risk mitigation as a value driver**, emphasising how it prevents bigger problems later. If you already struggled with prioritising tech investment to overcome tech debt, this may well empower you as tech debt can be described as a set of risks (or issues if left too long).

- **Tie Risks to Player Value**: Instead of saying, "We need to fix this because it's a high-risk issue", say, "If we don't fix this now, it will cause a delay in the launch of Feature X, which directly impacts player engagement".

- **Use Classes of Service** (if you use Kanban): Assigning risks different service classes can help teams prioritise them. For example, Expedite Class can be used for critical risks that require immediate attention, while Fixed Date Class is ideal for risks tied to an external deadline (e.g. platform certification requirements).

Class of Service	Example Risk	Action
Expedite	Build crashes during certification	Immediate task in current sprint
Fixed Date	GaaS content drop tied to season	Plan mitigation tasks 2 sprints ahead
Standard	Tool fragility with no hard deadline	Add to team backlog with review cadence

We cover this in more detail later. I realise that only a few of us out there use kanban and Classes of Service, so hopefully later chapters will convert you to the cause!

- **Work with Product Owners**: Producers, Product and Project Managers need to be on board with integrating risk-related tasks. Frame risk mitigation as a way to protect the project's success, rather than as a disruption. I often find that pointing out that we are all aware of the risks and issues now results in people realising that there is no longer a rug to sweep them under.

- **Use Risk Categories** to organise and prioritise actions to ensure that high-impact, high-likelihood risks are tackled first. More in Part III on this.

USING PROJECT MANAGEMENT TOOLS

Risk mitigation actions must be tracked, visible and consistently updated. The best way to achieve this is through project management tools that integrate risk-related tasks into the team's workflow.

- **Leverage Tracking Tools: Jira, Kanbanize, Trello, Asana** and so many more out there, allow teams to create risk mitigation tasks and track their completion.

- **Assign Risk Items Within Project Sprints**: Ensure that risk mitigation doesn't compete with feature work, but is embedded into development cycles. Since you are planning nice and early with many risks, this does not always have to rely on expediting, swarming or disrupting.

- **Use Automation**: Setting up reminders and tracking dashboards ensures that risk-related tasks are not forgotten.

Example: Using Jira for Risk Tracking

A development team handling an open-world game flags memory leaks as a significant risk. Instead of tracking them in a separate document, they:

- Create a Jira ticket assigned to engineering.

- Attach the risk to a specific sprint milestone.

- Define a success metric (memory usage reduced by 20% in crowded areas).

- If the engineer comes back and offers a cheaper solution or new information that alters the perspective of that risk, then we are witnessing success and why the regular risk reviews are so vital.

Jira also offers risk management plug-ins that allow issues to be created that are visualised on risk matrices, for example.

TRACKING PROGRESS AND ADJUSTING

Tracking risk actions is as important as identifying them. Otherwise, they become deprioritised or lost in the noise of daily development. How do we make sure risks stay on the radar?

- **Regular Risk Review Meetings**: Every sprint review, retrospective or milestone check-in should include an update on risk mitigation actions.

- **Visual Dashboards**: Using Miro, Confluence, or other visualisation tools can help teams see which risks are still open, which have been mitigated and which require new strategies.

- **Adjust Mitigation Plans as Needed**: If new information arises or a project shift occurs, risk mitigation plans should be updated accordingly.

Live Dashboard Advice: If you use Confluence or Notion, embed visual boards that update automatically from Jira/Asana statuses. Use tags like #risk-owner or #mitigation-open to filter what needs follow-up.

- **Reassess Risk Severity Periodically**: A low-priority risk may escalate due to unforeseen dependencies.

- **Document Changes in a Risk Register**: Keeping an updated record of risks and their mitigation progress ensures visibility across teams.

Example: Adjusting Risk Priorities Mid-Project

A multiplayer game team initially identified network latency as a medium-priority risk. However, as internal playtests revealed serious synchronisation issues, the risk was escalated to high priority and mitigation efforts were accelerated.

THE REALITY OF IMPLEMENTING RISK MANAGEMENT

At the project level, this is where risk management can feel like a real disruption. Teams are already under pressure to deliver features, fix bugs and meet milestones – so bringing risk actions into the mix can feel like adding more work rather than preventing bigger problems down the line.

To be effective, risk management must become part of the workflow, not an afterthought. Whether using Agile, Kanban, or any other methodology, teams need the right mindset: Managing risk is not extra work – it is part of building a stable, successful game.

CHANGE MANAGEMENT REFLECTION

Think of early risk implementation as culture-building. You will likely meet resistance. But as teams see that risk-based tasks prevent late crunch or leadership fire drills, adoption becomes easier.

- **Risk Mitigation Is an Ongoing Process**: It is not a one-time fix but requires continuous monitoring.

- **Integration into Team Culture Is Crucial**: Risk tracking should be second nature, not an additional burden.

- **Success Is Measured by Prevention**: The best risk mitigations prevent problems before they ever impact production.

In my experience, as time goes by and teams realise that they have been listened to and catastrophes have been averted, they become more and more bought into the process. Starting sooner reaps the benefits sooner. Do not wait for a perfect system to be in place.

CHAPTER 9

Step Five

Monitor and Review Risks

Y OU KNOW BY NOW that effective risk management in game development is not a one-time activity; it is an ongoing process that requires consistent monitoring and review. Risks evolve throughout the project lifecycle and new threats or opportunities can emerge at any stage. Therefore, it is essential to have a structured approach to reassessing risks and refining mitigation strategies.

REGULAR RISK REVIEW MEETINGS

One of the key methods for maintaining oversight of risks is to schedule regular risk review meetings. These should be integrated into existing project management cadences, such as sprint reviews, milestone assessments or executive status updates. Some kanban models already include risk meetings in their recommended cadence. The frequency of these meetings may vary depending on the project's complexity, but a biweekly or monthly cadence is often effective for game development projects. These may tie in to your sprint cadence, should you adhere to one.

Risk review meetings are often perceived as dull, but they are critical for fostering a proactive approach to risk management.

FRAMING TECHNIQUE

Frame risk review meetings as *"team contribution showcases"* – highlight progress, share mitigations completed and use phrases like:

- "Who needs help unblocking?"
- "Who saved the team time this sprint?"
- "What risks have we managed to reduce?"

Start with what has been *resolved*, not what is still wrong.

DOI: 10.1201/9781003646082-11

Instead of viewing them as mere checklist exercises, they should be framed as opportunities for teams to demonstrate accountability, share progress and seek support where necessary. When positioned this way, teams become more engaged and the meetings serve as a valuable communication tool. This becomes particularly true in remote or distributed teams where overcommunication is key.

I tell you this from direct personal experience – I always frame risk meetings as opportunities for team members and leaders to demonstrate what they have accomplished for the rest of us. After all, a risk averted, issue dealt with, opportunity seized, is a great moment for all of us to celebrate together. It is also psychologically more astute than playing blame games and accusing others of not completing agreed work – everyone in the room is a potential champion for building a positive risk culture so they must feel celebrated. They will want to come again and announce their accomplishments!

EMPOWERING EVERYONE THROUGH RISK MEETINGS

Purpose of Risk Meetings

Regular risk reviews provide structured opportunities for teams to:

- Monitor ongoing risks
- Identify new ones
- Report on mitigation efforts
- Keep all stakeholders aligned

These meetings are effective only if the right people attend. Too many and the discussion becomes unwieldy. Too few and crucial perspectives are missed.

One frequent problem is disengagement – when attendees assume risk management is someone else's job. Then, when a problem escalates, the same individuals are caught off guard despite having had an opportunity to speak up. Risk meetings are only useful when participants engage.

Engagement Structure

Assign rotating "risk champions" per sprint/review to ensure wider involvement. Their role: Update key risks, chase owners and raise blockers. Use a rotating model to avoid burnout and create distributed ownership.

At Bungie, risk management and issue flagging were formalised through regular meetings and tools, enabling developers across departments to surface interdependencies. In *Destiny*'s development, Bungie emphasised shared ownership and structured communication to align teams effectively and reduce misfires (Fane, 2018).

Best Practices for Risk Review Meetings:

- **Dedicated Time and Agenda**: Ensure that risk review meetings are separate from general status meetings to allow focused discussions on emerging threats and mitigation strategies. Time management is critical during the meetings – you must prepare beforehand and be ready to pinpoint what needs covering rather than simply going through a list of 50 items because they are there. If required, prepare ahead of time by visiting some of the key attendees and gaining quick updates on progress.

- **You do NOT Have to Cover Every Risk and Issue**: decide what is most important. As always with game production, knowing what to prioritise and what to ignore is an important part of ensuring these reviews go well. Where are the blockers? Which critical risks and issues require attention? Even then, if issues are being addressed already in other meetings or development cycles, move on quickly after a brief update.

- **Cross-Functional Involvement**: Risk reviews should include representatives from key disciplines, including production, design, engineering, QA, art and publishing so that all potential risks are accounted for. If possible, talk to them before the meeting so that risks and issues are up to date. If someone is not there, send them a summary afterwards. In fact, ensure you know who to inform and what they need to see.

Consider building a **Risk Review Attendee Matrix** template:

- Tracks roles and disciplines

- Flags if they missed the last review

- Helps you follow up on gaps in visibility

- **Risk Register Updates**: The risk register should be a living document, updated after every meeting to reflect new risks, changes in severity and progress on mitigations. I know it is tempting to update the Register during the meetings but **please, please, please only try this once** – believe me when I tell you that the meetings will grind to a halt, as deeply technical or specific knowledge is translated into the register. This is the best way to lose your audience and teach them to hate the meeting. Take notes and update afterwards and use follow-up meetings with individuals if the content is too technical or knowledge specific for you to make sense of at the time.

- **Accountability and Ownership**: Assign clear owners to specific risks and mitigation actions, ensuring follow-through and accountability. Ask them for updates and ensure they show up. How do you achieve this? Simply ensure that a very senior person always comes to the meeting and backs your involvement. Or ensure that a report is sent to them, where they agree to acknowledge and respond.

- **Kanban-Based Risk Tracking**: Optionally, using tools like Kanbanize can help visualise risks within a Kanban board, allowing hierarchical linking of risks from a granular level to broader categories. This makes it easier to identify commonalities, escalate risks appropriately and maintain transparency across teams. You can then easily share the screen and show everyone the risks and how they feed up, down and sideways. Somehow this is more comforting than an Excel spreadsheet. It is however a lot more work to set up.

In large studios with multiple teams working on a single project, it can be beneficial to have tiered risk reviews, where individual teams conduct risk assessments that are then rolled up into a higher-level game- or studio-wide review. Clearly, you need to be careful here to communicate progress to the correct stakeholders or silos may appear.

Creating a Structured Meeting Agenda

We all know that team leads, directors and the like are busy enough already, and they do not want to view the risk reviews as intolerable grinding meetings where they are forced to sit through a single person talking for 15 minutes about their pet risk. Prepare and plan accordingly, or your attendees will find themselves too busy with urgent matters to turn up again.

Suggested Agenda

- Begin with a one-slide visual summary:

  - Top 3 current risks

  - What has changed since the last review?

  - Any new, closed or escalated risks

- Review progress on mitigation actions

- Allocate time to surface new or emerging risks

- Assess the clarity and usefulness of risk reporting tools

- Encourage team input and open discussion

- Assign and agree ownership to the highest priority risks and issues

A clear agenda keeps meetings focused and prevents overrun. Over time, meeting formats should be refined to suit the team's needs.

Set time limits where needed.

As we covered, **do not cover a single risk for the entire length of a meeting**.

Stay focused on the future. If discussion drifts towards postmortems of resolved risks, guide it back to current and upcoming concerns.

Performance Indicators and Risk Metrics

Measuring the effectiveness of risk mitigation is critical to ensuring that risk management is not just a theoretical exercise but an actionable process. Key Risk Indicators (KRIs) can be established to gauge how well the team is addressing risks over time. However, it is important to introduce metrics progressively, particularly in studios still maturing their risk management practices (and let us be honest, that is 99% of them).

Common Risk Metrics in Game Development:

- **Risk Burndown Rate**: Tracks the rate at which risks are being mitigated or closed over time.

- **Production Stability Metrics**: Includes bug trends, failed builds and feature delays, which often correlate with risk exposure.

- **Budget Deviation**: Measures how risk factors (e.g. unexpected rework, scope creep) impact financial projections.

- **Player Sentiment and Market Risks**: If a game is live, monitoring community feedback, reviews and engagement trends can highlight emergent risks.

For teams still developing their risk processes, the simplest approach is to define clear success criteria for each identified risk, e.g. "We will consider this risk mitigated when X occurs". Over time, more sophisticated tracking methods can be introduced, such as visual risk matrices that demonstrate risk movement from high to low severity over multiple review cycles.

Visual Metric Examples

Examples of light-touch visual metrics:

- Colour-coded heatmaps (Miro/Excel)

- Trend on each risk's severity (↑, ↓, →)

- Burndown graph (remaining risks per week)

Use lightweight indicators unless your studio is already heavily metrics-driven.

Using dashboards or automated reporting tools can help visualise these metrics and make them accessible to stakeholders. Tools like Jira, Confluence or risk management software like ARM (Active Risk Manager) can assist in tracking these indicators in real time. Personally, I would stick with Miro or a slide with a heat map that you update each meeting. It does not greatly increase workload, even if there is some duplication of effort. I would not go near risk management software unless you are leading multiple studios across a plethora of products.

Documenting Lessons Learned

Each game project provides valuable lessons about risk management. A strong risk management process should include a formalised postmortem or retrospective process where risks and their mitigations are reviewed. The goal should be incremental improvement, much like the principles of Kanban – always refining the process a little at a time rather than attempting massive overhauls.

Key Elements of a Risk PostMortem:

1. **Risk Effectiveness Assessment**: Did our mitigation strategies work? If not, why?

2. **Emergent Risks**: What unexpected risks arose and how did we handle them?

3. **Process Improvements**: How can we refine our risk management framework for future projects?

4. **Knowledge Sharing**: Document lessons learnt in a central knowledge base to help future teams

PostMortem Template Prompt

Include three standard wrap-up questions in your postmortem forms:

1. What did we misjudge in our risk estimation?

2. Which mitigations worked better/worse than expected?

3. What would we do differently next time?

In AAA game development, I would like to believe that studios create internal reports that document risk handling from major releases. These reports, should they exist, would be used in onboarding new producers, refining production methodologies and improving risk culture across the organisation. Also, many program and portfolio issues and risks exist outside the life of any one game.

In many cases, risk registers serve as audit trails – detailing what went wrong, how priorities were set and what actions were taken to resolve issues. These provide proof of due diligence, demonstrating a structured approach to risk management rather than reactive firefighting. Do not forget to mention these in your career reviews.

Real-World Example: Risk Review in Action

Consider a large-scale game project where server stability was a significant risk leading up to launch. In the initial planning phases, mitigation strategies were set, including load testing, redundancy planning and fallback servers. However, during a routine risk review meeting, new data showed that certain geographic regions had much higher concurrency spikes than anticipated. This led to an additional escalation of risk priority, prompting last-minute scaling adjustments.

Because the studio had a structured risk review process, the issue was caught early enough to avoid a disastrous launch-day failure. This case highlights why regular monitoring and adaptive response are critical components of risk management.

Without this in place, imagine the crisis level conversations, potentially obscured escalation trails, lost opportunities to act early and a general feeling of disempowerment that might result. Those of us who have lived through these situations are well aware of the value that risk management brings once it is in place and running smoothly.

REFERENCE

Fane, L. (2018). *Wrangling the work of highly interdependent dev teams at bungie.* GDC Vault. Retrieved from: https://www.youtube.com/watch?v=ndPyhgorOKY

CHAPTER 10

Step Six

Communicate and Report Risks

W<small>E ARE NOW AT</small> Step Six – the final stage before re-entering the cycle of identify-ing new risks, analysing them and continuing onward through the cycle. This step focuses on the communication and reporting of risks – not always the most exciting part of risk management, but absolutely critical. We have already discussed how to review and monitor risks, but in this section we are interested in how we send the output of risk reviews and status outwards.

This does not mean producing a forty-page document that no one will read. A com-munication plan, in this context, simply means a clear, effective method for ensuring the right people or teams receive the correct information in the format they will best digest. It might take the form of quick, regular meetings with loose notes, a look over an actively maintained risk register, a regular view of a Miro board, etc. The format is not important. What matters is that it works for the team, the studio or the company and that it effectively conveys the necessary information. It must be directed with the audience in mind.

Here are some general tips.

ESTABLISHING A CLEAR COMMUNICATION PATH

Stakeholders – whether executives, publishing partners or internal leaders – must be informed about major risks and the mitigation efforts underway. These individuals either need to act on the information or stay informed. They must know what is happening.

Think of this as a way of applying Steps Four and Five in a transparent, structured manner. What risks are being tracked? What mitigation actions are in progress? What has escalated? What is new? If this information is already available, the next step is ensuring it is visible and comprehensible.

DOI: 10.1201/9781003646082-12

USE VISUAL DASHBOARDS TO SHOW THE RISK LANDSCAPE

Visual tools are powerful because they simplify complex information. They convey scope, urgency and focus quickly and clearly, making them invaluable in risk communication. You have likely seen heat maps, Miro boards, risk radars and similar tools. There are numerous templates available, and teams are free to develop their own. Anything that provides a transparent view of the current state is valuable.

Dashboards do not need to be elaborate, but they should:

- Clearly present top risks

- Provide an overview of mitigation progress

- Enable teams to identify patterns (for example, an unnoticed spike in technical risks)

Common tools include:

- Heat maps, which highlight critical risks

- Probability-impact matrices, which clarify how prioritisation decisions are made

- Risk dashboards, which track mitigation progress and provide an overview of project health

Whether using a Figma-based radar, a Notion template or an Excel layout, if it helps visualise risk effectively for the intended audience, it is the right tool. It is also worth standardising around the formats that work best in your environment – what matters most is that the information is timely, clear and actionable.

Tip: Embed visuals in risk registers, Miro boards or presentations – and keep them up to date. A detailed heat map from three sprints ago does not provide value today.

In *Cyberpunk 2077*, despite extensive use of project management and issue-tracking systems, internal dashboards failed to convey the true scope of technical debt and project readiness. As a result, stakeholders remained unaware of critical issues until it was too late, contributing significantly to the game's troubled launch (Thomas, 2020; Pelapkar, 2023). This illustrates that tools alone are not enough – visuals must be accurate, interpreted correctly and shared with the right people at the right time.

Tool Recommendation

If your team uses dashboards already, embed a section for **Top 5 Open Risks** updated weekly. In tools like Notion, use filters such as severity > 3 and status = open.

For Excel, use colour-coded conditional formatting on heat maps with arrows:

- ↑ Escalated this week

- → No change

- ↓ Mitigated/reduced

If your team has developed helpful templates, make them available. Useful tools should be shared, not hidden. It is particularly useful when it leads to standardisation where valuable, as this reduces the number of different methods teams are using to track and visualise risks.

Clarify Roles and Responsibilities

This is where communication intersects with ownership. Everyone must understand their responsibilities in identifying, managing and escalating risks. In practice, this often starts with team leads, producers and project managers asking questions such as: "How is this progressing?", "Has this changed?" and "Has this been flagged yet?".

Encourage teams to:

- Raise concerns early, before they escalate

- Keep risk conversations active

- Recognise when escalation is needed and know the appropriate channels

These habits must be encouraged and rewarded to become part of team culture. When it becomes easy and safe to report risks and when that process is respected, it becomes routine.

Risk Escalation Channels Template

You can find a template in the Appendix that defines:

- When a risk can be handled at team level

- When to raise it to project or exec leads

- Who to notify, and how (e.g. email, Slack, risk register field)

The early development of *No Man's Sky* highlighted how unclear roles and overextension in a small team can introduce major delivery risks. The limited team at Hello Games took on ambitious technical and marketing goals without fully delineated responsibilities, contributing to missed expectations at launch (Kuchera, 2016).

THE IMPORTANCE OF EFFECTIVE COMMUNICATION IN RISK MANAGEMENT

Communication is widely acknowledged as important, but in the context of risk management – particularly in game development – it can mean the difference between a manageable situation and a spiralling disaster.

This is not just about the ability to talk or send an email. It is about building awareness. Risks do not exist in isolation. Once they have been identified, the next step is to ensure the right people are aware, so that action can be taken, plans adjusted and that awareness cascaded across the team, the project, the program or the entire portfolio.

Communication Format Matching

Match message format to urgency and audience:

- **Critical**: Live call or ping to exec channel

- **High**: Raised in team review and flagged in register

- **Low**: Tracked, but bundled in summary reports

WHY COMMUNICATION MATTERS

An accurate and detailed **risk register** is of little value if no one sees it or responds to it. Effective communication:

- Ensures stakeholders are aware of potential risks and understand their impact

- Helps people contextualise those risks at the level they operate – whether project, program or portfolio

- Empowers teams to align their priorities and coordinate mitigation efforts

These conversations may happen in formal settings such as Scrum of Scrums, team check-ins or risk reviews. However, more often than not, they do not happen unless space is made for them. Without communication, people are unaware of what is brewing beneath the surface. That is when misunderstandings arise. Teams fall out of alignment. Before long, features fail to integrate properly, or departments end up working at cross-purposes.

CONSEQUENCES OF POOR COMMUNICATION

When people do not talk about risks, the result is not simply avoidance – it is an open invitation for those risks to escalate.

- Teams plough ahead based on assumptions

- Emerging issues go unnoticed because "we do not talk about that here"

- Individuals hesitate to raise concerns due to past negative experiences or fear of blame

Anthem provides a cautionary example (Polygon, 2019). Among its many development challenges, a critical one was the lack of clear communication around technical risks (Mikhailova, 2019). Teams were not aligned, assumptions were left unchallenged for too long and the end result was a product that failed to meet expectations, delayed its potential and ultimately fell short of the original vision (PC Gamer, 2019).

BUILDING A CULTURE OF TRANSPARENCY AND EMPOWERMENT

To manage risk effectively, teams must feel comfortable discussing it. This requires a culture in which:

- Team members feel safe raising concerns

- Everyone's voice is heard – from QA to design to leadership

- Knowledge is openly shared

Encouraging transparency builds trust. Trust, in turn, accelerates delivery.

Transparency is not just about visibility – it's about participation. Risk management should never rest solely with leadership. Everyone must have the opportunity to:

- Raise concerns

- Contribute perspectives from their area

- Take on risk ownership, linked to their role

Ownership, however, only works when accompanied by support. Assigning responsibility doesn't mean leaving someone to handle a problem alone. Teams must ensure that each risk owner has the tools, context and backing to take effective action. This includes making sure people know how and when to escalate, and that they'll be supported and not punished for doing so.

A strong example of this principle in action comes from *No Man's Sky*. After its rocky launch, Hello Games became a poster child for rebuilding trust through transparent communication. The studio began openly discussing roadmap changes, acknowledging issues and updating the community regularly. Over time, this steady, honest engagement transformed the game's reputation and restored confidence in the team (Hello Games, 2018).

Our goal in risk management is to foster that same level of internal trust and transparency. When teams feel safe, empowered and respected, they communicate more openly. And when they do that, risks surface sooner and before they escalate.

We will explore the broader theme of culture more fully in a subsequent chapter.

Strategies for Reporting Risks

Effective reporting can be transformative. Many professionals have experienced meetings where someone speaks at length about a risk, when all that is needed is: What is the problem? What is being done? Should anyone be worried?

Tailoring the Message

The way a risk is described must be adjusted to suit the audience:

- **Executives Need Concise Summaries**: Key risks, potential impacts, mitigation actions and implications for timelines or budgets

- **Developers Require Specifics**: Root causes, affected systems, mitigation tasks, estimates and dependencies

Example: For a mobile game launch, the executive team may need a brief update on the top three risks. The development team, however, must understand that the new SDK version is causing performance issues on older devices and know which workaround is being implemented.

Risk Report Template Example
Include a standard weekly risk summary (template in the Appendix) such as:

Title: Backend Latency on Xbox Build

Owner: Tech Director

Priority: High

Summary: Risk of missing trailer milestone due to unstable build under load

Mitigation: Load testing + Netcode patch scheduled

Escalation: Raised to VP Tech on 08 May

Frequency and Timing

Risk reporting must strike a balance. It must be frequent enough to maintain alignment, but not so frequent that it becomes noise:

- Weekly or bi-weekly reviews work well for project teams
- Monthly summaries are often suitable for executives and stakeholders
- Real-time updates are essential for critical risks, particularly if they threaten delivery

The key is consistency. People must know when risk reviews are happening and they must be expected to attend. If someone cannot attend, they must send a representative or follow up afterwards.

Champions are also important. The title "Risk Champion" may not appear on a job description, but when someone consistently leads the effort, it makes a difference. Start small, remain consistent and others will follow. Respect people's time by matching frequency and format to what they need.

Using Collaborative Tools

Risk discussions should continue outside meetings. Collaborative tools support this ongoing conversation:

- **Slack, Discord or Microsoft Teams**: Risk-specific channels where team members can raise concerns in real time

- **Jira, Trello or Kanban boards**: Integrate risk tracking directly into the development workflow

Example: A dedicated Slack channel for risk allows team members to raise potential issues quickly and ensures visibility across the team.

Tool Culture Warning

Slack/Discord are powerful – but also information can quickly become lost. Treat discussions there as **informal visibility,** not your system of record. Always migrate key items into your register or card system to track ownership and progress.

The Cycle of Risk Management

You have come to the end of the six steps, so now it is time to cycle back to the top and see this as an ongoing framework. Much like Agile and Kanban ceremonies, it is important to see this as a cycle of information gathering and analysis, review and reprioritisation. Risk management slots in alongside normal game development and simply aids in decision making and gifts you with an ever-improving method for empowering everyone to be heard and reducing the chaos and noise that so many of us have become so used to.

The rest of the chapters in Part II focus on how to optimise the risk management experience.

REFERENCES

ANTHEM

Mikhailova, V. (2019). Everything is wrong with the development of Anthem: How BioWare created their most failed game. *App2Top.ru*. Retrieved from: https://app2top.com/industry/everything-is-wrong-with-the-development-of-anthem-how-bioware-created-their-most-failed-game-138587.html

PC Gamer. (2019). Anthem community manager addresses player concerns at length, promises the game is 'here to stay'. *PC Gamer*. Retrieved from: https://www.pcgamer.com/anthem-community-manager-addresses-player-concerns-at-length-promises-the-game-is-here-to-stay/

Polygon. (2019). Recapping Anthem's messy road after launch. *Polygon*. Retrieved from: https://www.polygon.com/gaming/2019/5/7/18514310/anthem-bugs-delays-development-issues-bioware

CYBERPUNK 2077

Pelapkar, A. (2023). How agile rescued Cyberpunk 2077. *Medium*. Retrieved from: https://medium.com/@amruta.pelapkar/how-agile-rescued-cyberpunk-2077-8907ef0912a5

Thomas, T. (2020). Cyberpunk 2077 - Risk management lessons. *LinkedIn*. Retrieved from: https://www.linkedin.com/pulse/cyberpunk-2077-risk-management-lessons-tonny-thomas

NO MAN'S SKY

Hello Games. (2018). A message to the community. *No Man's Sky*. Retrieved from: https://www.nomanssky.com/2018/07/a-message-to-the-community/

Kuchera, B. (2016). No Man's Sky was a PR disaster wrapped in huge sales. *Polygon*. Retrieved from: https://www.polygon.com/2016/9/16/12929618/no-mans-sky-disaster-lies-lessons-learned

CHAPTER 11

Risk Registers in Practice

INTRODUCTION

A **risk register** is not a theoretical construct. It is a practical, living tool that enables teams to identify, track and mitigate threats across the lifecycle of a game project. Despite its potential value, the register is often misunderstood or dismissed in game development circles.

This chapter sets out to challenge that view. It provides a practical walkthrough based on real-world experience – mine – and showcases lean and usable alternatives. We close with guidance on RAID logs, an approach worth considering when risks alone are not enough.

A Practical Walkthrough of a Game Development Risk Register

This walkthrough began as a live demo for my **Game Production Academy** (www.game -production.com) and was later refined based on actual use in production environments. It is not perfect, but it worked, much like all of us. The aim here is not to show an idealised model from other industries, but to demonstrate a risk register that was used, adapted and still helps teams make better decisions.

I would encourage you to download the spreadsheet from the website here so that you can follow along painlessly:
https://www.game-production.com/riskbook

Starting Point: A Simple Project-Level Risk Register

The first version ("Simple Register" tab in the spreadsheet) is intentionally minimal, as we wanted to get started as quickly as possible. I am a keen proponent of the kanban philosophy in which we start with what we have and improve a step at a time. Here is how we started (I may have changed the names of the owners):

DOI: 10.1201/9781003646082-13

- Risk or Issue

- Title

- Impact

- Category

- Action Taken

- Owner

- Deadline

Example 1:

- **Title**: Railgun feature code to confirm if railgun is still achievable

- **Impact**: Very High

- **Category**: Game-wide issues

- **Action Taken**: Design change to remove the main technical risks

- **Owner**: Code Boss

- **Deadline**: End of May

Example 2:

- **Title**: Power-ups list incomplete

- **Impact**: High

- **Action Taken**: Overview updated to show three required power-ups. Design team to finalise the list.

- **Owner**: Design Boss

- **Deadline**: End of May

These examples show that even basic entries can spotlight meaningful risks. The use of colour coding (red for very high, orange for high) provides immediate visual cues. However, this format does not include probability, risk score or an audit trail. It mixes risks and issues and lacks structured phrasing. But it is functional and usable from day one, even by teams with no formal risk training. We knew we would have to improve over time and this is what we did.

A Structured Approach: Risk Scoring and If/Then Language

The second version ("Scored Register") adds core structure:

- ID
- Date Raised
- Risk Description
- Likelihood (1–10)
- Impact (1–10)
- Severity (calculated: Likelihood × Impact)
- Owner
- Mitigating Actions
- Contingent Actions
- Progress and Status

Hint: Risk Register Heat Map

You can add a heatmap to your register using conditional formatting:

- Red for severity > 64
- Orange for 36–63
- Yellow for 16–35

This lets you instantly visualise where your critical risks are, as long as you use the same numbering as I did (10x10=100)

A key improvement here is the use of **if/then** language to describe risks. For example:

Risk Description: If the railgun is not achievable, **then** we will need to find a new ranged weapon, **which will** impact schedule and design specifications.

This format separates cause from consequence and improves clarity. Vague entries like "railgun risk" become detailed and actionable.

Example Entry:

- **ID:** 001
- **Date Raised:** 10/05/2020
- **Risk Description:** (above)
- **Likelihood:** 8

- **Impact**: 8

- **Severity**: 64

- **Owner**: Bob the coder

- **Mitigating Action**: Change design to remove the main technical risk

- **Contingent Action**: Assign designer and coder to propose a replacement weapon; producer to assess impact

- **Status**: Investigating

Severity scores use conditional formatting. High numbers (close to 100) appear in red, making it easy to scan for priority items. Again, no specialist tools are needed. This is just Excel or Sheets using formula-based formatting.

Expanding the Model: Status Tracking, Comments, Residual Risk and Ownership
The "Detailed Register" adds the following enhancements:

- **Residual Risk**: The level of risk that remains after mitigation actions have been implemented. This allows the team to make conscious decisions about what level of risk is acceptable to carry forward. For example, a server latency issue might be mitigated with load testing and backup scaling plans, but the residual risk could still be medium if player numbers surge unpredictably.

Tracking residual risk encourages ongoing ownership and reassessment. It also supports better communication with leadership, who can weigh the costs of additional mitigation versus the likelihood and impact of the remaining threat.

- **Status**: Open, Investigating, Implementing, Escalating, Resolved, Issue

- **Internal/External Source**

- **Combined Mitigation/Contingency Column** (labelled M: or C:)

- **Updates and Comments**: Free-text log with date stamps

- **Accountable Person**: Named individual, not just a role

This provides auditability and narrative. You can now trace when a risk was raised, what actions were taken and how things changed. Here is an example comment:

Update Example:
"27/05: Became an issue after risk mitigation deadline reached without resolution. Design and code now working together".

ISSUES

When a risk becomes real, it becomes an issue. At this point, probability is no longer relevant. The language shifts from hypothetical to factual.

Risk Wording:
If the railgun is not achievable, then we will need a new ranged weapon.

Issue Wording:
As the railgun is not achievable, **we now need** a new ranged weapon.

The **status** is updated to "Issue". However, the original risk should not be deleted. Instead, it should be **archived**. The Excel file includes a tab titled **"Archive"** for exactly this purpose.

Archiving the risk allows the team to track its lifecycle – when it was first identified, what actions were taken and when it became an issue. This distinction matters. It provides insight into whether mitigation strategies were insufficient, or external factors overrode internal control.

IMPERFECT TOOLS STILL DELIVER VALUE

The spreadsheet presented here is far from perfect. It contains mixed levels of abstraction, vague categories and some terminology that I would now revise. However, it is practical. It was used in real projects. And it helped teams make better decisions.

You are encouraged to adapt the file to suit your own needs:

- Want to track assumptions? Add a new sheet.

- Prefer RAID (Risks, Assumptions, Issues, Dependencies)? Expand the tabs.

- Need a better status model? Define custom terms.

The only requirement is that the register is maintained, reviewed regularly and adapted as the project evolves. Even an imperfect register is better than none. It creates accountability, transparency and a shared understanding of where the biggest risks lie.

Also, what works is **Actions**. The Risks and Issues are interesting pieces of recorded data; **without actions attached to them** that reflect the Mitigation Strategy chosen, **nothing effective and real is happening**.

WHY RISK REGISTERS FAIL IN GAME DEVELOPMENT

In other industries like healthcare, defence or aerospace, **risk registers** are embedded into governance and audits. They are essential. But in game development, they often fail to take root. This can be due to:

- **Too much complexity.** Some companies build 60-column monsters that track every detail but offer no clarity.

- **Slow response.** Monthly governance cycles do not match the speed of dev teams. Executives are too busy to assist and cancel reviews.

- **No visual cues**. Compared to heatmaps, registers can feel hard to read and understand.

- **Poor integration**. Excel files are made, then ignored.

- **No ownership**. Items are tracked without anyone being accountable.

Instead of trying to copy highly regulated industries, game studios are better off with leaner, living documents. A **risk register** should:

- Capture key risks, not all risks – keep to the appropriate lens of the three levels

- Be updated weekly or biweekly, not monthly

- Be linked to sprint or milestone reviews

- Use tools like Jira, Miro or Trello where possible

Even a simple spreadsheet, if embedded in your sprint review process, is better than a risk register that no one opens.

Example: Live Game Risk Tracking

In this hypothetical example, a live-service game studio introduced a real-time risk register to manage post-launch risks. Instead of relying on a static spreadsheet, they embedded the register directly into their sprint tracking system. How would they do this? Well, if you use Jira, it is perfectly possible to create a Risk or Issue type, and Jira has multiple add-ons available that offer Risk Register capabilities.

Our example team was then able to:

- Track emerging technical issues based on real-time player telemetry (such as server spikes or login errors)

- Assign immediate ownership to developers or QA leads for investigation

- Prioritise mitigation and resolution activities dynamically, instead of waiting for monthly reviews

The register became part of the daily stand-ups and weekly sprint reviews. As a result, the studio significantly reduced the average time from issue detection to fix, improving both game stability and player satisfaction. Over the course of several updates, player complaints dropped, live ratings improved and negative reviews citing technical instability declined noticeably.

I have worked with several teams in more technically minded departments where this has proven effective. It does not completely replace the need for an accompanying risk register; however, as not all risks are part of game development at this level.

Understanding RAID Logs

A RAID log is a structured tool used to track four key elements that affect game projects:

- Risks

- **Assumptions**: Conditions you believe to be true, but that are not guaranteed. If these turn out to be false, they can trigger new risks or issues

- Issues

- **Dependencies**: External or internal constraints your project relies on. These could be partner deliverables, third-party tools or internal teams

Here are some examples.

Assumptions – Examples

Assumption: The console SDK version will remain stable throughout development.

- *If invalid:* A mid-project update requires rework on core systems, delaying integration

Assumption: The community team will provide timely player feedback on closed betas.

- *If invalid:* Lack of structured input leads to vague decision-making and late changes

Assumption: External localisation vendors will follow the same terminology guide.

- *If invalid:* Inconsistent terminology across languages causes confusion in UI/UX

Assumption: Your target platform (e.g. mobile hardware spec) will represent 80% of the user base.

- *If invalid:* Optimisation priorities are misaligned, leading to performance complaints on popular devices

Dependencies – Examples

Dependency: A backend platform (e.g. PlayFab or GameSparks) must deliver a new feature for inventory syncing.

- *Risk:* If delayed or deprecated, it blocks multiplayer progression and LiveOps readiness.

Dependency: Marketing relies on a working demo by a fixed date for trailer capture.

- *Risk:* Slippage means either delay to campaign or showcasing unstable assets.

Dependency: Your art team is waiting for the final shader pipeline from the rendering engineer.

- *Risk:* Artists build content on outdated assumptions, requiring rework.

Dependency: A porting partner is contracted to deliver console builds.

- *Risk:* Misaligned tooling or updates to engine version may create cascade delays.

The RAID format allows project teams to monitor not only future risks, but also what is currently happening and what might constrain them next. It supports a broader picture than a traditional risk register.

RAID logs are most useful when games or projects are complex, multi-threaded or involve significant collaboration across disciplines or studios. They can be updated frequently, reviewed in sprint meetings and integrated into tools like Confluence, Trello or Jira.

When RAID Logs Work Better

They tend to work better for:

- Multi-studio or vendor-heavy projects

- LiveOps games with lots of moving parts

- Projects involving legal, platform or publishing dependencies

Example: Outsourced Art Pipeline

Type	ID	Item	Owner	Status	Notes
Risk	R-03	Vendor may not meet shading standards	Tech Art Lead	Open	Shader complexity differs from vendor's process
Assumption	A-01	Vendor will use provided Maya rigs	Outsource Producer	Validated	Mitigated early through specification walkthrough
Issue	I-02	Two-week delay in asset delivery	External Producer	Resolved	Knock-on effects to integration
Dependency	D-01	Final character metrics needed from design team	Lead Designer	Blocked	Design blocked by animation prototyping

This RAID log may have lived in Confluence and would be reviewed every sprint. It would then help the production team escalate shading issues and track dependent decisions across design and tech art. It may also have sat inside a Miro board template instead or whatever format worked best.

WHAT NOT TO TRACK IN A REGISTER

Be careful not to include everything – some advice on what to avoid:

- Personal grievances or feedback ("X never replies to emails")

- Known, resolved issues (move these to archive)

- Extremely speculative risks that no one owns

Keep the register actionable. If it cannot inform a decision, it does not belong there.

START NOW

Do not over-engineer your register. Do not wait for perfection. Start simple, review often and make sure someone is accountable for each item. Use whatever format suits your team. A spreadsheet. A Jira plugin. A RAID board. A note pad. Start as simple as possible and build on that.

I am currently using a RAID log in a project and have added tabs to track Actions and Information Requests. The columns I am using are not strictly what I recommended. The content itself and the wording do not completely follow what I preach here either. This is because I am working on a high-pressure project with a very strict deadline and the team needs to be flexible and agile enough to pivot and deal with an ambiguous and potentially chaotic environment. It would make no sense for me to follow the doctrine to the letter, but jeopardise the project. The same is true of you – start with something, such as the template, but then go ahead and make it what you need it to be.

Please come and share your experiences on the Discord Server and we can enrich the templates on offer to reflect your own experiences.

Our Discord server is ready to welcome you: https://discord.gg/69nAY46A47.

CHAPTER 12

Fostering a Proactive Risk Culture

WHAT IS RISK CULTURE?

Risk culture refers to the collective attitudes, values and beliefs within a studio regarding how risks are perceived and managed. A strong risk culture ensures that risks are identified, discussed and addressed proactively. Conversely, a reactive risk culture only engages with risks once they have escalated into issues, often leading to costly delays and crisis management. In my experience, most studios fall into the latter category.

Many game studios do not have a formalised risk culture. Instead, they rely on experienced individuals to manage risks instinctively, often without recognition or structured processes. This informal approach may function in the short term, but it becomes a liability when a major issue arises unexpectedly – usually because risk was not openly discussed or tracked.

SIDEBAR: RISK CULTURE ≠ COMPLIANCE

It is easy to confuse risk management with box-ticking. But culture is not about policy – it is about what people say and do when leadership is not in the room. A studio has strong risk culture when risks are raised early, discussed openly and acted upon, without fear or bureaucracy. As I keep hearing, culture eats plans (or insert favourite example) for breakfast.

ASSESSING CURRENT RISK CULTURE

Understanding a studio's current risk culture involves asking key diagnostic questions:

- How frequently are risks discussed? Are they a routine part of team conversations, or only mentioned during crises?

DOI: 10.1201/9781003646082-14

- Is there transparency when raising issues? Can team members surface risks without fear of reprisal?

- Do individuals feel comfortable reporting risks? Or is there a tendency to remain silent and hope for the best?

In most studios, there is no kind of risk culture beyond intelligent knowledge workers doing the right thing quietly – and often getting into trouble for doing it. It is unofficial, and that makes it fragile.

SIDEBAR (VISUAL AID):

Self-Check: Culture Signals Grid

Behaviour Observed	Healthy Signal?	Concern?
Risks are raised in retros	☑ Yes	⊖ Only if urgent
Async discussions on risk topics	☑ Yes	⊖ Rare or discouraged
Execs reference risk in reviews	☑ Good signal	⊖ Never mentioned
People speak of "known unknowns"	☑ Cultural marker	⊖ Avoided conversations

TOOLS FOR EVALUATING RISK CULTURE

Unless it is already obvious, you might want to consider some methods, such as:

- **Surveys**: Anonymous feedback can reveal whether individuals feel safe raising concerns.

- **Interviews**: Speaking with team members across levels provides insight into how risks are handled.

- **Observation**: Paying attention to how teams respond to challenges can highlight whether risk management is ingrained or reactive.

You do not always need a formal survey. Just walk the floor (or the Slack channels). People already know what is wrong. They just assume no one is listening.

Facilitator Tip:
Ask team leads privately: "What's the one risk nobody's raising aloud but everyone knows is real?" This surfaces cultural blockages more quickly than surveys.

Often, a formal evaluation is unnecessary. Valuable insight can be gained by engaging teams in open dialogue and observing team dynamics. You may be surprised at the difference between teams. In my experience, some disciplines are much more used to questioning the status quo and challenging (as part of their effective function), whereas others will put their heads down and do what they are told, despite being convinced it is a bad idea.

This is not always obvious, but it will be revealed over time as risk management spreads across the teams.

EXAMPLES OF RISK CULTURE IN ACTION

Strong Risk Culture: A Studio's Success Story

In one studio I worked with, risk management was integrated into routine decision-making. Risks were openly discussed in planning meetings, not as an afterthought but as a structured agenda item. The studio visualised risks using dashboards and tracked mitigation efforts consistently. Raising a risk was viewed as contributing to problem-solving – not as negativity.

This mindset led to fewer surprises, better crisis response and more stable development cycles. It also led to increased morale and a sense that everyone was being offered a sincere opportunity to contribute positively to the growth of the studio and the success of its games. It spiralled out into other successes, such as Agile Guilds and a better uptake of learning path opportunities. Simply by realising that the leadership team was taking this seriously, a lot of related benefits spiralled through the studio.

SIDEBAR: SERVANT LEADERSHIP IN PRACTICE

Being a good producer or team lead includes admitting what you do not know. It means going to a senior dev and saying "I need help. How did you deal with this at your last studio?" That humility builds trust and brings solutions to light. Bring that humility into discussions on risks and issues.

Weak Risk Culture: A Case Study in Frustration

By contrast, I also encountered a studio where risks were ignored until they became unavoidable. There was no official tracking process. While teams discussed concerns informally, they lacked the ability to escalate them to leadership. There was a staggering amount of noise and disruption across Slack channels and in face-to-face conversations. At the time, most of the studio was working remotely, so tracking the true scope of these conversations was impossible. Take my word for it though, as in the first two weeks of my tenure, I was able to produce a report that highlighted countless problems that were being ignored by leadership. A culture of acceptance that nothing would change had infused the studio. I presented the situation to leadership *before* I even ran risk reviews – just to show them how much noise and waste was happening. That made space for the real work.

Management remained unaware until technical debt and delays made progress impossible. By pointing out that this was predictable and avoidable and that it was entirely possible to turn this around, we started to see progress. Often, people simply do not know what to do even though they accept the position and wish for it to change and improve.

When a risk management framework was finally introduced, it was met with relief. Team members had been aware of the issues but lacked a way to address them. Even basic processes transformed how the studio operated.

Time and again, the presence or absence of risk culture is what separates studios that ship polished games from those caught in last-minute chaos and years of noise and disruption.

BEST PRACTICES FOR A PROACTIVE RISK ENVIRONMENT

Encouraging Openness and Transparency

Cultivating an environment where team members feel safe discussing risks is fundamental. Too often, concerns are shared privately while official channels remain silent.

- **Open Communication Channels**: Risks should be visible and documented, not hidden in side conversations.

- **Regular Risk Reviews**: Scheduled meetings ensure concerns are heard and acted upon.

- **Psychological Safety**: Reporting a risk must be viewed as a contribution – not a liability. Let us not forget that since most studios purport to support the Agile approach, one of the pillars is a safe and secure working environment.

It is quite normal at first that team members fear raising concerns. Risks remain unspoken until they evolve into serious problems. Once structured reviews and open discussion are introduced, participation increases and overall project stability improves.

Involving All Levels of the Organisation

Risk management should not be limited to producers or project managers. Many of the most serious risks sit under the executive tier: It is the high-level workflows, service teams and gaps in coordination where things break first. That is where risks turn into blockers.

COMMON BLIND SPOTS BY LEVEL

Level	Commonly Missed Risks
Executives	• Broken or unowned workflows across Finance, HR, IT, Legal, Admin • Lack of operational tooling maturity (e.g. no version control on key templates) • Risks incorrectly "delegated away" without follow-up • Misaligned incentive structures (e.g. productivity targets that ignore technical debt) • Cultural silence: Risks are known but not surfaced due to power distance • No feedback loop between strategic decisions and downstream risk impacts
Middle Management	• Cross-team interdependencies (especially in hybrid organisations) • "Soft" risks: Morale, burnout, information asymmetry • The false belief that delivery pressure can be absorbed indefinitely • Invisible blockers arising from shared tools or environments • Blind trust in vendor/supplier estimates

Frontline Teams	• Systemic process weaknesses (e.g. lack of handover protocols) • Third-party constraints (certification, IP reviews, rating board delays) • Legacy system or pipeline limitations • Inconsistent documentation and tribal knowledge • Missing escalation paths

Everyone in the studio brings valuable insight:

- **Cross-functional Awareness**: Different disciplines spot different risks. Designers may flag feature creep. Developers see technical bottlenecks. QA identifies systemic patterns and so on.

- **Inclusive Discussion**: If only leadership is talking about risks, others feel excluded from key decisions.

- **Organisational Visibility**: Use tools like high-level Kanban boards to track risks across departments, not just within isolated teams.

Common Mistake: Risk conversations often happen in silos. For example, engineers may be discussing technical risk without design's knowledge, or QA might spot patterns in defects that leadership never sees. Integrated communication ensures a holistic view. Some specialised roles rely on these cross-departmental conversations happening already – ask a systems designer if they can work alone for example. The answer should be "no". If the culture reinforces open conversations, then it naturally spreads information and knowledge positively.

Rewarding Risk Awareness

Recognising those who identify and mitigate risks reinforces a proactive approach:

- **Public Recognition**: Acknowledge good risk management behaviours in team forums.

- **Meeting Integration**: Mention successful risk identification during regular updates.

- **Gamification**: Consider light incentives such as:

  - "Risk of the Month" awards for spotting high-impact risks early.

  - "Crisis Averted" stories that celebrate effective mitigation.

  - Be careful though, as this can feel a little forced and superficial.

Risk of the Month? Maybe not. Call it "Crisis Averted of the Month" or just thank them publicly. Avoid gamifying unless you really know your culture.

SIDEBAR: RECOGNITION IDEAS WITHOUT GAMIFICATION

- Include risk wins in weekly wrap-ups
- Private thankyous from leadership
- Highlight near-misses caught in time

STRATEGIES FOR CULTURAL CHANGE

Building Awareness and Training

Establishing a proactive risk culture requires deliberate effort:

- **Risk Training**: Host sessions using real project examples to demystify risk processes.

- **Make It Engaging**: Explain concepts in accessible language.

- **Core Topics**:

  - Recognising early warning signs

  - Understanding risk metrics and prioritisation

  - Using risk registers and visual tools

Lack of shared terminology hinders engagement. If team members do not understand the difference between a risk and an issue, or what a dependency means, they cannot fully participate. Training builds this shared vocabulary.

Establishing Open Communication Channels

Ease of communication is critical:

- **Dedicated Channels**: Use Slack or Teams channels focused on risk. I must say that I have never seen this succeed unless the channels are repositories of risks and issues, where the main conversations have already happened elsewhere. In other words, the channel is an escalation point in order to request that the risks are recorded and actioned.

- **Informal Options**: Allow drop-ins or asynchronous updates.

- **Lead by Example**: When leaders talk about risk openly, others follow.

If there is no visible discussion of risk, it will be seen as a management formality. Teams must view it as integral to development. The best method for convincing them is for action to be taken.

Leadership and Accountability

Cultural change is only sustainable if leadership sets the tone, reinforcing previous sections:

- **Leadership Buy-in**: Managers must consistently prioritise risk management. If your proactive risk culture is being undermined by a single leader, you have to name it. That is the risk. Leaders must model the behaviour, or the system breaks.

- **Empower Champions**: Support those naturally engaged in risk and amplify their influence.

- **Follow Through**: If risks are raised but ignored, engagement will vanish.

Your role is not to be a master problem-solver, but to facilitate solutions. The job is to combine experience, training and structure so others can operate safely. You seek to minimise chaos, surface risks and make sure people feel supported.

SIDEBAR: CHASING IS NOT A STRATEGY

Know your team and keenly observe behaviours – Invest time to understand their capabilities not just from technical/work perspective but as a personal/team player perspective

– PURVA GARG, SENIOR PRODUCER

Executive Reflection Exercise:
Ask your leadership team:

- Do we discuss risk in our planning meetings?

- Have we ever escalated a mitigation task ourselves?

- What risks do our teams believe we're ignoring?

CHAPTER 13

Implementing Crisis Management Strategies

A s THE FOCUS SHIFTS from general risk management into the realm of crisis management, the stakes become higher. Crisis management refers to the structured, immediate response required when a risk materialises into a serious, time-critical event. It is the difference between thinking, "There might be a server issue", and realising, "The servers are down. Players are angry. What is the next step in the next five minutes?".

A crisis is not just serious – it is urgent. It is when the priority becomes clear: Drop what you are doing and address this now.

SIDEBAR: FAST CRITERIA FOR IDENTIFYING A CRISIS

Ask:

- Is this materially affecting players right now?
- Does this block milestone progress or delivery?
- Are we at legal, reputational, or financial risk if we do not act?

  If YES to two or more, it is a crisis.

Crisis Management attempts to prepare us for these serious events that might happen. It also helps us when they are happening.

DEFINING A CRISIS

In game development, what constitutes a crisis is subjective to some degree, but its arrival is rarely ambiguous. A crisis is an acute event that poses a direct threat to project stability, company reputation, or team wellbeing.

DOI: 10.1201/9781003646082-15

Examples include:

- **Critical bugs** near launch that block delivery
- **Loss of key personnel** (e.g. a lead developer resigning mid-project)
- **Security breaches** exposing user data

A risk becomes a crisis when it transitions from potential to actual. It demands immediate, coordinated action to limit damage and stabilise operations.

IDENTIFYING POSSIBLE CRISES BEFORE THEY HAPPEN

Not every risk turns into a crisis, but many crises give early warning signs. By proactively scanning for and identifying potential crisis scenarios, studios can reduce the damage or avoid the event entirely.

Use Strategic Categorisation

Start by sorting risks into categories that reflect your studio's operations. We cover these in great detail in Part III, but here are some you might find useful:

- **Operational Failures**: e.g. build instability, missed deadlines, deployment outages
- **Reputational Threats**: e.g. staff misconduct, social media backlash, leaked content
- **Legal/Compliance Risks**: e.g. violations of gambling regulations, GDPR issues
- **Security Incidents**: e.g. hacking, ransomware, data theft
- **Financial Disruptions**: e.g. publisher withdrawal, underperforming monetisation
- **Staffing/Leadership Crises**: e.g. key resignations, team burnout, HR conflict, unionisation

This exercise alone can reveal blind spots in your planning.

FACILITATOR TOOL:

Run a "Could This Spiral?" workshop:

- List five current risks
- For each, ask: "What would make this worse, faster?"
- Map triggers, tripwires and early warning signs

You can plan ahead. The people who already know how these failures happen – such as IT, security and legal – will help you sketch what it looks like and how fast it goes wrong.

Scan for Early Warning Signs

Crises are rarely without warning signs. Ask yourself:

- Are deadlines consistently slipping?
- Are player complaints rising?
- Is any team visibly overwhelmed?
- Have external dependencies become unreliable?
- Are journalists or influencers asking unexpected questions?

This kind of signal detection can be incorporated into sprint reviews, weekly production updates, or leadership meetings.

CRISIS MANAGEMENT IN THE GAMES INDUSTRY: KEY CASE EXAMPLES

I think it is much easier to understand crisis management through examples, so here are some real ones.

Launch-Day Server Failures

Trigger: The release of highly anticipated online games like *Diablo III* (2012) and *SimCity* (2013) led to server overloads, rendering the games unplayable at launch (Alexander, 2013; Blizzard Entertainment, 2012).

Impact: Players faced login errors (notably *Diablo III*'s "Error 37") and connectivity issues, leading to widespread frustration and negative publicity (Alexander, 2013).

Response: Blizzard and EA issued apologies and worked to stabilise servers, but the initial damage to reputation was significant (Blizzard Entertainment, 2012).

Lessons Learned: The importance of robust server infrastructure and stress testing before launch cannot be overstated.

Security Breaches and Data Leaks

Trigger: CD Projekt RED suffered a ransomware attack in 2021, compromising internal data and source code. Riot Games faced a similar breach in 2023 involving *League of Legends* source code (CD Projekt RED, 2021; McKinnon, 2023).

Impact: Sensitive data was leaked online, posing risks to company operations and player trust.

Response: Both companies acknowledged the breaches, refused to pay ransoms and worked to mitigate the damage.

Lessons Learned: Implementing strong cybersecurity measures and having a crisis response plan are essential.

Regulatory Challenges Over Loot Boxes

Trigger: EA faced legal scrutiny in Belgium over the use of loot boxes in games like *FIFA*, with authorities deeming them a form of gambling (Esports Insider, 2018).

Impact: The company was under criminal investigation and faced potential fines and reputational damage.

Response: EA eventually ceased the sale of FIFA Points in Belgium to comply with regulations (Graft, 2019).

Lessons Learned: Adhering to regional laws and ethical considerations in game monetisation is crucial.

Workplace Culture and Harassment Allegations

Trigger: Reports emerged of toxic workplace environments at companies like Riot Games and Ubisoft, including allegations of harassment and discrimination (Condis, 2021; France 24, 2024).

Impact: These revelations led to lawsuits, employee walkouts and significant public backlash.

Response: Riot agreed to a $100 million settlement. Ubisoft executives faced legal proceedings and increased scrutiny.

Lessons Learned: Fostering a respectful and inclusive workplace culture is both ethical and vital for sustainability.

Leaked Game Content

Trigger: In 2020, significant plot details and gameplay footage of *The Last of Us Part II* were leaked online ahead of its official release (Reddit, 2020).

Impact: The leaks sparked controversy and debates among fans, potentially affecting the game's marketing strategy.

Response: Naughty Dog and Sony addressed the leaks publicly, urging fans to avoid spoilers and promising a complete narrative experience on launch (Hernandez, 2020).

Lessons Learned: Strengthening internal security and managing communication effectively are key in such scenarios.

Monetisation Backlash

Trigger: *Star Wars Battlefront II* faced severe criticism for its loot box system, which many perceived as "pay-to-win" (Kuchera, 2017).

Impact: The backlash led to plummeting sales, negative press and regulatory debates around gambling in games (Kain, 2017).

Response: EA temporarily removed microtransactions and overhauled the progression system.

Lessons Learned: Transparent and fair monetisation practices are essential to maintain player trust.

Bug-Ridden Game Launches

Trigger: *Cyberpunk 2077* launched with numerous bugs and performance issues, especially on last-gen consoles (Hern, 2020) (IGN, 2020).

Impact: The game's reputation suffered, leading to widespread refunds and removal from the PlayStation Store.

Response: CD Projekt RED issued apologies and committed to post-launch fixes, pushing multiple large patches (CD Projekt RED, 2021).

Lessons Learned: Ensuring a polished product at launch is critical. Rushing to market can create long-term brand damage.

Political Controversies

Trigger: Blizzard Entertainment banned a professional *Hearthstone* player for expressing support for Hong Kong protests during a live stream (VanDerWerff, 2019).

Impact: The decision led to global criticism, boycotts and heated debates around freedom of speech and corporate neutrality (Gamma Law, 2019).

Response: Blizzard reduced the player's suspension and issued public statements to explain their position.

Lessons Learned: Companies must navigate geopolitical sensitivities carefully, balancing market access with internal values and external expectations.

Use these as case prompts in team retros or simulation prep. Ask: "What would we do if this happened to us?"

KEY COMPONENTS OF CRISIS MANAGEMENT

Every effective crisis response comprises three core phases:

1. Preparation

This is about laying the groundwork before anything goes wrong:

- Establish a crisis response team and assign clear roles
- Identify necessary stakeholders (legal, IT, production, PR, etc.)

- Define protocols: What steps must be followed and who is contacted at each stage?

While these actions may seem mundane, they prove invaluable when a crisis strikes. When I have sat in on security breaches involving data leaks, I was extremely relieved that such preparation had been undertaken prior to me joining the company. Information was sent to the right people at the right time and we all understood our roles.

2. Response
When the crisis occurs:

- **Triage the Situation**: What exactly is the crisis?

- **Contain the Impact**: How can the situation be prevented from worsening?

- **Communicate**: Who needs to be informed and what is the message?

One useful component of your communication plan is a **holding statement**. This is a short, pre-approved message acknowledging that something has gone wrong, while buying time for a fuller update. These can be drafted in advance and adapted quickly.

Example: "We are aware of performance issues affecting matchmaking. Our teams are working to resolve the issue, and we will share more details shortly".

These statements reduce panic, maintain credibility and give your internal teams breathing space during high-pressure incidents.

Clear, structured action is only possible when preparation has been thorough.

3. Recovery
After the immediate crisis:

- Stabilise systems, personnel and processes

- Conduct retrospectives to identify what succeeded and what failed

- Update protocols based on new insights

This final point is easy to skip over, but it is critical. You must update your protocols if any improvements are spotted or information that proves incorrect.

CRISIS MANAGEMENT PLANS

A crisis plan is a tailored playbook for the most challenging days of development. It combines risk foresight with operational readiness. It will slow down any impending heart attacks, and you will be proud of the team involved when such a plan is in place and everyone cracks on with what they need to do.

Essential components include:

- **Crisis Risk Assessment**: Identify which risks could escalate into crises

- **Escalation Paths**: Define who is informed, in what order and at what threshold. For clarity, link these escalation paths to your existing RACI matrix. This ensures everyone understands not just who is informed, but who is expected to act, approve, or support decisions.

  Example: A risk affecting legal compliance might trigger an escalation to the Director of Compliance, who is marked as *Accountable* in the RACI. This clarity prevents hesitation and finger-pointing in fast-moving situations.

- **Communication Strategies**: Plan messages for internal stakeholders, legal obligations and public channels

  Example: If preparing for the launch of a multiplayer game, server instability should be anticipated:

- **Assign Roles**: Who manages infrastructure, player communication and platform coordination?

- **Prepare Backup Actions**: Can server capacity be scaled instantly?

- **Draft External Communications** in advance, including breach notification templates

Legal and security experts should contribute to defining these plans. If such teams are not available, know where to seek assistance and be prepared to pay for the services to be brought in. It will prove cheaper in the long run. Plans must be created before they are needed – they are not meant to be drafted in real time under pressure.

CRISIS RESPONSE PLAYBOOK

A structured, reusable guide to crisis handling. Includes:

- Roles and escalation contact list
- Crisis type triggers and thresholds
- Pre-written messages and holding statements
- Technical fallback procedures (e.g. rolling back builds, pausing liveops)
- External contact protocols (e.g. platform holders, PR firms, legal)

This is the wiki page that someone grabs when everything goes sideways. It is most valuable when it has been rehearsed, not just written.

Simulating Crisis Response: Pressure-Testing the Team

Crisis simulations are one of the most effective ways to prepare. These are not about box-ticking, but they are exercises in pressure-testing people, plans, and systems. They are far more enjoyable and effective than you might think.

You bring in the right people and say: Here is a situation. You do not have a perfect plan. What is your move? Role-play who leads, who informs, who triages. It is like Apollo 13, only with less chance of dying.

Tabletop Exercises and Simulated Scenarios
Simulations allow teams to rehearse their response before a real crisis hits. Tabletop exercises present realistic, fast-moving scenarios where participants must decide how to react under pressure.

- Game-breaking bug discovered at launch
- Player data leaked from a security breach
- Server overload halts multiplayer functionality

During these exercises, facilitators should prompt discussion:

- What are our first three actions?
- Who takes the lead?
- What will we tell players, stakeholders, or the press?

Live Role-Play: Practising Real-Time Decision-Making
To heighten realism, assign specific roles, such as:

- Producer
- Lead engineer
- Community manager
- Supporting roles

Provide situational updates in real time:

- Three hours post-incident: What is the current status?
- Players are posting complaints online: What is the message?
- Do you push a hotfix or roll back?

These simulations often surface practical gaps such as missing tools, unclear ownership, or misaligned escalation paths. Capturing these insights live can lead directly to improved crisis protocols. Teams may begin documenting real crisis workflows during the session itself.

Simulation Debrief: Embedding the Learning

After each exercise, hold a structured debrief:

- What went well?
- What failed?
- What changes are required?

This is often where the most valuable insights emerge. Teams may realise:

- Social media messages can be pre-written
- Escalation paths need clarity
- Real-time visibility tools must be improved

Simulations not only prepare teams, but they also strengthen cohesion. Teams that practise navigating chaos are more effective during actual emergencies.

The real value of crisis is cultural: You build trust, resilience, and reflexes. A good crisis response builds pride, not shame.

In the Appendix you will find:

- Crisis Day Agenda (hour-by-hour prompts)
- Roles and personas (e.g. CM, QA lead, platform liaison)
- Situational cards (incident escalation triggers)

CAPTURING LESSONS LEARNED FROM CRISIS RESPONSE

Every crisis leaves behind lessons. Capturing those insights is vital – not just for preventing repeat errors, but for refining how a studio operates under pressure. Instead of simply listing tasks, this section encourages teams to see lessons learned as an evolving system of improvement.

Post-Crisis Review: What Actually Happened?

After a crisis, it is easy to move on too quickly. But without proper review, your team misses the opportunity to improve. Hold structured, facilitated reviews that look at:

- What occurred?
- What was effective?
- Where did processes fail?

Useful tools for this phase include structured team debriefs, process evaluations, and visualised timelines of how the crisis unfolded. These help separate perception from reality.

Reviews should be blameless, forward-looking, and grounded in psychological safety. The goal is not to assign fault, but to identify what can be improved. This is the perfect time to hear out ideas, have valuable but safe arguments, and take away actions to investigate further anything that cannot be resolved immediately.

From Debrief to Documentation

Once insights are gathered, formalise them in a simple shared document. Good documentation answers:

- What would be done differently?

- What immediate changes are required?

- What should other teams know?

Example Entries:

- Consider phased patch rollouts to reduce the risk of widespread regressions

- Allocate contingency budget for QA tooling during pre-launch crunch periods

This documentation becomes a foundation for future planning and improvement.

Continuous Improvement: Turning Lessons into Action

The final phase of learning is action. It is not enough to identify issues, but you need to apply what you have learned. Teams should review prior crises during roadmap planning or milestone retrospectives. Focus on practical changes that reduce fragility:

- Update playbooks

- Improve detection mechanisms

- Add simulation scenarios

Not all improvement requires more tools, of course. Sometimes it is about making better decisions.
   Example: If server issues were repeated, the response may include:

- Expanding server capacity

- Investing in load testing

When teams take the time to analyse crises, they gradually build resilience. They become not only better at recovery, but faster and calmer in the face of future challenges. A resilient studio is not one without problems, but it is one that knows how to handle them.

A crisis is not failure. It is learning in fast forward. What you capture here can build QA headcount, unlock tool budgets, or streamline future go-lives. Capture it or repeat it.

RECOMMENDED TEMPLATES AND RESOURCES

These may not be immediately suitable, but they can be modified:

1. Smartsheet Crisis Management Templates

Smartsheet offers a suite of free, downloadable templates – including crisis management plans, communication checklists, and tabletop exercise guides. These templates are well-suited for adapting to game studio needs, covering aspects like team roles, escalation paths, and communication protocols. https://www.smartsheet.com/content/crisis-management-templates

2. HubSpot Crisis Communication Kit

HubSpot provides a comprehensive crisis communication plan template, complete with sections for stakeholder mapping, messaging strategies, and post-crisis reviews. This resource is particularly useful for managing public relations during crises. https://blog.hubspot.com/service/crisis-communication-plan

3. Change the Game Academy's 7-Step Crisis Plan

This resource offers a straightforward, step-by-step guide to building a crisis management plan, focusing on risk assessment, response strategies, and evaluation. While designed for non-profits, its principles are broadly applicable. https://www.changethegameacademy.org/shortmodule/crisis-management-plan/

4. NCJFCJ Crisis Management Plan Template (DOCX)

This editable Word document provides a structured format for developing a crisis management plan, including prompts for identifying risks, defining response teams, and outlining communication strategies. https://www.ncjfcj.org/wp-content/uploads/2022/03/crisis-management-plan-template.docx

Adapting Templates for Game Development

When customising these templates for the games industry, consider incorporating elements specific to your operations:

- **Technical Infrastructure**: Detail protocols for server maintenance, load balancing, and emergency patches.

- **Community Management**: Establish guidelines for moderating forums, social media responses, and player communication during crises.

- **Regulatory Compliance**: Include procedures for adhering to data protection laws and industry regulations.

- **Postmortem Analysis**: Plan for conducting thorough reviews after a crisis to identify lessons learnt and improve future responses.

By integrating these industry-specific considerations into a general crisis management framework, you can create a comprehensive plan tailored to the unique challenges of game development.

REFERENCES

Alexander, L. (2013). SimCity launches to critical acclaim and crippling server problems. *The Verge*. Retrieved from: https://www.theverge.com/2013/3/14/4103140/simcity-launch-and-server-problems

Blizzard Entertainment. (2012). Blizzard apologises for Diablo 3 launch server problems. *Reddit Discussion*. Retrieved from: https://www.reddit.com/r/Diablo/comments/trfdd/blizzard_apologises_for_diablo_3_launch_server/

CD Projekt RED. (2021). *Security breach update*. Retrieved from: https://www.cdprojekt.com/en/media/news/security-breach-update/

Condis, M. (2021). Riot Games agrees to pay $100M in gender discrimination lawsuit. *Axios*. Retrieved from: https://www.axios.com/2021/12/28/riot-games-agrees-to-pay-100m-in-gender-discrimination-lawsuit

Esports Insider. (2018). *EA under criminal investigation in Belgium due to loot boxes*. Retrieved from: https://esportsinsider.com/2018/09/ea-under-criminal-investigation-in-belgium-due-to-loot-boxes

France 24. (2024). *Former Ubisoft bosses on trial in France over alleged harassment*. Retrieved from: https://www.france24.com/en/live-news/20250310-former-ubisoft-bosses-on-trial-in-france-over-alleged-harassment-1

Gamma Law. (2019). *Blizzard's controversial 'blitzchung' ruling*. Retrieved from: https://gammalaw.com/blizzards-controversial-blitzchung-ruling/

Graft, K. (2019). EA amends FIFA loot boxes in Belgium after regulators increase pressure. *Game Developer*. Retrieved from: https://www.gamedeveloper.com/business/ea-amends-i-fifa-i-loot-boxes-in-belgium-after-regulators-increase-pressure

Hern, A. (2020). Cyberpunk 2077: Sony pulls game from PlayStation store after complaints. *The Guardian*. Retrieved from: https://www.theguardian.com/games/2020/dec/18/cyberpunk-2077-sony-pulls-game-from-playstation-store-after-complaints

Hernandez, P. (2020). Even if you saw the leaks, you are not prepared for 'The Last of Us Part II'. *The Washington Post*. Retrieved from: https://www.washingtonpost.com/video-games/2020/06/12/i-saw-leaks-thought-i-knew-i-was-still-not-prepared-last-us-part-ii/

IGN. (2020). *Cyberpunk 2077's best bugs and glitches* [YouTube video]. Retrieved from: https://www.youtube.com/watch?v=wPcPDanmeCQ

Kain, E. (2017). EA shares plummet after 'star wars: Battlefront II' loot box fiasco. *Forbes*. Retrieved from: https://www.forbes.com/sites/erikkain/2017/11/28/ea-shares-plummet-after-star-wars-battlefront-ii-loot-box-fiasco/

Kuchera, B. (2017). Star Wars Battlefront 2's loot crate controversy. *Polygon*. Retrieved from: https://www.polygon.com/2017/11/13/16646692/star-wars-battlefront-2-loot-crate-controversy-ea

McKinnon, D. (2023). Riot Games says League of Legends' source code stolen in cyberattack. *Axios*. Retrieved from: https://www.axios.com/2023/01/24/riot-games-league-of-legends-source-code-cyberattack

Reddit. (2020). *The last of Us Part II: A look back at the major leaks & rumours*. Retrieved from: https://www.reddit.com/r/Games/comments/i81yab/the_last_of_us_part_ii_a_look_back_at_the_major/

VanDerWerff, E. (2019). Blizzard Hong Kong controversy: What happened and why it matters. *Vox*. Retrieved from: https://www.vox.com/2019/10/8/20904433/blizzard-hong-kong-hearthstone-blitzchung

CHAPTER 14

Three Levels – Project, Program and Portfolio

OVERVIEW: THREE LENSES = THREE OVERLAPPING CONVERSATIONS

When we talk about risk management across game development, it is not just one conversation that covers all levels. Three overlapping conversations happen at three levels: Project, program and portfolio. I like to see these three levels as lenses. As you move up, the lens widens – from executing work, to managing complexity, to steering strategy. The conversation changes. So does the responsibility. As you move from project up to portfolio, the lens zooms out: Each level seeing more, involving more and requiring a different flavour of discussion and decision-making.

At a Glance: Three Levels Compared

Lens	Primary Focus	Core Risk Types	Common Responsibilities
Project	Tactical execution and delivery	Technical, resource, scope, scheduling	Feature development, sprint planning, issue response
Program	Coordination and interdependency	Cross-team blockers, misalignment	Roadmapping, dependency mapping, stakeholder alignment
Portfolio	Strategic alignment and viability	Market, investment, governance	Diversification, M&A, strategic pivots

PROJECT-LEVEL RISK MANAGEMENT

Lens Overview

Project level is where the action happens. This is about the now – the sprints, the builds, the features. When you are in it, you are not just managing risk; you are living it. You are inside the trees, not up in the helicopter. At this level, risk management is survival – tactical,

DOI: 10.1201/9781003646082-16

immediate and crucial. You are in the weeds. The issues you surface are already live. What changes with the introduction of risk management is that you structure your cry for help and hence turn escalation into a process.

Focus
Specific, tactical risks within a single game development project.

Core Activities

- Identifying relevant risks.
- Implementing targeted mitigation strategies.
- Communicating risks clearly to those affected.

Common Examples

- Building a new feature.
- Implementing an art pipeline tool.
- Delivering a marketing campaign.
- Managing outsource deliverables.

Deep Dive: Execution-Level Risk in Action
As I often say when teaching the accompany online course on Udemy – you are working "in the weeds" here. You are not theorising about what might go wrong months from now, you are dealing with issues that are already happening. Performance bugs, scope drift, technical gaps – they are live. You need to act.

Risk management here is how you think, how you plan, and how you get help. Instead of raising your voice and hoping someone notices a blocker, you have structure. You have escalation paths. You have ways of saying, "This is serious", without needing a crisis to prove it.

This is the front line – bugs, blockers, shifting scope. You do not just track risk – you live it.

Identifying Risks: Use retros, planning sessions, Jira boards and check-ins to flag:

- Bugs and performance issues
- Staffing gaps or burnout
- Scope creep and blocked dependencies

Mitigating Risk: Practical techniques include:

- Testing protocols (unit, integration, UAT)

- Contingency plans and resource buffers

- Prioritising by risk level and team capacity

Communicating Risks:

- Daily standups

- Transparent risk tagging in project tools

- Status updates that include risk – not just progress

Examples from Practice:

- One studio embedded risk reviews into their sprint planning to spot and address memory leaks early

- Another reduced stakeholder misalignment by inviting marketing and execs into bi-weekly sprint demos

Conclusion: At project level, risk management is survival. You fix problems before they become failures.

PROGRAM-LEVEL RISK MANAGEMENT

Lens Overview

The program lens is where coordination dominates. This is where production directors, lead producers and discipline heads live. Program conversations are dominated by interdependencies. Pull one thread, ten others tighten. You manage the ripple effects before they become blockers. Risk management here is about juggling interdependencies and seeing the knock-on effects before they cause damage.

Focus

Managing risks across multiple, related projects – where interdependencies live.

Core Activities

- Navigating interdependencies and resource allocation

- Aligning stakeholders and delivery plans

- Tracking cross-team blockers

- Monitoring and adjusting program-level roadmaps

- Visualising and dealing with dependencies

Common Examples

- Coordinating multiple departments to ship a game

- Delivering shared backend services across studios

- Aligning liveops, marketing and support

SIDEBAR: WEEKLY PROGRAM RISK REVIEW – SAMPLE AGENDA

1. Dependency check
2. Staffing overlaps
3. Cross-team blockers
4. Stakeholder alignment review

Deep Dive: Coordinated Complexity

Program-level conversations are dominated by one word – interdependency. You do not just manage delivery; you manage the ripple effects between teams, functions and sometimes even studios.

You feel this most when a tool is not ready, and downstream teams grind to a halt. Or when marketing is promoting a feature that engineering quietly de-scoped three weeks ago. Good risk management at program level means people are not surprised. It means decisions have backup plans and blockers have pathways.

Programs are about orchestrating people, priorities and progress across shifting landscapes – balancing teams and deadlines while ensuring alignment across the moving parts.

Key Techniques:

- **Dependency mapping**: Understand what relies on what

- **Capacity mapping**: See who is overextended

- **Shared calendars and dashboards**: Create program-wide visibility

Stakeholder Risk: One of the most critical program risks is misalignment. Prevent it by:

- Communicating strategic vision early and often

- Ensuring team leads understand their part in the whole

- Escalating risks before they impact milestones

Feedback Loops:

- Run program-level risk reviews regularly

- Adapt your roadmap based on changing player feedback or team velocity

Conclusion: Program-level risk is about orchestration. It is not only what's being built, but how it all fits together.

PORTFOLIO-LEVEL RISK MANAGEMENT

Lens Overview

Think of portfolio level as the outer layer of the onion – the wrapper that holds everything else together. This is executive territory: Strategic bets, investor relations, governance. It is less about making the game and more about making sure the business behind the game survives and thrives. At this level, you deal with existential risk. These are the calls that keep studios alive – or sink them. It is not sexy. But this is the real work of strategic steering.

> **SIDEBAR: RISK QUESTIONS FOR EXECS**
> - "Where are we overexposed?"
> - "Which bets depend on unproven platforms or teams?"
> - "Are our incentives aligned with our risk tolerance?"
>
> You do not need a crisis to justify strategic change. Use risk reviews to challenge 'sacred cows' such as projects, platforms and pipelines that no longer fit your future.

Focus

Strategic, long-range risks across the entire studio or company.

Core Activities

- Balancing risk and return

- Diversifying products and platforms

- Aligning initiatives with company strategy

- Monitoring external trends and compliance risks

Common Examples

- Studio-wide investment decisions

- Transformation programs

- Strategic M&A or market entry

- Platform diversification

Deep Dive: Big Bets and Existential Risk

At portfolio level, you are dealing with the existential stuff: Where are we going, and are we putting the right resources behind the right risks? I have sat in board meetings where delays at the feature level sparked investor concern – because those delays were not just timeline blips, they were forecast-impacting, trust-breaking events.

Portfolio risk management is deciding whether to diversify platforms, whether to restructure, whether to cut a game that is 18 months into development because market trends have shifted. These are the decisions that make or break companies.

And yes, I have also seen those "random executive ideas" filter down – like pivoting an entire art style based on a trend video. Silly in isolation, but powerful if unchecked. Risk management here gives you a framework to challenge ideas early, with structure and data behind you.

These are high-stakes risks – the kind that determine whether a business thrives, pivots or folds. They are not just about what's being made, but about how the entire enterprise steers through uncertainty.

Strategic Techniques:

- Risk-adjusted ROI and scenario planning

- Aligning IP and monetisation strategies with brand and audience

- Rebalancing investment between core franchises and innovation

Environmental Risk Awareness:

- Regulatory changes (e.g. loot box legislation)

- Talent market shifts

- Tech platform consolidation (e.g. engine dependencies)

WHAT HAPPENS WHEN RISK IS NOT MANAGED

38 Studios – The Cost of Overreach (Wikipedia, 2024a)

- Raised $75 million in public funding

- **Released *Kingdoms of Amalur*:** *Reckoning* but failed to complete their MMO *Project Copernicus*

- Collapsed under financial strain from poor portfolio-level planning and overextension

- No clear staged investment gates or strategic contingency paths

Risk Insight: A gated investment model and clearer risk tolerance could have preserved capital and prevented collapse.

Blizzard's *Odyssey* – Sunk by Engine Risk (Wikipedia, 2024b)

- Cancelled after six years of development due to reliance on a proprietary engine
- Massive technical overhead slowed progress and led to escalating delays
- Ultimately deemed unviable despite internal investment

Risk Insight: Program-level risk reviews, technical feasibility assessments and transparent escalation could have surfaced engine concerns earlier, enabling a pivot or reset.

Conclusion: Portfolio risk thinking is how you stay viable – not just efficient. It is how studios survive the next wave.

INTERCONNECTION BETWEEN LEVELS

There is a great deal of interconnectivity – and realising that is empowering. Risks do not stay in their lane. A delayed backend feature can ripple into art, outsource and schedule collapse. And it can end in a boardroom apology if investors were promised delivery. What starts as a seemingly minor issue – a broken feature pipeline – can spiral into a full program derailment, outsourcing chaos and ultimately, portfolio-level delays.

I have sat in board meetings where executives were forced to revise investor updates because game timelines shifted. That level of exposure – when someone senior has publicly committed to a release date – cannot afford surprises. Risk has to be surfaced early. You might have to spend money to fix it. You might need to isolate a person or team so they can get work done without interruptions. Whatever the solution, you need to act before it explodes upward.

But this flow is not one-way. Strategic decisions cascade down too. A portfolio-level pivot – like cancelling a genre due to market forecasts – can instantly derail multiple in-flight programs and invalidate months of project-level work. Sometimes these decisions are well-informed. Sometimes they are "we watched a YouTube trend video and now everything's red and gold". Either way, risks need to be surfaced early and fed back – risk management empowers you to influence decisions before they create chaos.

And remember, some risks lie dormant. You might sit on an external dependency for months, powerless. But when it breaks, it can trigger a cascade. That's why communication channels matter so much.

Effective Communication Channels

- **Regular Reporting**: Everyone keeps talking to each other across the levels, utilising existing or newly formed channels
- **Aggregated Summaries**: Digestible risk snapshots for executive audiences
- **Audience Awareness**: Executives are flooded with input. If you want support, make it easy for them to see the big risks and act.

The goal is to shape your communication so others can help. If you do not escalate, they cannot support. If you do not simplify, they will not absorb.

COLLABORATIVE RISK MANAGEMENT AND INTEGRATION

A cohesive strategy for risk is not written in a binder – it is lived across levels. And it only works when people collaborate.

I often say this: A shared risk appetite, escalation logic and proactive plan are not abstract ideas. They are the foundations of psychological safety. Teams feel empowered to surface problems because they know they will not be punished for telling the truth. That only happens with transparency and shared understanding.

What This Looks Like:

- Alignment on strategy and appetite from execs to teams

- Empowered, safe-to-speak-up culture

- Visible, evolving risk logs embedded in workflow tools

Benefits of Integration:

- You avoid silent bottlenecks

- You reduce surprise pivots

- You respond, adapt and learn continuously

I have seen the opposite too. Where people did not speak up, or did not realise it was their job to raise concerns, and everything crashed because of it. Your best defence is a shared culture where risk is normal, not taboo. And where everyone – from sprint teams to the boardroom – knows how to speak the same risk language.

SIDEBAR: THE OWNERSHIP VACUUM

One of the most common pitfalls I've seen in my career...is unclear ownership...Without a clear 'this is mine' moment, the momentum stalls...A simple fix is to always ask "who owns this?"...Assigning a single point of accountability early on – even if others take supporting roles – saves a huge amount of pain later on.

– SHAUN BOND, SENIOR PRODUCER/PROJECT LEAD

Managing risk relies on transparency, shared responsibility and a culture where surfacing problems is safe and expected.

What This Looks Like:

- Shared taxonomies and templates across teams
- Escalation paths that make sense
- Tools that link project boards to program dashboards and portfolio KPIs

Integrated Framework Benefits:

- Smoother delivery
- Sustainable workflows
- Better cross-level decision-making
- Lower failure rate on big bets

When Integration Breaks, Organisations Suffer from:

- Siloed teams
- Conflicting priorities
- Missed signals and duplicated work

Fixing it often starts with portfolio-level leadership and systemic tooling.

Summary: Why This Structure Matters

This chapter introduced a practical and scalable model for understanding and communicating risk through three interrelated lenses:

- **Project**: Where risk is immediate, executional and tactical
- **Program**: Where risk is relational, coordinated and systemic
- **Portfolio**: Where risk is strategic, existential and business-defining

Each level must speak to the others – because when they do not, risks grow unnoticed, mitigation comes too late and alignment collapses. That's why the lens model matters: It doesn't just help you see risk – it helps you see who needs to hear about it and when.

REFERENCES

Wikipedia. (2024a). *38 Studios*. Retrieved from: https://en.wikipedia.org/wiki/38_Studios
Wikipedia. (2024b). *Odyssey (cancelled video game)*. Retrieved from: https://en.wikipedia.org/wiki/Odyssey_(cancelled_video_game)

PART III

Game Development Risks

Introduction

L ET ME BE CLEAR up front: game development is messy. It is exciting, creative, unpredictable and full of hidden traps. I have seen brilliant ideas fall apart not because of a lack of vision or talent, but because of risks or issues that were never named, never tracked and never owned. And the tools we borrow from other industries – construction, manufacturing, even mainstream software – do not always help.

Game development is not a factory line. You are building something with emergent properties – part software, part art, part service. It is a cultural product, perhaps a work of art, with commercial constraints. It is iterative, collaborative and filled with uncertainty. This single game can take three or more years to turn from an idea into a released product. That product changes while it is being built. The target audience evolves. Sometimes even the platform shifts beneath your feet.

In this world, traditional risk management practices fall short. You cannot Gantt chart your way out of systemic dysfunction. You cannot manage risk like a spreadsheet. You need situational awareness, cultural literacy and, above all, communication across disciplines.

One of the things that fascinates me most about game risk is how invisible it is until it is too late. I have worked with teams who did not realise they were in trouble until the demo failed live. It was not because of one person, but rather because everyone assumed someone else had flagged the risk. Or that if no one had raised it, it must be fine. We confuse silence with safety.

I have also seen studios with the opposite problem: every team flags everything, but nothing gets resolved. Risk becomes noise. Nobody owns the register. Nobody follows

DOI: 10.1201/9781003646082-17

through. It just becomes another dashboard people ignore until the raging fires can no longer be ignored.

This section of the book is about surfacing those risks.

Here is what makes risk in games unique:

- You are innovating with incomplete information.

- You are judged by an audience that does not care how hard it was.

- Your most risky features are often the ones leadership is emotionally invested in.

- Your pipelines and tools are often mid-evolution.

- Your staff are often overworked, under-resourced and told to hit a moving target.

A seemingly good decision – like giving the design team more freedom – can create unmanageable scope unless it is framed, documented and timeboxed. A platform deal might look strategic, but if the SDK is not ready, it introduces months of technical fragility. A leadership reshuffle might sound benign, but it can stall sign-offs and introduce stakeholder drift.

Games are volatile, creative, late-binding systems. They do not behave like enterprise apps or mechanical supply chains. They break quietly and collectively. And the better the team, the more likely they are to silently absorb risk – until they cannot.

As explained in Part II, categorising risks assists us in better understanding some of the common types and mitigation strategies within those categories.

Due to the overlapping nature of making a game and running studios, we can expect some duplication in these sections and references back and forth. I felt this was more useful for you, my busy reader.

How to Read the Sections

Each section is structured using a consistent and reader-friendly format designed to support both deep learning and practical application. This structure was developed specifically for game development professionals and reflects real-world challenges encountered across studios, platforms and production scales.

The sections follow this format:

1. Section Introduction

2. A short explanation of the relevance of the risk area and its impact on games industry outcomes.

3. Common Risk Triggers

4. Bullet-point breakdowns of the most frequent or high-impact causes, often drawn from lived industry experience.

5. Mitigation Strategies

6. Practical, actionable approaches for teams, producers and leadership. Where appropriate, strategies are grouped (e.g. by tooling, process, or cultural factors).

7. Real-World Examples

8. Verified case studies drawn from published sources or professional experience, with proper citations provided in the References section. These tend to be integrated within the section but sometimes have their own section.

9. Key Risk Patterns *(where applicable)*

10. Recurring antipatterns or "named failures" with mitigation checklists. These are particularly useful for initial risk identification workshops, postmortems, retrospectives and team training. There is more explanation below.

11. References

12. Full citations of all examples, data points and external sources, so you can explore them further.

Key Risk Patterns

In this part of the book, you will find many recurring sections titled *Key Risk Patterns*. These are structured frameworks based on common failure modes observed across the games industry. Inspired by software design patterns, Agile antipatterns and scientific research (see *Part VI's Anti Pattern Risk Deck*), each one includes:

- A short definition of the risk archetype
- A concrete example drawn from real-world or case studies
- A mitigation checklist to support practical application

These patterns are not theoretical. They are distilled from studio retrospectives, postmortem reports, developer blogs and first-hand industry experience. Their purpose is to:

- Help studios name and recognise high-risk patterns early
- Enable producers and leads to standardise responses
- Serve as training artefacts for cross-functional development teams

These patterns are designed to help teams break the cycle of repeating the same behaviours of others, without recognising that there is another way.

CHAPTER 15

Technical Risks

Technical risks are some of the most common and challenging issues faced in game development. They are also often the most immediate and tangible. They arise due to the complexity of modern game engines, platform requirements, the wish to push barriers and the constant evolution of technology.

COMMON RISK TRIGGERS

- **Game Engine and Middleware Issues**: The game engine is the foundation of development and any instability, lack of support or integration challenges can have a major impact. Middleware tools for physics, AI or networking may introduce unforeseen compatibility problems. Choosing the wrong middleware can lead to massive inefficiencies down the line.

- **Engine Upgrades**: Changing from one engine to another mid-development (e.g. moving from Unity to Unreal) can introduce massive risks in asset compatibility, rendering and performance. Upgrades can lead to delays and unexpected newly discovered bugs *(Epic Games, 2021)*.

- **Platform Compatibility**: Developing for multiple platforms introduces risk in terms of optimisation, certification requirements and performance discrepancies. A feature that works on one platform might break on another, and certification failures can delay releases significantly.

- **Hardware Limitations**: Optimising for multiple platforms (PC, console, mobile) introduces performance risks, particularly when cross-platform parity is required.

- **Software Integration**: Risks associated with integrating third-party software (e.g. asset management, physics engines, multiplayer services) that may not function as expected.

- **Server Stability:** Multiplayer and live service games rely on robust server infrastructure. Poor scalability, unexpected player spikes or security vulnerabilities can result in game-breaking issues post-launch. Many studios underestimate the server load on launch, leading to frustrating downtime and a reputational hit.

- **Release Management and Deployment Failures**: Failed builds, issues with digital distribution platforms or mismanaged day-one patches can lead to disastrous launches. If deployment pipelines are not automated and properly tested, last-minute issues can result in broken builds (*GDC Vault, 2020*)

- **Security Risks**: Cheating, hacking and data breaches can damage player trust and compromise game integrity, leading to negative publicity and potential legal action. Games with poor anti-cheat or weak security protocols can become easy targets for exploiters, leading to long-term reputation damage.

- **Online Infrastructure Risks**: Server stability, netcode reliability and live-service backend scaling are high-risk factors, as seen in many botched online launches.

Example: A studio builds a game on a proprietary engine that lacks support for large open-world streaming. Late in development, they realise the engine struggles to handle dynamic asset loading, causing severe performance issues. Retrofitting a solution takes months of unplanned development time.

Table: Technical Risk Trigger Matrix

Trigger Type	Common Risks	Detection Method	Mitigation Prompt
Engine/Tech	Engine instability, upgrade impact	Performance profiling, build time anomalies	Early prototyping, version control
Platform	Cert failure, missing platform specs	Submission dry-runs, dev kit flags	Pre-cert planning, lock targets early
Server	Netcode spikes, infra overload	Load test simulation	Throttle points, prelaunch shadow runs

Always ask: "Are we assuming something will 'just work'?" That is where risk hides.

THE CREATIVE VS TECHNICAL BALANCE

Unlike many industries where risk assessment focuses solely on technical feasibility and financial stability, game development introduces a creative layer of unpredictability:

- **Creative Vision Conflicts**: What a designer envisions may not be technically feasible or it may change based on playtesting feedback.

- **Iterative Gameplay Tuning**: Unlike traditional software, where a product is built to meet specifications, fun is subjective and requires ongoing iteration.

- **Player Expectations**: Market trends shift rapidly. What was innovative a year ago may feel outdated upon release.

Are designers asking for the impossible? Are engineers pretending it is possible, or are they over-enthusiastic? If yes, you may be on fire and not know it yet.

Example: *No Man's Sky*

When *No Man's Sky* was announced, its ambitious vision of procedural planets, deep exploration and endless possibilities generated huge excitement. However, upon release, several promised features were missing, leading to a backlash. The risk wasn't just technical – it was the gap between expectations and reality. Over time, the developers worked to deliver on their vision, but the initial launch demonstrates how creative ambition can create major risk exposure if not managed properly *(Digital Foundry, 2016)*.

Case Study: *The Last Guardian*

The extended development of *The Last Guardian* wasn't just about technical hurdles – it was a perfect storm of multiple risk factors that compounded over time. The game's delays were not due to a singular issue but rather a combination of:

- **Technology Limitations**: The original PS3 hardware could not handle the complex physics and AI-driven behaviours planned for the game, leading to multiple engine overhauls.

- **Shifting Development Priorities**: Internal restructuring at Sony meant that the game was deprioritised at certain stages, leading to a loss of momentum.

- **Leadership and Team Changes**: The project lost key staff over time, requiring retraining of new team members and a steep learning curve to adapt to the previous work.

- **Project Scaling Risks**: Moving from PS3 to PS4 was not just a technical shift – it required rebuilding core systems, which added years to the timeline *(Leadbetter, 2016; Schreier, 2017)*.

Lesson: Crisis emerges from compound risks – none are fatal alone, but together they are hugely destabilising.

This also highlights how development risks are not always clear-cut. A technical challenge might start as a medium-severity risk, but over time, its impact can snowball into something far more disruptive. This is why continuous risk assessment is essential; a seemingly small issue at the start of development can evolve into a full-blown crisis if not managed proactively.

MITIGATION STRATEGIES

- **Modular System Design**: Use modular architecture to isolate components and reduce systemic failures.

- **Technical Prototyping**: Build early tech prototypes for core systems (e.g. procedural terrain, large-scale multiplayer).

- **Infrastructure Load Testing**: Simulate launch-day concurrency for multiplayer/backend systems.

- **Version Locking and Rollback Pipelines**: Build safety nets for tools, middleware or engine upgrades.

- **Cross-Platform Testing Early**: Begin certification checklists and performance testing early in development *(MSDN, 2023; Sony Interactive Entertainment, 2022; Nintendo Developer Portal, 2023)*.

- **Security Audits and Anti-Cheat Planning**: Schedule penetration testing and invest in backend analytics to detect suspicious behaviour.

Do not just list these. Choose one per quarter or per month and test it. For example, simulate rollback on a hotfix branch.

PLATFORM AND HARDWARE SPECIFICATIONS

Platform risks stem from changing hardware capabilities, unexpected platform requirements and cross-platform development complexities.

Common Hardware and Platform Risks

- **Mid-Project Platform Additions**: A game initially targeting PC and PlayStation might later be required to launch on Nintendo Switch 2, introducing performance and optimisation risks.

- **Evolving Hardware Specs**: New GPUs or next-gen console hardware may change performance expectations, requiring adjustments late in development.

- **Certification and Compliance Risks**: Sony, Microsoft and Nintendo each have unique submission requirements and failing certification can delay launch by months *(MSDN, 2023; Sony Interactive Entertainment, 2022; Nintendo Developer Portal, 2023)*.

Managing Hardware and Platform Specification Risks

- **Early Communication with Platform Holders**: Ensure that developers understand hardware constraints early.

- **Scalable Game Design**: Building with flexible scalability options prevents late-stage performance bottlenecks.

- **Proactive Performance Testing**: Regular profiling on target hardware ensures compatibility before certification deadlines.

INADEQUATE TECHNICAL SPECIFICATIONS

Technical specifications define performance targets, engine capabilities and system requirements. However, at the beginning of development, many of these details are uncertain because they rely on ongoing discovery and iteration.

Challenges of Incomplete Tech Specs

- **Unclear Performance Targets**: Teams may initially set vague performance goals (e.g. frame rates, resolution) without knowing if they are achievable.

- **Engine and Middleware Choices**: Early decisions on using Unreal Engine, Unity or proprietary engines can later lead to rework if limitations emerge.

- **Evolving System Design**: Engineers may require early collaboration with designers to determine what is technically feasible, but this takes time to solidify.

The Risk of Rework

Because technical specs often evolve, teams may have to redo significant work, leading to schedule delays. For example, an AI system built for open-world pathfinding may need to be rebuilt entirely if the game later shifts to mission-based linear design.

Balancing Flexibility and Documentation

While over-documenting technical specifications too early can be counterproductive, some boundaries must be defined to prevent scope creep. A clear negotiation between tech leads, designers and producers is essential to ensure that:

- Decisions are recorded and communicated effectively.

- Performance expectations are realistic.

- Scope creep does not introduce unsolvable technical challenges.

Key Risk Patterns
The Mid-Dev Engine Switch
A project changes engines or rendering pipelines mid-development.

- **Impact**: Loss of tooling, asset incompatibility and retraining.

- **Mitigation**: Lock engine decisions early. Only change if survival depends on it.

Underspecified Toolchains

Teams build core features without a clear toolchain or automation plan.

- **Impact**: Rework, manual bugs and poor scalability.

- **Mitigation**: Align technical design with production pipelines.

Over-Promise/Under-Deliver Tech

Leadership commits to a feature (e.g. 1000-player MMO battles) without validating feasibility.

- **Impact**: PR damage, scope cuts, morale hits.

- **Mitigation**: Build vertical slices and validate assumptions before announcement.

REFERENCES

Digital Foundry. (2016). No Man's Sky: Technical analysis of the PC and PS4 versions. *Eurogamer.* Retrieved from: https://www.eurogamer.net/digitalfoundry-2016-no-mans-sky-face-off

Epic Games. (2021). *Migrating from UE4 to UE5: Technical considerations.* Unreal Engine Documentation. Retrieved from: https://docs.unrealengine.com

GDC Vault. (2020). *Avoiding day-one disasters: Lessons in launch infrastructure.* Game Developers Conference. Retrieved from: https://www.gdcvault.com

Leadbetter, R. (2016). The last guardian: The digital foundry verdict. *Eurogamer.* Retrieved from: https://www.eurogamer.net/digitalfoundry-2016-the-last-guardian-tech-analysis

Microsoft Developer Network (MSDN). (2023). *Certification requirements for Xbox developers.* Retrieved from: https://learn.microsoft.com/en-us/gaming

Nintendo Developer Portal. (2023). *Certification guidelines and launch considerations.* [Access required]

Schreier, J. (2017). *Blood, sweat and pixels: The triumphant, turbulent stories behind how video games are made.* Harper Paperbacks.

Sony Interactive Entertainment. (2022). *PlayStation submission process: Technical checklist and TRCs.* Developer Support Portal. [Access required]

CHAPTER 16

Design and Art Risks in Game Development

INTRODUCTION

Game development thrives on creativity, but creativity without constraints is a production risk. Both design and art disciplines are inherently iterative and subjective, making them powerful sources of innovation but also potential destabilising forces. This chapter treats design and art risks as separate categories, each with their own triggers and consequences, while acknowledging their frequent points of crossover.

Producers, directors and leads must learn to recognise where design and art decisions become delivery risks: Where unvetted ambition undermines feasibility, or where misalignment between intent and implementation generates waste. The goal here is not to teach you how to design or paint, but to show how these functions can derail production if not managed carefully.

It is imperative to acknowledge that it is possible to make a game without giving complete freedom to either discipline. It is also impossible to make a game without giving some freedom to both. Discovery and development can go hand in hand, with boxed time constraints in place for the innovation and exploration that are required. However, firm control must be exerted, along with often difficult decisions actioned; otherwise, the path of making a game can swiftly career out of control.

In my experience, producers and planners are not trained how to handle feature creep, visionary creative directors overreaching, the shift of a design away from the original without gauging impact, untested style guides and Art Bibles, the impact of late changes on Art assets. The list goes on and on. I hope that, by utilising risk management foundations, you and your team can be in control more of the time and at least possess a foundation within which to make transparent these risks and issues.

DOI: 10.1201/9781003646082-19

DESIGN RISKS

Common Risk Triggers

- **Feature Creep**: New mechanics or systems are added late in development in response to market trends or internal ambition, destabilising core systems.

- **Balance and Progression Failures**: Poor pacing, reward structures or difficulty curves, often due to insufficient playtesting or interdependent systems.

- **Innovation vs Familiarity**: Striking the wrong balance can alienate players. Lack of audience research compounds this risk.

- **Visionary Overreach**: A lead designer or exec with a brilliant but unbuildable vision pulls the team off track.

- **Shifting Design Goals**: Changing pillars mid-production invalidates prior work, especially in UX, writing and systems design.

- **Live Game Design Debt**: Feature layering in live games creates complexity and undermines the player journey.

Key Risk Patterns

Feature Creep Loop

Unchecked addition of features leads to scope churn, downstream bottlenecks, QA overload and team burnout.

Mitigation:

- Lock major features by Alpha; require impact review for late additions.

- Maintain a public "Not This Project" list.

- Appoint a Scope Gatekeeper with veto power.

Feedback Fuzz Loop

Multiple stakeholders give conflicting or vague feedback, leading to unclear iteration goals and design churn.

Mitigation:

- Consolidate feedback through a single Product Owner or Review Lead.

- Use structured design review formats (e.g. **Miro** boards with pinned annotations).

- Require written design intent before accepting feedback.

Visionary's Curse
Charismatic or senior leaders push for unscoped ideas based on taste or nostalgia, regardless of production impact.

Mitigation:

- Require feasibility sign-off from tech and production leads.
- Use pre-prototype review gates with playable validation.
- Tie every feature to a player-facing outcome or business goal.

Over-Benchmarking Trap
Designs are overly influenced by competitors, leading to incoherent or Frankenstein mechanics.

Mitigation:

- Define design pillars early and filter benchmarks through them.
- Treat competitor analysis as input, not blueprint.

Mitigation Strategies

Activity	Tool/Method	Outcome
Design Lock Milestones	Confluence milestone policy	Limits feature instability
UX Testing and Telemetry	Playtest + analytics dashboards	Validates design clarity
Single Source of Design Truth	Notion or **Miro** Design Wiki	Reduces ambiguity and misalignment
Arbitration for Design Conflicts	Design Board with voting power	Avoids endless debates

As repeatedly noted in GDC Vault production talks, maintaining clear feature-lock milestones and structured design reviews is central to avoiding scope churn (GDC Vault, Multiple Years).

REAL-WORLD EXAMPLE: *ANTHEM* (BIOWARE)

Design changes to core systems (e.g. flying, loot) were made repeatedly without feasibility checks. Technical and art teams were blindsided, leading to crunch and poor player experience (Schreier, 2020).

MINI CASE: AUDIENCE MISMATCH

In a AAA project funded by a major platform, the design team built an action title with deep lore, only to find out late that the publishers envisioned it as a casual co-op game. No player data had been gathered, and contradictory feedback from marketing created chaos. The project was eventually shelved.

ART RISKS

Common Risk Triggers

- **Changing Art Direction Midstream**: Revisions to tone, rendering style or lighting invalidate approved assets.

- **Inadequate Style Guides**: Lack of concrete reference points leads to misaligned outputs.

- **In-Engine Betrayal**: Assets that look great in Photoshop fall apart under in-game lighting, scale or motion.

- **Vendor Drift**: Outsourced teams misinterpret intent or build to outdated specs.

- **Stylistic Erosion**: Gradual degradation of visual coherence due to expanding teams, late features or DLCs.

Key Risk Patterns

Creative Misalignment Triangle

Design, Art and Tech interpret the same concept differently, causing expensive rework.

Mitigation:

- Cross-discipline reviews with shared artefacts.

- Playable grey boxes that show spatial and tonal intent.

Stylistic Drift

Visual style erodes due to miscommunication, lack of consistent review or leadership changes.

Mitigation:

- Lock style pillars early.

- Use benchmark scenes and style bibles.

- Re-review key screens quarterly.

In-Engine Betrayal

Concept art does not translate due to shader or lighting constraints.

Mitigation:

- Use live engine test scenes during the concept phase.

- Review in multiple lighting conditions and contexts.

Vendor Visual Bottleneck
Outsourced teams work without aligned reference or feedback cadence.

Mitigation:

- Audit outsource readiness (style guide, tools, onboarding).

- Assign an Art Vendor Manager role.

Mitigation Strategies

Activity	Tool/Method	Outcome
Art Bible with Animation Tests	Figma/Notion + embedded gifs	Aligns style across teams
Look Dev Test Scene	Unity/Unreal sample scene	Validates shader, lighting, tone
SyncSketch or **Miro** Reviews	Asynchronous visual feedback	Speeds iteration, reduces misfire
Vendor Readiness Checklist	**Jira** or Sheet Tracker	Prevents drift before contracts start

Real-World Example: Outsourced Animation Drift
A UK studio outsourced animation to an Eastern European vendor. Halfway through production, internal art direction changed. Approved animations no longer matched the new look, but the vendor was still on retainer. Weeks of paid work were rendered unusable.

Cross-Discipline Risk Points
Where design, art and tech meet, ambiguity thrives. These crossover points are where risks often emerge:

- **Interpretive Drift**: Different disciplines translate briefs differently.

- **Unscoped Cross-Dependency**: Designers require assets that break the art pipeline; art relies on tech features that are not locked.

- **Ownership Confusion**: No clear lead on experiential fidelity (e.g. who owns how it "feels").

Mitigation:

- Assign joint review gates with mutual veto.

- Ensure design documents explain *why*, not just *what*.

- Build vertical slices early to validate convergence.

Producers may wish to use a Creative Triad Worksheet (see Toolkit) to surface disagreements between design intent, artistic direction and technical feasibility early, before rework accumulates.

Vision Alone Is Not Enough

Design and Art risks are not just about missed deadlines or broken pipelines. They are often the consequence of a well-meaning vision that lacks the constraints and scaffolding needed to deliver it. Sometimes they are simply the overwhelming of production and project management through the sheer weight of chaos and noise. That is where strong Design and Art leadership needs to step up and assume their own part of the production responsibilities.

As someone said, "Ideas are cheap. Execution is hard". As we know, execution under pressure, with incomplete references, evolving tech and external stakeholders is where risk lives. If you want to preserve creative ambition, you must invest in the operational foundations that support it: Clear documentation, shared artefacts, mutual sign-offs and a culture of alignment, with great risk management in place.

REFERENCES

GDC Vault. (Multiple Years). *Postmortems and production talks on feature lock, art direction, and outsourcing.* Retrieved from: https://www.gdcvault.com

Schreier, J. (2020, April 20). How bioware's anthem went wrong. *Bloomberg.* Retrieved from: https://www.bloomberg.com/news/articles/2020-04-20/how-bioware-s-anthem-went-wrong

CHAPTER 17

Operational Risks

Note to the Reader: Although this entire book covers game production risks across disciplines, this chapter is the closest thing to a central hub for operational production risk. We cover planning, scheduling, dependencies and change control, all of which are core concerns for producers. If you are a game producer, programme lead or operations director, this is your chapter. You will find practical guidance across the book, but this is the anchor point for the most common risks you will manage.

O PERATIONAL RISKS INVOLVE THE management and coordination of teams, resources and processes. These risks often stem from poor planning, communication failures or external factors outside the studio's control. When left unmanaged, they lead to delays, quality issues or even project failure.

The classic example is when a team starts off thinking it is working on a two-week feature, then someone realises halfway in, "this could be brilliant, if we just..!" and the scope explodes. Unfortunately, the window you boxed it into does not stretch without huge impact on dependent features and teams.

However, there are plenty of occasions when best intentions and plans meet the enemy, then we realise that information was missing, or assumptions made were incorrect. This is simply life and we will never solve that – we can use risk management to soothe the pain though and make sense of the actions required to take control back. That is my gift to you, gentle reader.

In this section we bundle Operational, Dependency and Change Management Risks. These traditionally fall under the remit of game production but can appear in any team at any level, in many cases.

COMMON RISK TRIGGERS

- **Resource Management Issues**: Misallocating resources, such as overloading one team while another is underutilised, leads to inefficiencies and burnout. Poor coordination between teams can create bottlenecks that stall entire departments.

- **Outdated Pipelines and Tooling Friction**: As teams scale rapidly, existing workflows and tools may no longer serve their purpose. I have seen this first-hand when studios scale up in the number of people they hire but forget that workflows and processes that worked for a team of 45 do not serve their purpose when the team doubles or triples in size. When pipelines do not evolve, tool misalignment and process bottlenecks create friction, rework and morale damage.

- **Coordination Between Teams and Departments**: Large projects require synchronisation across multiple disciplines, and misalignment between teams can cause major bottlenecks. If outsourcing partners fail to deliver on time, or internal teams work in silos, progress slows significantly.

In Bioware's *Mass Effect: Andromeda*, development was distributed across multiple studios, including BioWare Montreal and BioWare Edmonton. The lack of cohesive leadership and shared pipelines led to coordination problems, especially in animation and narrative implementation. According to postmortems, late-stage crunch and misalignment between the teams were significant contributors to the game's underwhelming launch (Schreier, 2017).

- **Timeline Adherence and Scheduling Problems**: Unrealistic deadlines, scope creep or underestimating development complexity can cause project delays. If a team is forced to work on a rigid schedule without room for adjustments, even minor setbacks can have catastrophic knock-on effects.

The 2019 launch of *Anthem* was plagued by years of shifting scope and unclear direction. As reported by Kotaku, the team often had to reset large chunks of work following leadership indecision, with key design decisions happening less than a year before launch. Unrealistic milestones and rigid timelines forced late pivots, leading to crunch and a product that underdelivered (Schreier, 2019) (Takahashi, 2019).

- **Failure of Internal Processes and Systems**: Outdated or inefficient workflows, lack of documentation or reliance on legacy systems can slow down development and create unnecessary obstacles. Studios that do not invest in proper pipeline tools may find themselves bottlenecked by inefficient processes.

Similarly, proponents of Game Design Documents may enforce old-fashioned rules around preparing all documentation in advance of any design and discovery work, rather than seeing them as live and evolving.

- **External Events and Dependencies**: Game development is affected by factors beyond a studio's control, such as vendor delays, third-party API changes or unstable software dependencies. If a core piece of software used in development is discontinued, the team may have to scramble for an alternative. Always ensure that you audit your third-party tool providers, for instance, particularly if they are small or rely only on a few clients.

- **Outsourcing Risks**: Relying on third-party contractors or external studios for art, QA or development work introduces risks related to quality control, missed deadlines or communication breakdowns. When an outsourced team underperforms or delivers subpar assets, the internal team is left with the burden of fixing or redoing work at additional cost. There is also considerable management overhead with co-development partnerships which introduce their own risks.

- **Infrastructure Failures**: Server outages, data loss or cyberattacks during development or after launch can disrupt game progress or cause reputational damage.

- **Testing and QA Failures**: Insufficient or poorly managed quality assurance (QA) processes may lead to undetected bugs and instability in the game.

Although highly anticipated, *Cyberpunk 2077* released in 2020 with widespread performance and stability issues – especially on older consoles. Despite a long development cycle, the QA pipeline reportedly lacked sufficient time and transparency. The studio later admitted that internal testing underestimated the severity of the problems (CD Projekt Red, 2021; Schreier, 2021).

Operational Trigger Map

Trigger	Typical Source	Risk Outcome
Resource mismanagement	No load balancing, unclear ownership	Team burnout, idle time
Outdated pipelines	Rapid headcount growth	Tool friction, rework
Coordination breakdowns	Siloed teams, outsource delays	Cross-discipline bottlenecks
Scheduling fragility	Over-commitment, no buffer	Missed milestones, crunch
Internal process failure	Legacy tools, poor documentation	Rework, dev slowdown
External dependency failure	Vendor/API disruption	Missed deadlines, integration risk
Outsourcing underperformance	Quality drift, misaligned objectives	Costly rework, morale issues
Infrastructure breakdown	Server or data failure	Workflow disruption, reputational damage
QA integration gaps	Late QA engagement, low coverage	Bugs at launch, player backlash

UNPLANNED SCOPE CHANGES RISKS

We mention scope creep a great deal in this part of the book. Scope creep is one of the biggest risks in game development, often creeping in gradually through well-intentioned requests that accumulate over time.

How Scope Creep Happens

- **Passionate Developers Adding Features**: A developer experiments with an unapproved mechanic over the weekend, and suddenly it is expected to be in the game. Well-meaning leads or producers let it through, as they do not wish to hurt feelings – or, of course it genuinely improves the game. But at what cost?

- **Leadership Requests**: Design leads or executives may keep asking for "just one more thing" without evaluating the impact.

- **Market Pressure**: If a competitor launches a similar feature, studios may rush to implement a counter-feature, derailing planned work.

I highly encourage you to adopt the Butterfly Effect mantra – repeat after me: "A small change in a complex system can affect the behaviour of the entire system, eventually".

Managing Scope Changes Effectively

- **Assess Impact Before Approving Changes**: Any new feature should be evaluated for time, budget and resource implications.

- **Maintain a Scope Change Log**: Documenting scope changes ensures the team understands why adjustments were made.

- **Clear Approval Processes**: Producers should ensure all major changes go through proper review rather than being added informally.

Facilitator Tip:

If a weekend experiment becomes a feature request, stop and ask: *Where is this tracked? What does it replace or delay?*

SIDEBAR: FEATURE DELIVERY WITHOUT BUFFERS

When I joined, the team was nearing the end of a feature plagued by scope creep and unsustainable 60–80 hour work weeks... Production schedules across all features lacked any buffer for added or discovered work... To break this cycle, always assume that even the smallest features will encounter unforeseen technical challenges... Track how much added work typically arises for your team and build in a realistic buffer.

- LEAD GAME PRODUCER

Example: Volcanic to Ice Biome Shift

In one project, leadership decided late in development to overhaul an entire biome environment, shifting from a volcanic world to an ice world. This change meant that textures, lighting and level design all had to be redone, delaying the game's launch by several months. Proper risk assessment before approving the change would have highlighted the consequences early.

BROKEN PLANNING SYSTEMS: WHEN PRODUCERS ENABLE RISK INSTEAD OF MANAGING IT

It would be difficult to ignore the propensity for poor planning throughout the game development lifecycle. This is partly linked to the lack of production staff training across most studios in how to plan at project and programme level (covered in Chapter 14). It is also often linked to impossible asks based around too little time, not enough budget and a general squeeze on resources. Most companies have too little, not too much. Those with too much are finding themselves with too little in recent years (see the Trends chapter).

In this section we take a look at some common factors at play and offer mitigation strategies that go beyond generic project management advice. As I often tell students, these are the kinds of issues that quietly strangle a game long before they explode into visible crises. I could write a whole book on this topic, but for now we will focus on general advice.

Common Risk Triggers

Broken Planning Systems

One of the most damaging operational risks is poor planning, especially from producers who schedule work without acknowledging the chaos and emergence that define creative software projects. Schedules often look clean and linear, but the real world does not behave that way. There is always iteration, especially in legacy or shared codebases. You build something, you test it, it breaks, someone suggests a better idea and suddenly the neat box you drew for that feature cannot contain the actual work. I have seen this over and over, including when teams treat Jira boards as if they were set in concrete rather than a conversation starter. You are asking for repeated last-minute crunch and burned-out teams.

Unplanned Scope Changes

As mentioned frequently, because it is so important, scope can change: Features evolve, stakeholders change their minds or discoveries are made during development. Without structured change management, teams are forced into reactive mode. Poor documentation or lack of impact assessments exacerbates this. Worse than all of this is poor communication, leading to shocks after the fact.

Dependency Risks

Covered in this chapter in greater detail, dependencies are everywhere. Reliance on other teams, tools or external vendors creates fragile interlocks. If a dependency fails or slips, it can derail downstream work. Dependencies are often hidden or poorly tracked.

Change Management Chaos

Also covered in this chapter, rapid pivots are sometimes necessary – but without a structured change control system, chaos replaces momentum. Teams waste time chasing the latest "urgent" directive without alignment or clarity.

Inadequate QA Integration

QA is often brought in too late or given too few resources, resulting in unstable builds and low confidence in releases. This amplifies operational fire-fighting late in development. See Part V: "Risk Reduction Through User Testing and Embedded QA".

Process Misfit

As covered in the *"Agile, Lean and Kanban Risk Management"* chapter, ceremonies are applied without understanding. Waterfall is declared dead but remains in spirit and indeed in truth in the form of Stage Gates. Teams perform rituals without outcomes – stand-ups, retros and demos become box-ticking exercises.

IRONY CHECK

Agile practices were supposed to replace the rigidity of waterfall development: No more locking away teams for years without stakeholder feedback. Yet in many AAA environments today, large-scale games are hidden from public view for two or more years, sometimes longer. Stand-ups, retros and demos become empty rituals, as the only audience is internal. Most teams do not do retros or regular demos anyway as they are too busy. Waterfall was mocked for isolating teams from users, yet in practice, we often recreate those same dynamics. We may have changed the lexicon, but many games still fail because they are not exposed to real players early enough to inform their development.

Mitigation Strategies

Plan for Emergent Work

Track how much additional work arises in each sprint or milestone. Use this data to inform minimum buffer thresholds. Require producers to include a "risk reserve" in all estimates, validated via historical data, not gut feel. It is worth emphasising: Schedules should not be forecasts of what we *hope* happens – they should be defensive buffers against what we *know* will try to happen.

Schedule Audits

Introduce periodic audits of sprint plans and milestone roadmaps. Look for signs of zero-buffer assumptions, one-shot deliverables or magical thinking. Train leads to spot "risk blind spots" in their teams' plans. These audits spark conversations that go deeper: If you say, "I need support to mitigate this risk" and the answer is "those people are booked elsewhere", now you are discussing prioritisation, resource limits and what trade-offs actually mean.

Real-Time Risk Monitoring Tools

Use burndown and cumulative flow diagrams not just to visualise progress, but to detect risk emergence. Annotate charts with emergent work trends to refine estimation over time. Remember: If your early burndown looks too good, it probably is. It should account for discovery and feedback, not ignore them.

You can also use Miro and other visualisation tools to track progress on roadmaps and track milestone confidence. Use RAG ratings; use whatever works for you and your team.

Embed QA Early and Fully

Operational risk is reduced when QA is present from the start – writing test plans, contributing to user stories and evaluating risk exposure as code is written. I always tell teams: If QA only shows up at the end, you are not testing – you are firefighting and your quality is being eroded as you leave bugs to build up. We have a whole chapter on this later in the book.

Strengthen Change Control

Create a lightweight but consistent change review system. All mid-cycle scope shifts should include an impact assessment, including resourcing, dependencies and testing impact. This is not about saying no – it is about making the cost visible. The best studio leads and production directors I ever worked with all introduce this intuitively and ensure that their production staff and team leads think in this way. If you know the cost and the value, you can make informed decisions and prioritise.

Empower Producers as Systems Thinkers

Train producers not just in tools or methods, but in system dynamics. Encourage them to model feedback loops, dependency chains and team fatigue as part of planning. It is not just about identifying risks; it is about learning from them and feeding that back into the system. Anyone can remain a reporter, observer or critic, but what we need here is a champion representing the team and the truth. Champions speak up.

SIDEBAR: REAL-WORLD PERSPECTIVE – PLANNING FOR REALITY

When I joined, the team was nearing the end of a feature plagued by scope creep and unsustainable 60–80 hour work weeks. I quickly realized that production schedules across all features lacked any buffer for added or discovered work. This led to repeated last-minute crunches, which had become ingrained in team culture. Developers who couldn't or wouldn't sustain the pace often churned, resulting in frequent backfilling and loss of experienced talent.

To break this cycle, always assume that even the smallest features will encounter unforeseen technical challenges – especially when working in shared or legacy code – and expect rounds of critical feedback due to inevitable misalignments. Track how much added work typically arises for your team and build in a realistic buffer. Early burndown charts may appear overly optimistic; that's intentional. They should absorb the impact when, not if, additional work emerges.

- LEAD GAME PRODUCER

KEY RISK PATTERNS

Blind Scheduling Optimism
Planning based on ideal paths, ignoring emergent complexity.

Impact: Schedules collapse under the weight of unexpected iterations, feedback loops or code integration issues. Often results in late-stage crunch and systemic team burnout.

Mitigation: Include historical buffers in planning, track emergent work trends and establish a culture of revisiting assumptions.

The Crunch Cycle Trap
Team culture that relies on unsustainable effort to meet milestones.

Impact: Leads to chronic overwork, talent attrition, morale decline and long-term productivity loss (Parkin, 2015). Creates a cycle where critical work only gets done through crisis mode.

Mitigation: Normalise realistic pacing. Track team load versus effort. Reward pace-setting, not burnout endurance.

Reactive Change Chaos
Frequent changes without structured impact review.

Impact: Creates delivery instability and confusion, derailing committed work and burning sprint credibility.

Mitigation: Establish light-touch change control, require resourcing impact assessments for all scope additions.

Invisible Dependencies
Untracked or misunderstood links between teams, tools or vendors.

Impact: Downstream teams blocked by unmet upstream expectations. Last-minute coordination failures.

Mitigation: Use dependency mapping, daily integration check-ins and toolchain visibility reviews.

Process Theatre
Ritualised but ineffective Agile or Waterfall practices that do not reduce risk.

Impact: Teams go through the motions (stand-ups, retros, demos) without extracting value or insights. Feedback is delayed or suppressed.

Mitigation: Align process rituals with actual decision-making needs. Ensure retros lead to visible improvements. Evaluate meeting ROI regularly.

DEPENDENCY RISKS

Dependencies in game development arise from strategic decisions and interconnected workflows across multiple teams. **They are inevitable.** Agile and Lean methodologies may tell you to minimise and remove as many as possible, but that is rather like trying to hold grains of sand in your hand by squeezing harder. Dependences are everywhere as we are working across functions, across teams, across studios sometimes and almost certainly across outsourcers and co-dev partnerships. We all depend on each other, and that needs to be tracked and taken into account.

As noted previously, dependencies tend to be exposed most at programme level, where the job of the production director, development director or producer is to make sense of them all and move across the various teams, both internal and external. Dependencies at project level tend to be escalated to the programme level, unless they can be dealt with directly and quickly.

Common Types of Dependencies

- **Strategic Dependencies**: Creating a game trailer for a major event (e.g. a publisher showcase) is dependent on having gameplay-ready content. If core mechanics are not functional, the marketing team cannot build the trailer.

- **Platform or Publisher Dependencies**: If the game relies on the support of external publishers or platforms (e.g. Steam, PlayStation Store), changes to their policies or delays could affect your game's launch or distribution.

- **Cross-Team Dependencies**: Large studios often have 30+ teams working on different features that must seamlessly integrate. A delay in one feature (e.g. AI behaviour coding) can stall multiple other teams, creating a ripple effect.

- **Producers and Communication**: Producers must ensure clear cross-team communication to track and manage dependencies so that one team's delay does not derail the entire project. Most studios and teams benefit from overcommunication.

Dependency Risk Types

Dependency Type	Risk	Example
Cross-team	Integration failure	Rig not delivered → animation team blocked
Strategic	Upstream failure	Marketing campaign relies on gameplay that is not yet functional
Platform / Publisher	Policy or SDK changes	Platform TRC failure delays certification and launch
External / Vendor	Delivery inconsistency	Outsource studio misses milestone → asset rework and delays
Communication / Producer	Misalignment or missed handoff	One team unaware of dependency → schedules desynchronise silently

If a single team misses a milestone, bottlenecks emerge, affecting multiple teams. For example, in a multi-studio project, the animation team in Studio A might be waiting for rigged character models from Studio B. If Studio B runs into delays, Studio A is blocked, leading to wasted time and a backlog of unfinished work. This is where strong dependency tracking and risk monitoring come into play. Without them, game development can quickly grind to a halt.

Tip: Use a RACI chart to visualise dependency risk – do we know who is responsible *and* accountable for each link in the chain?

SIDEBAR: DEPENDENCY IS NOT JUST TECHNICAL

"Our Technical Artist was based in Brazil and was part time, while the rest of the art team worked UK hours. I agreed with him that he will make time for collaboration based on UK hours even if it was 30mins a day. I expected responsiveness since he had access to our Slack channels, sync meetings and he had tasks prioritized and organised for him. The situation was a risk from a collaboration perspective already but it was made worse because my assumption that he will make time for collaboration and will be a pro-active communicator was proven wrong. This led to a hidden cost of 3 highly paid seniors (Art Director, Art Lead and Myself) wrangling him for an answer to a chaser let alone a proper update. We were returned silence even though he was working on high stakes work which he was fully aware of".

- PURVA GARG, SENIOR PRODUCER

Example: Project Copernicus by 38 Studios

Project Copernicus, an ambitious MMORPG developed by 38 Studios, was plagued by dependency issues. The game's development relied heavily on the success of its single-player counterpart, Kingdoms of Amalur: Reckoning, to fund ongoing work. When Reckoning underperformed financially, it disrupted the funding pipeline for Copernicus. Additionally, the complex interdependencies between various development teams led to coordination challenges. These issues, combined with financial mismanagement, ultimately resulted in the studio's collapse and the cancellation of Project Copernicus. (Wikipedia)

CHANGE MANAGEMENT RISKS

Game development is inherently complex and complicated (I use *chaos* below as this is often interpreted in that way). With so many moving and interlocking parts, much like the insides of a watch, you need to be very careful what you touch, add or remove. This is change management. Without effective processes in place, changes can lead to delays, miscommunication or scope creep that threaten project stability. Understanding how to handle change efficiently is key to ensuring smooth development.

Change Management is a field of foundational knowledge within project, program and portfolio management. We do not attempt to touch on that here, beyond introducing you to the idea that you can actually manage change – it does not have to be something that "just happens" outside of your control.

Follow the advice in this book, set up your risk management processes and you will see that you are already far more able to effectively spot and control change.

Why Development Chaos Exists

- **Unpredictable Iteration Cycles**: Unlike traditional software, game features need to be tested for fun and engagement, leading to constant iteration.

- **Cross-Team Dependencies**: A single change in physics or AI behaviour can ripple across multiple departments.

- **Shifting Industry Trends**: Market demands change and studios must adapt mid-project to stay competitive.

Mitigating Chaos with Structured Change Management

- **Document Key Changes**: Risk registers and structured logs prevent undocumented shifts that cause confusion.

- **Kanban Boards for Tracking**: Using their toolsets, teams can create a living record of decisions, blockers and outcomes and track the actions.

- **Decision-Making Frameworks**: Establishing clear processes for approving changes ensures they are evaluated and communicated properly.

SIDEBAR: WHAT GOOD CHANGE MANAGEMENT LOOKS LIKE

- The change is proposed, not assumed
- It is logged, with impacts discussed
- It is approved, with escalation triggers defined
- It is communicated, with rationale and ownership

Example: *L.A. Noire* by Team Bondi

The development of L.A. Noire by Team Bondi is a notable example of poor change management. The project underwent numerous changes in direction, with frequent shifts in design and technology choices. These changes were often implemented without adequate communication or planning, leading to extended crunch periods and high staff turnover. The lack of structured change management processes contributed to a toxic work environment and delayed the game's release (Wikipedia).

Let us not pretend that this is unusual and specific to Team Bondi, however, it is the norm rather than the exception.

Personal Example

I have successfully implemented Kanban boards to track blockers, decisions and resolutions in real time. This allowed my teams to search past changes and understand why a decision was made – preventing repeated discussions and uncertainty. We used this very effectively to empower and inform at the highest level of the company, as we had rock solid evidence of decisions made and an audit trail. It was very satisfying and not a lot of extra work.

Change Management can be this light; it does not have to be about change control rules and over-complicated processes pushed at teams.

Key Risk Patterns
Decision Drift

Definition: When important project decisions are made verbally, revisited without documentation or reversed with little communication. This leads to confusion, misalignment and rework.

Mitigation Checklist:

- Assign clear decision owners per discipline.

- Maintain a live decision register with rationale and date.

- Share changes in team-wide channels and project management tools.

> **SIDEBAR – CHECKLIST: SPOTTING DECISION DRIFT**
> - Decisions verbally made off Slack/Teams/Discord with no record
> - Roadmaps change, but backlogs do not
> - Different teams believe different versions of the plan

Integration Bottleneck

Definition: Where teams or departments operate in isolation until late-stage convergence, only to discover significant misalignment during integration. This often results in crunch or rewrites.

Example: In *Mass Effect: Andromeda*, animations and narrative content were developed in parallel across studios. Without shared pipelines, integration issues surfaced too late, leading to poor polish and late rework (Schreier, 2017).

Mitigation Checklist:

- Plan regular vertical slice reviews involving all disciplines.

- Align milestones with cross-functional deliverables.

- Use automated pipelines and shared environments early.

Example Integration Risk Timeline
T0: Feature kicks off
  T+3 weeks: Silence
  T+6 weeks: Team 2 attempts integration – fails
  T+8 weeks: Fire drill + weekend work

Mitigation:
Run vertical slices every two or three weeks with Art, Tech, QA and Production present. Do not wait for "polish" before you test integration.

Unrealistic Recovery Planning
Definition: Project leadership assumes minor setbacks can be "made up" later without adjusting scope or milestones, often resulting in crunch or cascading delays.

Example: A studio encountered a month-long delay due to unexpected engine performance issues. Instead of rescheduling, leadership insisted on maintaining launch dates, triggering unsustainable overtime.

Mitigation Checklist:

- Adjust timelines or scope immediately after confirmed delay.

- Include buffer time in milestone planning.

- Escalate and document recovery trade-offs early.

You cannot "make up" a month, unless you cut something. If you do not, you are just moving the crisis downstream.

I hate to think how many times I have seen this Risk Pattern emerge. Despite all evidence to the contrary, people seem wired to believe that time is on their side and there will be savings elsewhere. Or they think that developers who are sitting around idle near the final phase of making the game can step in to sort it all out.

This is particularly true of critical bugs that QA teams and engineers raise that are inconvenient at the time and moved to the "we will fix that at the end". It will often not end well.

Shadow Gatekeeping – the Wise Hermit

One individual holds undocumented knowledge critical to a system, pipeline or process, creating fragility if they leave, take leave or reprioritise. They are nearly always needed on too many jobs, due to their deep specialised knowledge.

Example: A senior audio engineer controls the entire voice-over ingest pipeline. When they leave, the studio loses three weeks rebuilding workflows no one else understood.

Mitigation Checklist:

- Map key systems and assign backup owners with access and training

- Tie documentation milestones to sprint acceptance criteria or performance reviews

- Create a cadence for peer walkthroughs or "second pair" reviews of high-dependency systems

REFERENCES

CD Projekt Red. (2021, January 13). Cyberpunk 2077 — Our commitment to quality. CD PROJEKT Group. Available at: https://www.polygon.com/2021/1/13/22229626/cd-projekt-apology-cyberpunk-2077-post-launch-roadmap-patch-107

Parkin, S. (2015). The human cost of destiny's success. *The Guardian*. Retrieved from: https://www.theguardian.com/games/2020/jan/13/destiny-bungie-human-cost-success

Schreier, J. (2017). The story behind mass effect: Andromeda's troubled five-year development. *Kotaku*. Retrieved from: https://kotaku.com/the-story-behind-mass-effect-andromedas-troubled-five-1795886428

Schreier, J. (2019). How BioWare's anthem went wrong. *Kotaku*. Retrieved from: https://kotaku.com/how-biowares-anthem-went-wrong-1833731964

Schreier, J. (2021, January 16). Inside Cyberpunk 2077's disastrous rollout. Bloomberg News. Available at: https://www.bloomberg.com/news/articles/2021-01-16/inside-cyberpunk-2077-s-disastrous-rollout-and-why-it-couldn-t-be-stoppedhttps://www.bloomberg.com/news/articles/2021-01-16/inside-cyberpunk-2077-s-disastrous-rollout-and-why-it-couldn-t-be-stoppedhttps://www.bloomberg.com/news/articles/2021-01-16/inside-cyberpunk-2077-s-disastrous-rollout-and-why-it-couldn-t-be-stopped

Takahashi, D. (2019). What went wrong with anthem. *VentureBeat*. Retrieved from: https://venturebeat.com/games/biowares-anthem-postmortem-what-went-wrong/

CHAPTER 18

Financial, Legal, Regulatory and Compliance Risks

INTRODUCTION: BUSINESS-SIDE RISK IS PRODUCTION-CRITICAL

Creative ideas and technical ambition are rarely enough to sustain a studio. Financial and legal risks, compliance blind spots and monetisation missteps can derail even the most promising project. These risks live outside of Jira and Trello, but they affect every milestone, hiring plan and release decision. Game producers, executives and department leads must understand the business-side terrain to prevent silent project killers.

Recent industry trends show an increasingly unforgiving environment: game investment has dropped, layoffs are surging and regional regulation is expanding rapidly. There is no production safety without business fluency.

FINANCIAL RISK TRIGGERS

Budget Overruns and Underruns

Most studios focus on cost overruns, but underruns are dangerous too. Underspending can signal staffing gaps, overpromised deliverables or deferred risks. Both lead to delivery failure if left unmanaged.

Cash Flow and Burn Rate Exposure

You can hit your milestone and still miss payroll. Burn rate tracking is not just for finance teams – it should inform sprint velocity and hiring plans. Teams that overhire after a funding round often find themselves shrinking months later. More production teams need to be exposed to the budgets and burn rates.

DOI: 10.1201/9781003646082-21

Milestone Dependency

Payment often comes only after deliverables are approved. When milestones are vague or unrealistic, studios enter cash flow freefall. QA bottlenecks, scope pivots or feedback loops can delay those deliverables and wreck the studio's timeline.

Funding Model Instability

VC investment in games dropped significantly from 2022 to 2024 (GameSpot, 2024). Studios reliant on equity rounds, token sales or publisher advances are exposed to shifts in investor confidence or genre fashion. Co-development funding models can also collapse when one party withdraws.

Cost Inflation and Salary Pressure

Salaries have surged in major game hubs. Inflation in Europe and North America affects everything from motion capture bookings to localisation (Schreier, 2021) (CD Projekt Red, 2021). This silently extends your cost-to-complete runway. There is also a huge salary expectation from the older veteran game professionals who may have been in the industry for 20+ years. Risk assessments of replacing them with inexperienced staff or outsourcing/co-dev partnerships can prove interesting.

Forecasting Fragility

Studios often forecast based on success-case monetisation. That is dangerous. Overestimating LTV (lifetime value), retention or ARPU creates brittle roadmaps (Schreier, 2019). I have seen this first-hand in pitch decks that assume wild conversion rates and launch day sales with no evidence.

LEGAL RISK TRIGGERS

IP Infringement and Grey Areas

Many indies borrow too liberally from established franchises. Even UI layouts or colour schemes can attract cease-and-desist letters.

In 2020 and beyond, Nintendo issued takedown notices for several fan-made monster battler games on platforms like itch.io and Game Jolt, citing infringement due to similarities in naming, character design and gameplay style (Kuchera, 2020). Some developers were forced to remove their games post-release or undergo complete rebranding efforts to avoid legal action.

Music and Asset Licensing Pitfalls

Using unlicensed fonts, sound libraries or freelance art without a clear transfer of rights is a common early-stage oversight. These bite hardest right before release.

Contractual Ambiguity

Poorly written contracts with co-dev studios or freelancers lead to scope disputes, ownership confusion and expensive rework (Schreier, 2017). Boilerplate NDAs and agreements are not enough.

Employment and Outsourcing Legal Gaps

Different jurisdictions treat contractors, interns and full-time staff differently. Misclassification can lead to fines or forced contract revisions.

Trademark and Brand Clashes

Even accidental name collisions with existing media or international brands can delay release. Always do regional trademark searches – your harmless game title might be banned in Brazil or South Korea. I would share accidental names and hilarity ensuing in other languages, but fear they would be a little crude for a book.

REGULATORY AND COMPLIANCE RISKS

Data Protection Laws

Games aimed at children must comply with COPPA. Any user data must comply with GDPR. Consent management and opt-in systems need to be built from day one and not tacked on.

The FTC fined Epic Games a record-breaking $520 million (Federal Trade Commission, 2022). This included $275 million for violating COPPA (collecting data from children without proper consent) (US Federal Trade Commission, 2019) and $245 million for using deceptive interfaces to trick players into making unintended purchases.

Age Ratings and Content Restrictions

PEGI, ESRB and Chinese authorities all have distinct rules (PEGI, 2023). A single blood effect or word choice can trigger an 18+ rating or outright ban. Schedule time for regional compliance, especially for launch builds.

Ratings systems vary wildly. A horror game with a child NPC might pass in Europe, be age-gated in the US and banned in Brazil. Plan regional compliance paths early, especially if relying on revenue from specific markets.

Red Candle Games' *Devotion* was pulled from Steam globally after players discovered a hidden in-game image mocking Chinese president Xi Jinping (Yin-Poole, 2019). Though initially unrelated to ratings, the incident highlighted the political and regulatory volatility of publishing games in sensitive regions.

Monetisation Regulation

Loot boxes, gacha mechanics and randomised rewards are under scrutiny. Belgium and the Netherlands have banned them outright. Countries like the UK and US are debating legislation (UK Parliament, 2023). Studios that ignore these trends risk retroactive takedown.

Governments in Belgium and the Netherlands declared loot boxes illegal under gambling law (BBC News, 2018). This led to multiple publishers, including EA, having to disable certain features in games like *FIFA* in those territories or face penalties. Blizzard's Diablo Immortal was not released in these regions due to its loot box monetisation, which would have violated local gambling legislation (Yin-Poole, 2022).

Platform Compliance

Console platforms have complex and evolving technical requirements checklists (TRCs). These affect game logic, error messaging, save systems and UI. Certification failures cause delays and can force painful last-minute patches. It often makes sense to break down and map these TRCs into actual milestones in the game development lifecycle.

Accessibility Compliance

While not yet legally enforced in all regions, players and platforms expect accessibility standards. Titles that ignore this risk criticism, platform rejection or viral backlash.

MONETISATION MODEL RISKS

Revenue Model Volatility

Ads, IAPs, premium pricing, battle passes – each model has risks. Studios that mix multiple models without a clear strategy often alienate their core audience.

Game Pass Dilemma

Subscription platforms boost discoverability, but revenue may plateau. You must plan for what happens after the initial deal or showcase exposure. Many titles fail to monetise past their featured week.

Ethics vs Revenue

Push too hard and players leave. Push too softly and you miss targets. This is especially hard for LiveOps games where F2P dynamics are culturally sensitive and regionally diverse.

Platform Terms and Retroactive Changes

Sony, Apple, Steam and others may change policies post-launch. A monetisation strategy that was compliant on day one might become non-compliant within six months.

Sony attempted to retroactively enforce PSN account linking for *Helldivers II* players on Steam (Tassi, 2024). This sparked community backlash and led to the game being delisted in countries without PSN availability. After protests and refunds, Sony reversed the requirement, but not before significant brand damage.

Community Trust Collapse

When players feel tricked or exploited, no monetisation model survives. Studios that bake in psychological dark patterns tend to face massive backlash.

MITIGATION STRATEGIES

- Include legal and compliance experts early – not just at release
- Use licence tracking sheets and asset usage audits throughout development
- Forecast burn rate with pessimistic and fallback scenarios
- Define clear milestone criteria in funding contracts

- Include platform and rating requirements in milestone definitions
- Build for age ratings and content policy from the start
- Test monetisation strategies with real players and regions
- Monitor laws in target markets and maintain a compliance update calendar

KEY RISK PATTERNS

Key Risk Patterns

Funding Instability Loop
Studios assume best-case monetisation and guaranteed funding rounds. When one element shifts, such as a delayed milestone, investor withdrawal or platform deal falling through, the entire financial model collapses, leaving teams unable to sustain development.

Mitigation:

- Build revenue models with conservative estimates and stress-tested scenarios
- Secure multiple funding sources where possible
- Ensure contractual clarity around milestone terms and payment timing

Compliance Oversight Trap
Legal and regulatory requirements are delayed until the end of production. At that point, fixes require major rework, such as re-implementing age gating, altering monetisation mechanics or rebuilding backend data handling, all under deadline pressure.

Mitigation:

- Involve legal advisers at concept and pre-production stages
- Maintain a live compliance checklist for all active regions
- Integrate regulatory audits into milestone exit criteria

Retroactive Policy Whiplash
Platforms change terms or enforcement expectations after submission or launch. Studios must suddenly re-certify, remove features or delay patches to meet new guidelines they were not prepared for.

Mitigation:

- Monitor platform policy updates continuously
- Avoid brittle dependencies on platform-specific monetisation models

- Build patch buffers into your schedule to allow for resubmission if needed

Legal Afterthought Syndrome

Legal considerations are excluded from core development decisions. Teams work under the assumption that "someone else will handle it", resulting in cumulative legal debt; these include anything from unlicensed assets to ambiguous contracts and territorial risks.

Mitigation:

- Make legal review part of every major contract, feature and asset decision
- Track usage rights and IP obligations in shared documentation
- Establish escalation paths for unresolved legal ambiguity

Case Study: *Club Penguin*

Club Penguin launched in 2005 as a child-friendly MMO and was acquired by Disney in 2007 for over $350 million. It implemented strong moderation tools, safe chat filters and a subscription-based monetisation model. However, maintaining a safe, compliant environment for millions of young players proved increasingly resource-intensive.

In 2017, Disney shut down the original game and attempted to migrate its audience to a new product, Club Penguin Island. This move failed to gain traction and sparked community backlash.

This case illustrates multiple interwoven risks:

- **Compliance and Child Safety Costs**: Ongoing moderation demands were large and non-optional
- **Platform Transition and Community Risk**: Shuttering the original alienated users and fuelled piracy
- **Legacy Security Exposure**: Data tied to Club Penguin was reportedly involved in later security breaches
- **Monetisation Risk**: Subscription model faced attrition as free-to-play competitors dominated
- **Brand Sustainability Risk**: Relaunch attempts failed to recapture the original's loyal audience

Following the shutdown, fan-run clones proliferated, some of which were later involved in serious moderation failures and data breaches. *Club Penguin Online* was a fan-hosted private server emulating the original. While it drew hundreds of thousands of nostalgic users, it operated without Disney's approval, violating IP rights and exposing minors to severe safety risks.

In 2020, investigative reports by the BBC and The Verge uncovered rampant unmoderated behaviour, including racist messages, simulated sex acts and allegations of paedophilic activity by moderators. Disney issued a DMCA takedown and the site was permanently shut down.

This case illustrates multiple interwoven risks:

- **IP and Licensing Risk**: Fan-made servers infringing on Disney's copyright

- **Compliance and Child Safety Failures**: Violations of COPPA and lack of moderation

- **Platform and Hosting Risk**: Disney had no direct control but bore reputational consequences

- **Legal and Regulatory Exposure**: BBC and Verge investigations leading to public backlash

- **Community Trust Breakdown**: Toxic behaviour, e-sex and racial slurs across servers

- **Brand Erosion and Franchise Risk**: Disney's need to defend the brand led to takedowns

(Kelly, 2020; Engadget, 2020; BBC News, 2018; The Independent, 2022; Bleeping Computer, 2022; Awesome Games Wiki, 2024; Yin-Poole, 2017; Alexander, 2017; TechCrunch, 2007)

COMPLIANCE IS CRITICAL

Financial and legal risks are often seen as the domain of specialists – but they are production-critical. Whether you are budgeting your roadmap, contracting an artist, forecasting revenue or preparing to launch globally, you are navigating this space. Failure to engage early could mean the game your team has been working on for the last three years never actually ships.

REFERENCES

Alexander, L. (2017). Why club penguin shut down. *Polygon*. Retrieved from: https://www.polygon.com/2017/1/31/14456272/club-penguin-shut-down-disney-island

Awesome Games Wiki. (2024). *Disney shuts down Club Penguin online*. Summary of moderation failures, racism, and grooming allegations. (Archived and paraphrased community reporting)

BBC News. (2018). *Belgium declares loot boxes illegal under gambling law*. Retrieved from: https://www.bbc.com/news/technology-43906306

BBC News. (2018). *Club Penguin fan servers expose children to abuse and hate speech*. Reported via BBC investigation, frequently cited in subsequent moderation and safety analyses.

Bleeping Computer. (2022). *Disney hit by data leak allegedly tied to legacy Club Penguin assets*. Retrieved from: https://www.bleepingcomputer.com/news/security/disney-data-leak-exposes-legacy-assets-club-penguin/

CD Projekt Red. (2021). *Cyberpunk 2077 developer postmortem presentation*.

Engadget. (2020). *Disney shuts down Club Penguin clone plagued by racism and 'e-sex'*. Retrieved from: https://www.engadget.com/disney-shuts-down-club-penguin-clone-131820741.html

Federal Trade Commission. (2022). *FTC finalizes orders against epic games, imposing $520 million penalty for COPPA and dark patterns.* Retrieved from: https://www.ftc.gov/news-events/news/press-releases/2022/12/epic-games-settles-ftc-allegations

GameSpot. (2024). *The collapse of game investment: Why 2023 was so brutal.* Retrieved from: https://www.gamespot.com/articles/the-collapse-of-game-investment-2023

The Independent. (2022). *Club Penguin rewritten fan server shut down following arrest of staff and investigation.* Retrieved from: https://www.independent.co.uk/tech/club-penguin-rewritten-shut-down-arrest-b2060547.html

Kelly, M. (2020). Club Penguin Online shuts down after receiving copyright claim from disney. *The Verge.* Retrieved from: https://www.theverge.com/2020/5/15/21260122/club-penguin-dmca-disney-takedown-cponline-online

Kuchera, B. (2020). Nintendo cracks down on fan-made Pokémon games hosted on itch.io and Game Jolt. *Polygon.* Retrieved from: https://www.polygon.com/2020/6/10/21286825/nintendo-pokemon-fan-game-takedown-dmca

PEGI. (2023). *Age rating guidelines for digital distribution platforms.* Retrieved from: https://pegi.info/pegi-age-ratings

Schreier, J. (2017). The story behind mass effect: Andromeda's troubled five-year development. *Kotaku.* Retrieved from: https://kotaku.com/the-story-behind-mass-effect-andromedas-troubled-five-1795886428

Schreier, J. (2019). How BioWare's anthem went wrong. *Kotaku.* Retrieved from: https://kotaku.com/how-biowares-anthem-went-wrong-1833731964

Schreier, J. (2021). Inside Cyberpunk 2077's disastrous rollout. *Bloomberg.* Retrieved from: https://www.bloomberg.com/news/articles/2021-01-16/the-inside-story-of-cyberpunk-2077-s-disastrous-rollout

Tassi, P. (2024). Sony's PSN requirement for helldivers II sparks massive backlash and regional delistings. *Forbes.* Retrieved from: https://www.forbes.com/sites/paultassi/2024/05/05/helldivers-2-delisted-on-steam/

TechCrunch. (2007). *Disney buys club penguin for $350 million.* Retrieved from: https://techcrunch.com/2007/08/01/disney-buys-club-penguin-for-350-million/

UK Parliament. (2023). *Loot boxes and video game monetisation.* Digital, Culture, Media and Sport Committee. Retrieved from: https://committees.parliament.uk/publications/3896/documents/38987/default/

US Federal Trade Commission. (2019). *FTC imposes $170 million fine on YouTube for COPPA violations.* Retrieved from: https://www.ftc.gov/news-events/news/press-releases/2019/09/ftc-youtube-coppa

Yin-Poole, W. (2017). Disney is shutting down Club Penguin. *Eurogamer.* Retrieved from: https://www.eurogamer.net/disney-is-shutting-down-club-penguin

Yin-Poole, W. (2019). Devotion pulled from Steam after backlash over hidden Winnie the Pooh reference. *Eurogamer.* Retrieved from: https://www.eurogamer.net/devotion-pulled-from-steam-after-backlash-over-hidden-winnie-the-pooh-reference

Yin-Poole, W. (2022). Diablo immortal won't launch in the Netherlands or Belgium due to loot box laws. *Eurogamer.* Retrieved from: https://www.eurogamer.net/diablo-immortal-wont-launch-in-the-netherlands-or-belgium

CHAPTER 19

Marketing and Audience Risks

INTRODUCTION

There is no shortage of ways to announce a game today. Trailers, festivals, showcases, social ads, creator campaigns and let us not forget our friends travelling the conference circuit to push their games. But there is a fundamental difference between getting your game seen and building momentum with the people who might actually play it.

Marketing risk is not just about messaging. It is about whether the people you need to reach are actually listening, whether the format suits the audience, and whether your discovery strategy aligns with how those players find and assess new games.

As touched on in Chapter 4 (Risk Landscape) and Chapter 27 (Mobile Game Risks), the ecosystem of discovery is volatile, fragmented and hard to control.

COMMON RISK TRIGGERS

Platform-Controlled Discovery

PC and console games are largely at the mercy of Steam visibility algorithms, Xbox/PlayStation store placement and showcase event invites. Mobile titles rely heavily on App Store rankings and user acquisition performance.

Genre Saturation and Fatigue

Some genres, including survival crafting or card battlers, are so oversaturated that even excellent titles struggle to differentiate.

Mismatch Between Game and Target Audience

When the art style, tone or gameplay loop is not aligned with audience expectations, conversion rates suffer. This is especially dangerous when pitching to a player base unfamiliar with your studio or IP.

DOI: 10.1201/9781003646082-22

Overreliance on Paid UA (Mobile)

Mobile games often spend tens of millions on user acquisition. Post-Apple ATT, this model is fragile. Studios without first-party data pipelines face rising CPIs and decreasing ROI (Perez, 2021).

Late Discovery or Delayed Marketing

Marketing left too late often means the audience is not primed for launch. This can kill wishlists, soften day-one impact or make influencer partnerships harder to secure.

Streamer Dependence Without Fit

Some games chase Twitch visibility without being "streamable". Narrative-heavy titles with slow pacing do not generate highlight moments and may flop despite marketing.

Platform Tone Mismatch

PC players expect deep systems. TikTok audiences want novelty and humour. If your messaging is wrong for the platform, players will scroll past or bounce.

Monetisation Pushback

A game may be mechanically sound but rejected if players perceive the monetisation as exploitative. This often happens when mobile IAP models are copied onto PC/console.

Mobile vs Console/PC: Different Discovery Battlegrounds

Factor	Mobile	PC/Console
Discovery Drivers	Paid UA, App Store ranking, cross-promotion	Wishlists, trailers, influencer streams
Monetisation Norms	IAP, ads, subscriptions	Premium, DLC, Battle Pass
Risk of Overreach	ATT and rising CPI, ad fatigue	Algorithm opacity, limited organic exposure
Player Expectation	Short loops, re-engagement mechanics	System depth, content volume, quality polish
Platform Control	Heavily dictated by Apple/Google policies	Showcase-driven, Valve/Sony/Microsoft discretion

Case Study: Knockout City/MultiVersus
Both *Knockout City* and *MultiVersus* launched with strong early traction and publisher backing. Their visibility benefited from Game Pass inclusion, Twitch streams and launch-week buzz. However, both titles failed to retain users long-term. In each case, LiveOps content cadence slowed, player engagement dropped, and monetisation plans struggled to keep up (Makuch, 2023).

This illustrates the risk of mistaking initial discovery for sustained retention. A strong launch window is not enough without deep player resonance and ongoing value.

Case Study: MindsEye – When Production Star Power Isn't Enough

MindsEye, developed by Build a Rocket Boy and helmed by Leslie Benzies (ex-Rockstar), launched June 10, 2025 on PC, PS5, and Xbox Series X/S to widespread criticism. Despite pre-launch buzz tied to Benzies's pedigree, it was reviewed as "unfinished", "bug-ridden" and technically broken, even on PS5 Pro. Player complaints included frame-rate drops well below 30 fps on PS5 Pro, buggy AI, stuttering and crashing (Scullion, 2025).

Around launch, communication missteps followed: Review codes were withheld, streams were abruptly cancelled and developers outwardly accused critics of orchestrating "smear campaigns" or deploying "bots"(Saed, 2025). Leadership upheaval compounded the problem, with two key executives departing just days before launch (Dinsdale, 2025). Within 24 hours, player numbers plummeted by approximately 75%, indicating a failing retention strategy and reactive post-launch patching (Hernandez, 2025).

Lessons Learned:

- **Audience Misfit + Discovery Failure:** High-profile marketing cannot compensate for a lack of early community engagement or audience alignment.

- **Process Misalignment:** Late or opaque marketing (no review copies, cancelled streams) damaged trust and revealed fragmentation between development and audience-facing teams.

- **Platform and Community Expectations Mismatch:** Pursuing streamer exposure without proper engagement (or providing playable builds) alienated influencers, press and players.

MindsEye remains a cautionary tale: Even with big names and solid backing, a game still needs player alignment, transparent marketing and technical readiness to survive its opening weekend.

MITIGATION STRATEGIES

Risk Area	Strategy
Late or Weak Discovery	Build wishlist early, test trailers, attend festivals
Genre Saturation	Position with unique hook or hybrid twist
Audience Mismatch	Conduct audience personas, test messaging on platform-native audiences
Paid UA Fragility (Mobile)	Build first-party data funnel, diversify creative, A/B test rigorously
Monetisation Pushback	Perform sensitivity testing with communities prior to launch
Platform Cert Timing	Secure showcase invites and platform alignment months before gold build

KEY RISK PATTERNS

Trend-Chasing Collapse

A studio rushes to build the next viral genre (e.g. deckbuilder, vampire survivor, cosy farm sim) without understanding audience saturation. Launch visibility is decent, but long-tail interest disappears within weeks.

Mitigation:

- Analyse competitor player retention, not just sales
- Build audience engagement loops distinct from trend base
- Soft launch to test stickiness

Mismatch Monetisation Burn

Mobile-inspired monetisation (IAPs, gacha mechanics) ported to PC/console causes player backlash and negative reviews.

Mitigation:

- Adapt pricing and feature visibility to audience platform norms
- Watch platform-specific community sentiment and monetisation acceptance

Delayed Discovery Trap

Studios prioritise dev over audience-building until the final months. Wishlist numbers are low, awareness is weak, and influencers are already booked by competitors. Visibility on platforms like Steam is tied closely to wishlist activity and visibility rounds, so without early player interest, your game may never surface organically (Valve, 2020).

Mitigation:

- Build trailers and playable builds early
- Grow community via devlogs, sneak peeks, festival demos

Platform Tone Mismatch

Game tone and messaging do not resonate with the discovery platform's audience (e.g. too slow for TikTok, too shallow for Steam).

Mitigation:

- Tailor content to each platform's native consumption style
- Use microcontent testing (shorts, memes, influencer reactions) as signal

BUILDING COMMUNITIES BEFORE CODE

In recent years, a clear pattern has emerged across many of the studios I have worked with: Community cannot be an afterthought. More and more teams are recognising that their biggest marketing advantage is not a splashy trailer, but rather a player base that is already invested. In some cases, such as with *Nyan Heroes*, the community came first. The concept gained traction, early supporters rallied around it, and the game was built in partnership with those players. That kind of support is not just a nice-to-have; it shapes everything from wishlist momentum to development asset drops and promises of demos to keep future players interested.

This is not just anecdotal. There is increasing consensus across the industry:

- A Reddit post on r/gamedev explains that early communities directly impact Steam algorithm exposure, stating: "When you have a community of 500 people, and 300 of them buy it on release day…Steam will push it higher" (Reddit, 2024).

- New games like *Supervive* are using Discord not only for engagement but as part of their product discovery and playtest pipeline (Alexander, 2024).

- Marketing firms like ELO now explicitly market themselves as building "community-first" campaigns for games in development (VentureBeat, 2024).

- Guides from platforms like Medium and Enjin note the strategic shift towards player inclusion early in development, using community polling, devlogs and progressive reveals to gain trust (Medium, 2023; Enjin, 2023).

Studios are returning to a mindset not dissimilar to the old Kickstarter era: Establish audience proof, then scale. Developer diaries, progress updates, public playtests and community polls have become standard practice, not fringe experiments. If you are not showing your game until launch, you are almost certainly too late. What does this mean for the traditional model of *hide until launch*? A great deal.

REFERENCES

Alexander, J. (2024). How supervive is using discord to build a game before launch. *Polygon*. Retrieved from: https://www.polygon.com/

Dinsdale, R. (2025). Two executives depart build a rocket boy ahead of MindsEye launch. *GamesIndustry.biz*. Retrieved from: https://www.gamesindustry.biz/two-executives-depart-build-a-rocket-boy-ahead-of-mindseye-launch

Enjin. (2023). *Building a community-first strategy for indie games*. Retrieved from: https://enjin.io/blog

Hernandez, P. (2025). MindsEye player count plummets 75% within 24 hours. *Kotaku*. Retrieved from: https://kotaku.com/mindseye-player-count-drop-launch-1851543217

Makuch, E. (2023). Knockout City shutting down after two years. *GameSpot*. Retrieved from: https://www.gamespot.com/articles/knockout-city-shutting-down-after-two-years/1100-6511270/ $1

Medium. (2023). *Game marketing 101: Don't forget your community*. Retrieved from: https://medium.com/

Perez, S. (2021). Apple's ATT prompts massive shifts in mobile marketing. *TechCrunch*. Retrieved from: https://techcrunch.com/2021/09/01/apple-att-impact-mobile-marketing/

Reddit. (2024). *How to build steam visibility through early community engagement.* r/gamedev thread. Retrieved from: https://www.reddit.com/r/gamedev/

Saed, S. (2025). MindsEye dev cancels streams and blames bots amid negative launch. *VG247*. Retrieved from: https://www.vg247.com/mindseye-stream-cancellations-dev-response

Scullion, C. (2025). MindsEye launches to poor reviews on PS5 and PC. *VGC*. Retrieved from: https://www.videogameschronicle.com/news/mindseye-launches-to-poor-reviews-on-ps5-and-pc/

Valve. (2020). *Steamworks documentation – Visibility rounds and wishlists.* Retrieved from: https://partner.steamgames.com/doc/marketing/visibility

VentureBeat. (2024). *Community-first marketing and the rise of discord-native development.* Retrieved from: https://venturebeat.com/

CHAPTER 20

Strategic Risks

INTRODUCTION: STRATEGIC DRIFT IS NOT JUST A LEADERSHIP PROBLEM

Strategic risks are often the most damaging and least visible threats to game development. They tend not to arrive dramatically. Instead, they emerge as a slow erosion of direction, a misalignment of assumptions or a shift in stakeholder intent that is never properly surfaced. These risks rarely show up in Trello, but they shape every milestone, investment pitch and hiring decision.

What makes strategic risk so dangerous is how quietly it builds, and how hard it can be to name. Teams often know something is wrong, but cannot pin it to a single feature or moment. Unlike bugs or budget gaps, this is the kind of risk that accumulates invisibly until something breaks: Morale, funding or the future of the game itself.

This area is slightly different from other categories, so I have played fast and loose a little with the structure of the chapter, particularly in the room granted to the Case Studies.

SIDEBAR: WHY STRATEGIC RISKS ARE RARELY LOGGED

- Feels too abstract or "above your pay grade"
- Risk owners are often the ones making the strategic decisions
- Raising it may be seen as political or disloyal
- There is no clear trigger event – just drift over time

COMMON STRATEGIC RISK TRIGGERS

Trigger	Likely Outcome
Leadership fixated on milestone events	Crunch, tech debt, faked demos
Genre or product pivot midstream	Lost assets, incoherent player experience
New exec or stakeholder partway through	Shifting priorities, morale drop
LiveOps or monetisation push late	System rework, design mismatch

DOI: 10.1201/9781003646082-23

Trigger	Likely Outcome
Vision not shared or understood	Parallel efforts, decision friction
Reacting to market trends blindly	Studio identity loss, poor fit with audience

Industry Trends That Exacerbate Strategic Risk

The following trends (see Chapter 4: "Risk Landscape") increase the chance that studios will drift or pivot for the wrong reasons.

Trend	Strategic Risk Amplified
Decline in investor confidence	Studios chase safer genres, lose distinctiveness (GameSpot, 2024)
Publisher consolidation and exits	Project re-scoping, instability in long-term partnerships
Multi-platform as default	Strategy must account for more variables from day one (Polygon, 2025)
LiveOps pressure	Teams forced into service models they are not structured to support (Game Developers Conference, 2025)
Lack of leadership training	No framework for evaluating trade-offs or pivot risks (IGDA, 2023)
Monetisation expectations	Creative goals get overruled by short-term revenue thinking

MITIGATION STRATEGIES

Mitigation	Benefit
Strategic risk reviews	Create a rhythm for examining key assumptions and pivots
Roadmap confidence modelling	Exposes fragile timelines, risky feature clusters
Embed commercial leads in dev teams	Aligns creative and business intent early
Transparent decision logs	Reduces forgotten pivots and hindsight bias
Cross-functional review panels	Enables senior staff to flag risks outside their usual domain

Prompt Box:

Has your game changed audience, monetisation or genre in the past year? If so, has the roadmap changed too? If not, you are likely carrying strategic debt.

KEY RISK PATTERNS

Showcase-Driven Development

What it is: Resources are diverted to polished vertical slices or trailer content to meet press or investor events.

Impact: Short-term wow factor, long-term tech debt and missed deadlines.

Mitigation: Prioritise real progress over optics. Only show what is close to real game quality.

Strategic Whiplash

What it is: Leadership changes, publisher requests or market fads cause repeated changes in direction.

Impact: Waste, morale erosion, delivery incoherence.

Mitigation: Require pivot impact reviews. Log each pivot formally with rationale and risk.

Innovation Paralysis

What it is: Teams want to push boundaries but do not feel safe to fail.

Impact: Bland execution, missed market opportunity.

Mitigation: Run protected discovery sprints. Make space for risk-taking early on.

SIDEBAR: INNOVATION PARALYSIS – DIAGNOSTIC TOOL

Symptom	What It Suggests
All features feel "safe"	Culture of caution, no permission to fail
Recycled systems from past games	Innovation by imitation – low trust in new ideas
No postmortem on failed ideas	Teams are not learning from creative risk

EXPANDED CASE STUDIES: STRATEGIC RISKS IN PRACTICE

I felt it necessary to explore the case studies here in more detail than in other chapters. This is because strategic risks are so important to understand, particularly their impacts on hundreds of employees.

Also, please do not think that strategic risks are easy to solve, or necessarily even possible to solve. Some are so difficult to predict and understand, given their nature, that it would be almost impossible. However, I firmly believe that risk management grants us the processes and audit trails to stand more of a chance.

Case Study: *Babylon's Fall* (PlatinumGames and Square Enix)

Babylon's Fall launched in 2022 as a live-service action RPG developed by PlatinumGames and published by Square Enix. Despite Platinum's reputation for high-quality combat design, the game received widespread criticism for weak visuals, shallow systems and a lack of identity. It felt like a single-player game that had been awkwardly refitted into a live-service model late in production, likely to meet Square Enix's monetisation goals (GamesIndustry.biz, 2023) (IGN, 2023).

Internally, reports suggest teams struggled with unclear direction and minimal player-facing rationale for core mechanics. Post-launch support was minimal, and player counts plummeted. Servers were taken offline in less than 14 months.

This is a clear case of strategic misalignment between the studio's creative strengths and the imposed business model. Leadership failed to correct course despite poor early feedback and low interest during testing. (Schreier, 2019)

Factor	Risk Type	Impact
Genre misfit and unclear USP	Vision and product strategy	Failed to build a compelling audience
Pushed live-service model (Polygon, 2022)	Business model misfit	Poor retention, critical backlash
Minimal marketing support	Publisher alignment	Confused launch, commercial failure

Case Study: *Battlefield 2042* (DICE and EA)

Released in 2021, Battlefield 2042 was intended to modernise the iconic franchise, but strategic missteps undermined the project from the early stages. Reports point to repeated internal shifts, including the removal of the campaign mode and late-stage changes to the core multiplayer formula (Eurogamer, 2022). These pivots came with little time to rebuild infrastructure, yet the game was released to meet end-of-year financial goals.

The outcome was a widely panned launch, rife with bugs, absent features and confused gameplay systems. Despite player feedback, initial post-launch recovery efforts were slow and poorly targeted. EA later acknowledged issues and restructured the Battlefield leadership team (Schreier, 2022).

This case reflects the danger of adjusting strategic direction without recalibrating production expectations. Directional decisions were made without adequate governance or bottom-up feasibility assessments.

Factor	Risk Type	Impact
Leadership pivot midstream	Strategic whiplash	Rebooted systems, poor cohesion
Rushed to meet market window	Marketing vs readiness	Major bugs, player backlash, lost trust
Post-launch roadmap failure	LiveOps misalignment	Player base collapse, content drought

Case Study: *Redfall* (Arkane Austin and Bethesda/Xbox)

Redfall, released in 2023, was positioned as a co-op vampire shooter. But the project began as a more traditional single-player immersive sim. Midway through development, Xbox leadership reportedly directed a shift towards multiplayer and live-service features (GamesIndustry.biz, 2024). This did not match Arkane's strengths in narrative and systems design, and internal teams reportedly struggled to retrofit their toolsets.

At launch, Redfall faced strong criticism for weak AI, repetitive encounters and low production values (IGN, 2023). Its poor reception led to reputational harm and internal morale issues. The failure was not due to laziness or underinvestment, but to strategic shifts imposed without alignment or resourcing (Bloomberg, 2023).

The result: A studio producing a type of game it was not suited to build, without the tools, culture or structure to support it.

Factor	Risk Type	Impact
Genre pivot during development	Strategic whiplash	Shallow systems, confused design
Xbox mandate to build co-op	Platform strategy misalignment	Misuse of studio strengths
Post-launch fallout	Brand damage, commercial loss	Player distrust, internal morale drop

STRATEGY IS NOT SET-AND-FORGET

Strategic risk is often treated as a one-off: A choice made during the pitch phase, locked in at greenlight. In reality, it is a moving target. The market shifts. New people join. An entire game pillar is removed or added. A feature goes viral. A partner exits. There is a very public data breach. Covid happens. Life is about change, and we need to include our strategy within that truth. Strategic goals are allowed to shift and, in fact encouraged to, if properly thought through, discussed, and communicated.

In my experience, many execs who have grown up in the games industry do not necessarily understand what strategy is and how to utilise strategic best practices. That is not their fault – they have not been exposed to the cut and thrust of the business world. However, that does put them at its mercy. Highlighting strategic risks can help all of us learn how to control them.

REFERENCES

Bloomberg. (2023). *Why redfall was dead on arrival.* Retrieved from: https://www.bloomberg.com/news/articles/2023-05-09/redfall-xbox-failure-arkane-bethesda

Eurogamer. (2022). *Inside battlefield 2042's development chaos.* Retrieved from: https://www.eurogamer.net/inside-battlefield-2042s-development-chaos

Game Developers Conference. (2025). *GDC 2025 state of the industry.* Retrieved from: https://gdconf.com/news/gdc-2025-state-game-industry-devs-weigh-layoffs-ai-and-more

GamesIndustry.biz. (2023). *Square enix and the live service strategy that didn't work.* Retrieved from: https://www.gamesindustry.biz/articles/2023-04-12-square-enixs-live-service-strategy

GamesIndustry.biz. (2024). *What redfall means for xbox strategy.* Retrieved from: https://www.gamesindustry.biz/redfall-and-the-future-of-xbox-game-strategy

GameSpot. (2024). *The collapse of game investment: Why 2023 was so brutal.* Retrieved from: https://www.gamespot.com/articles/the-collapse-of-game-investment-2023

IGDA. (2023). *Developer satisfaction survey: Training, education and career growth.* Retrieved from: https://igda.org/resources/research-reports/

IGN. (2023). *Arkane staff speak out on redfall's failure.* Retrieved from: https://www.ign.com/articles/redfall-arkane-inside-story

IGN. (2023). *Why Babylon's fall failed.* Retrieved from: https://www.ign.com/articles/why-babylons-fall-failed

Polygon. (2022). *Babylon's fall: A live-service misstep.* Retrieved from: https://www.polygon.com /23057246/babylons-fall-review-square-enix-live-service

Polygon. (2025). *The video game industry's 2025 turning point.* Retrieved from: https://www.poly-gon.com/gaming/512115/2025-video-games-big-events-releases

Schreier, J. (2019). How BioWare's anthem went wrong. *Kotaku.* Retrieved from: https://kotaku .com/how-biowares-anthem-went-wrong-1833731964

Schreier, J. (2022). *What went wrong with battlefield 2042.* Retrieved from: https://www.bloomberg .com/news/articles/2022-01-24/ea-s-battlefield-2042-s-launch-problems

CHAPTER 21

Reputational and Public Trust Risks

INTRODUCTION: REPUTATION AS A SYSTEMIC RISK

Reputational risk is often mischaracterised as a communications issue or the result of a poor launch. In practice, it is rarely caused by a single moment. It tends to build quietly over time, emerging from a combination of delivery shortfalls, misaligned messaging and player-facing decisions that were not properly stress tested.

It is important to recognise that reputation is not a marketing asset. It is a fragile outcome of how consistently a studio behaves, communicates and delivers against expectations. Reputational damage usually arrives late but begins early, often rooted in unacknowledged risks in development, production and leadership. We have covered many of these in previous chapters.

Most teams do not intend to overpromise. Most bugs are not ignored maliciously. Most poor reviews are not caused by a single design flaw. But once players begin to lose trust, the situation becomes very difficult to contain. This is especially true in the current environment, where social media sentiment can shift rapidly, and where platform holders and press are quick to respond to public criticism.

This chapter does not treat reputation as a branding concern. Instead, it frames reputational risk as a reflection of deeper systemic issues. We will look at how expectation gaps are created, how player trust erodes and how internal misalignment often results in very public consequences.

COMMON RISK TRIGGERS

- **Dissatisfied Players**: In multiplayer and live-service games, if a large enough segment of the player base becomes frustrated – whether due to balancing issues, server outages or technical problems – word spreads fast. A million players can be lost in a matter of days.

- **Poor Launch Experience**: If a game launches in a buggy, broken state, with unplayable multiplayer or poor optimisation, it leads to negative reviews, mass refund requests and a loss of goodwill that is difficult to recover from. It can take years for games to recover, or they are shut down.

- **Perceived Unethical Practices**: If players believe a company is engaging in exploitative monetisation, misleading advertising or anti-consumer behaviour, they will take to social media, Reddit and Metacritic to make their frustrations known.

- **Weak Community Support**: If a studio's community engagement team is under-resourced or poorly managed, it can lead to mistrust, toxic forums and PR disasters

- **Market Saturation**: Releasing a game in a highly competitive genre could lead to a lack of visibility and poor sales.

- **Audience Mismatch**: Misjudging the target audience, either through incorrect genre targeting or poor communication in marketing efforts.

- **Expectation-Delivery Discrepancy**: When pre-release promises don't match the final product, reputational fallout is almost guaranteed.

Trigger	Primary Signal	Outcome
Player dissatisfaction	Spiking refund rates, negative sentiment	Loss of player base, review bomb
Poor launch experience	Bug reports, refund requests, unmet specs	Metacritic crash, negative PR
Unethical practices	Social media discourse, watchdog media	Platform penalties, brand damage
Weak community support	Silent forums, late responses, mod toxicity	PR crises, lost trust
Genre saturation	Wishlist stagnation, high CPI	Poor conversion, revenue failure
Audience mismatch	Confused reviews, poor engagement	Failed market positioning

Example: Blizzard's Warcraft III: Reforged

Marketed as a definitive remaster, *Reforged* was released with missing features, altered terms of service and visual downgrades from previews. The game received record-low user scores on Metacritic and became a cautionary tale of overpromising and underdelivering (Makuch, 2020).

Example: A studio assumes nostalgia will drive sales, creating a sequel without researching modern audience expectations. The game flops due to outdated mechanics and failure to evolve with the market.

Example: Aliens: Colonial Marines

The game was marketed using high-fidelity demo footage that did not reflect the final release. The discrepancy triggered accusations of false advertising and a class-action lawsuit, becoming a prime example of misaligned marketing and delivery (Chalk, 2013).

MITIGATION STRATEGIES

- **Transparent Pre-Launch Communication**: Avoid overhyping. Share realistic gameplay previews, roadmap caveats and feature limitations.

- **Technical Readiness Reviews**: Ensure platform compatibility and stress test multiplayer functionality before launch.

- **Dedicated Community Team**: Invest in trained professionals with escalation protocols. Moderate forums actively and respond to critical issues promptly.

- **Market Timing and Audience Research**: Conduct genre saturation analysis and competitor release calendars. Validate feature expectations via closed alphas, surveys or focus groups.

- **Post-Launch Crisis Protocols**: Prepare contingency plans including refund processes, hotfix staffing and public statements.

- **Proactive Community Moderation**: Implement active moderation practices to remove toxicity and ensure a healthy discourse environment (Duggan & Smith, 2023).

SIDEBAR: WHY REPUTATIONAL RISK IS STUDIO-WIDE

- Engineers think it is a PR problem.
- PR thinks it is a dev problem.
- Execs think it is a player problem.

Reputation risk tends to be cumulative: it starts with scope creep, poor tooling, unspoken changes. Eventually, it shows up at launch, but it *started* months earlier.

Ask: "Where in our process can we still catch reputational damage before it happens?"

KEY RISK PATTERNS

Review Score Spiral

Definition: The cascade of negative reviews triggered by early bugs, unmet promises or performance issues.

Example: *Cyberpunk 2077*'s console performance at launch led to poor Metacritic scores, which were amplified by YouTubers and social media commentary, causing refunds and temporary delisting on the PlayStation Store (Schreier, 2021).

Mitigation Checklist:

- Ship a stable build for all platforms.

- Ensure aligned marketing expectations.

- Prepare patch communication and press response plans.

Monetisation Misfire

Definition: Implementing revenue strategies that are viewed as exploitative or opaque.

Example: *Star Wars Battlefront II* faced severe backlash for loot boxes perceived as pay-to-win. The controversy led to widespread media coverage and a sharp response from EA, who restructured the entire monetisation model prior to launch (Yin-Poole, 2017).

Mitigation Checklist:

- Conduct ethical reviews of monetisation systems.

- Include consumer advisory boards or user research.

- A/B test systems in limited geo-releases where possible.

Absent Community Engagement

Definition: Failure to acknowledge or address legitimate community feedback in a timely manner.

Example: *No Man's Sky* suffered from poor communication in its early post-launch months, fuelling player frustration. It took over a year of consistent updates and improved engagement to begin restoring goodwill (Murray, 2017).

Mitigation Checklist:

- Establish community engagement protocols and staffing.

- Publish patch notes, dev diaries and roadmap updates.

- Address high-traffic forum issues and provide visibility into resolutions.

Expectation-Delivery Discrepancy

Definition: A significant gap between pre-release marketing promises and the actual product delivered.

Example: *Aliens: Colonial Marines* heavily promoted impressive demo footage that didn't represent the final product, leading to consumer backlash and a lawsuit (Chalk, 2013).

Case	Risk Type	Outcome	Lesson
Warcraft III: Reforged	Expectation-Delivery Discrepancy	Record-low user scores	Overpromise kills legacy trust
Aliens: Colonial Marines	Marketing vs Product Mismatch	Class action lawsuit	QA your marketing assets
Star Wars Battlefront II	Monetisation Misfire	System overhauled pre-launch	Ethical monetisation matters
No Man's Sky	Communication Failure	One-year recovery	Dev silence deepens backlash

Connecting Reputation Risk to Upstream Failures

Reputation collapses are rarely "surprises" inside a studio. The warning signs exist, but they live in different systems. Below are examples of public-facing risk outcomes and their typical upstream origins:

Public Risk Outcome	Underlying Root Cause(s)
Review Score Spiral	Technical debt, late-stage crunch, QA deprioritised
Monetisation Misfire	Siloed economy design, no user testing, leadership pressure
Absent Community Engagement	Understaffed or unsupported comms teams, unclear escalation routes
Expectation-Delivery Discrepancy	Leadership drift, pivot without marketing coordination, cut features
Toxic Forum Backlash	Inactive moderation, vague patch notes, poor transparency post-launch

Studio Lesson:
Your trailer, monetisation plan, patch cadence and community tone are all public reflections of internal alignment (or the lack of it). Players can smell it out.

MITIGATION CHECKLIST

- Align marketing materials closely with the final product.
- Vet demos and trailers through QA to ensure consistency.
- Maintain records of design changes and disclose major shifts early.

REFERENCES

Chalk, A. (2013). Aliens: Colonial Marines lawsuit ends with settlement. *PC Gamer.* Retrieved from: https://www.pcgamer.com/aliens-colonial-marines-lawsuit-ends-with-settlement/

Duggan, M., & Smith, A. (2023). *Online harassment 2023.* Pew Research Center. Retrieved from: https://www.pewresearch.org/internet/2023/07/13/online-harassment-2023/

Makuch, E. (2020). Blizzard apologizes for *Warcraft III: Reforged*'s problems. *GameSpot.* Retrieved from: https://www.gamespot.com/articles/blizzard-apologizes-for-warcraft-3-reforgeds-problems/1100-6473191/

Murray, S. (2017). No man's sky: Foundation update. *Hello Games Blog*. Retrieved from: https://www.nomanssky.com/foundation-update/

Schreier, J. (2021). *Press reset: Ruin and recovery in the video game industry*. Grand Central Publishing.

Yin-Poole, W. (2017). The story behind Star Wars Battlefront 2's loot box controversy. *Eurogamer*. Retrieved from: https://www.eurogamer.net/articles/2017-11-21-the-story-behind-star-wars-battlefront-2s-loot-box-controversy

CHAPTER 22

Collaboration and Partnership Risks in Game Development

INTRODUCTION

Game development frequently involves a complex network of partnerships: Co-development studios, outsourcing vendors, tool providers and internal studios following mergers or acquisitions. While these collaborations offer the promise of increased productivity, efficiency and access to specialised skills, they also introduce considerable risk across alignment, communication, delivery and cultural compatibility.

What we often call "external" partnerships are not truly external anymore. Post-acquisition studios, offsite co-dev teams, even subsidiaries with different pipelines – they act like vendors in terms of risk, even if they sit under the same organisation chart. Dangers come from assuming we are compatible and will slip into each other's processes and culture.

UNDERSTANDING COLLABORATION RISKS

Internal vs External Partnerships

Not all "external" collaborations are truly external. Sometimes, newly acquired or restructured internal studios function independently – with different systems, pipelines and expectations. This can make them just as risky to collaborate with as third-party outsourcers.

Just because a partner is internal on paper does not mean they are risk-free. Mergers, acquisitions and reorganisations create pseudo-external conditions: Teams with different cultures, expectations and capabilities. If you force uniformity too fast, it fails.

DOI: 10.1201/9781003646082-25

Examples of Risk Factors:

- **Company Culture Clashes**: A rigidly hierarchical studio may struggle to work with a team that favours a flat structure and autonomy.

- **Process Misalignment**: One team may use Scrum; another, Kanban. Integration becomes difficult without clear interface protocols. Process goes way beyond this example and can end up creating so much misalignment that it requires major intervention.

- **Capability Gaps**: Discrepancies in technical maturity, tool proficiency or creative standards can cause delivery breakdowns.

According to the IGDA Developer Satisfaction Survey (2021), mismatched production methodologies and unclear expectations were among the top three causes of tension in external partnerships.

Key Collaboration Risks

- **Readiness Gaps**: Internal teams might not be prepared to work with external partners due to recent restructuring or unclear roles.

- **Miscommunication**: Lack of shared context, poor documentation and language barriers lead to delays and rework.

- **Workflow Incompatibility**: Different pipelines or toolchains can cause production bottlenecks.

- **Undocumented Risks**: If risk is not openly shared across partners, surprises emerge late in the development cycle.

Risk Type	Real Example	Outcome
Readiness Gaps	Internal leads redeployed due to emergency task	Partner onboarding fails
Time Zone Asymmetry	Feedback loop stretched 48 hrs	Asset rework cycle
Process Misfit	One team uses Unreal, the other Unity	Failed integration or redundant work
Role Ambiguity	No RACI matrix for signoff	Assets stuck in approval limbo

MITIGATION STRATEGIES

Risk Transparency and Role Clarity

- **Shared Risk Registers**: Collaboratively maintained documents that track known risks, owners and status across all partners.

- **Use of RACI Matrix**: Assign roles as Responsible, Accountable, Consulted and Informed to reduce confusion over ownership (Wikipedia contributors, 2024).

Example: In a GDC 2017 session, representatives from EA and Bioware detailed how they used structured role definitions (akin to a RACI matrix) when coordinating between internal teams and external vendors on Mass Effect: Andromeda. This clarified handoff responsibilities and reduced friction around asset delivery and approval loops (GDC Vault, 2017).

Frequent and Honest Communication

- **Structured Check-Ins**: Weekly stand-ups or milestone reviews across teams ensure friction points are surfaced early.

- **Operational Dashboards**: Shared tools (e.g. Jira, Miro, Confluence) allow real-time visibility into backlog, feedback and blockers.

GDC presentations have frequently highlighted the importance of aligning tooling and dashboards between studios to improve visibility and decrease reliance on informal updates (GDC Vault, 2020).

Adaptive Workflows

- **Do not Force Uniformity**: Aim for interoperability, not conformity. Let each partner use their preferred tools and formats as long as delivery specs are clearly defined.

- **Prototyping Expectations**: Validate shared understanding early with small-scale deliverables or technical tests.

Vendor and Outsourcing Risks

One of the biggest issues leading to vendors' failure occurs when we fail to prepare for them.

Causes of Vendor Delays

- **Overcommitted Workloads**: Outsourcers often juggle multiple clients. Your project may not be their top priority.

- **Approval Loops**: If asset reviews are slow or inconsistent, entire production pipelines can stall. Do not let your internal art director block asset flow by insisting on personally reviewing 1,000 assets – that is a bottleneck. Systemic risk hides in over-centralised approval loops.

- **Time Zone Barriers**: Feedback cycles are prolonged when teams are 10+ hours apart without asynchronous tools.

Example: A vendor issue was discussed during a GDC 2019 talk by Anna Kipnis (then at Double Fine), where poor bug triaging practices led to QA teams overwhelming development backlogs with low-priority issues. By restructuring triage workflows and introducing asynchronous prioritisation reviews, the team reduced critical issue turnaround time and improved communication between QA and development (GDC Vault, 2019).

Mitigation Approaches

- **Contractual Clauses**: Define SLAs, revision timelines and penalties for missed deadlines upfront.

- **Contingency Planning**: Maintain relationships with alternative vendors or in-house teams that can be activated in emergencies.

- **Regular QA and Integration Cycles**: Avoid deferring acceptance testing until late stages – validate early and often.

Misaligned Expectations

Misalignment occurs even in the presence of contracts. Differences in interpretation around quality, timelines and definitions of "done" lead to unnecessary rework and tension.

They want to do a good job for you, yes. But they also want to spend as little time as possible so they can make a margin. That is not malicious – it is commercial logic. If you do not factor that in, you will get a delay and disappointment.

Producer Prompt:
Have you defined what "done" means? For both parties? If not, expect to be surprised.

Why It Happens

- **Differing Incentives**: Vendors may seek efficiency over excellence to preserve margins.

- **Ambiguous Documentation**: Briefs that rely on assumptions rather than clarity.

- **Insufficient Oversight**: Late feedback or approval bottlenecks introduce delays.

Preventing Misalignment

- **RACI Matrices**: Reduce ambiguity by clearly defining who signs off on what.

- **Early Sample Reviews**: Catch misunderstandings before they affect 100 assets.

- **Written Agreements for Quality Benchmarks**: Specify frame rate, texture resolution, collision fidelity – whatever is relevant.

KEY RISK PATTERNS

The following are recurring risk patterns that emerge when collaboration lacks structural support. These are common failure modes across vendor, partner and internal team relationships.

1. Feedback Fog

Definition: Collaboration proceeds without timely, specific or reliable feedback.

Risk: Teams waste time guessing expectations, leading to rework, resentment and morale drift.

Real-World Marker: A partner sends an update and hears nothing back for a week. When feedback finally arrives, it is vague or contradictory.

Mitigation:

- Set clear expectations on feedback turnaround and format.

- Use asynchronous tools with versioning where possible.

- Escalate absence of feedback explicitly as a risk and not a politeness issue.

2. The Illusion of Alignment

Definition: Two teams believe they are working together, but are actually operating in parallel with diverging assumptions.

Risk: Gaps are discovered only at integration points. Trust erodes quickly.

Real-World Marker: Dependencies are missed, ownership is unclear and both sides blame the other for delay.

Mitigation:

- Create a single source of truth for shared priorities.

- Agree jointly on definitions of "done" and release readiness.

- Track whether integration time is growing silently.

3. Deferred Friction

Definition: Disagreements, delays and mismatches are downplayed to "keep things friendly".

Risk: Pressure builds behind the scenes until collaboration breaks down.

Real-World Marker: Everyone knows the delivery is slipping, but no one is willing to say so.

Mitigation:

- Build escalation into the contract or working agreement.

- Assign a named person responsible for managing relationship health.

- Review not just delivery, but collaboration quality in retros.

4. Silent Vendor Syndrome

Definition: A vendor or partner delivers late or off-target, but has not raised blockers in advance.

Risk: Issues are discovered only at review or drop stage. Recovery costs escalate.

Real-World Marker: Status reports are always "green" until the day the milestone is missed.

Mitigation:

- Require regular status updates or live demos, not just tracking documents.

- Include responsiveness and transparency in vendor evaluation criteria.

- Use dry runs or partial drops to detect divergence early.

CO-DEVELOPMENT RISKS

Co-dev is not just large-scale outsourcing. It is shared delivery and often on core systems, within the same build pipeline, and with overlapping areas of ownership. The risks are deeper, and the damage from misalignment is often higher.

Pipeline Drift

Different studios evolve internal tooling, workflows or practices over time. If integration checkpoints are infrequent, drift accumulates until reintegration becomes non-trivial.

Example: AI or animation logic forks between co-dev and internal teams, and so reintegration causes bugs and wasted QA.

Mitigation:

- Shared integration cadence.

- Appoint a tech alignment lead on each side.

- Run compatibility checks mid-sprint, not just at milestone gates.

Ownership Ambiguity

When multiple studios co-develop features, clarity over who owns the final polish, integration or bug fixing often disappears.

Example: Both teams assume the other will handle final pass QA or adapt to a system refactor.

Mitigation:

- Write shared definitions of system ownership and release responsibilities.

- Track work status *by integration state*, not just completion.

- Run regular "ownership refresh" sessions during major scope changes.

Cultural Divergence

Co-dev teams often work under different assumptions about communication, escalation and visibility. Silence does not always mean agreement.

Example: A partner studio interprets constructive critique as criticism, withdraws from meetings and morale collapses.

Mitigation:

- Schedule co-dev onboarding sessions, including team culture and comms styles.

- Assign internal champions to monitor health and tone of partnership.

- Build a rhythm of informal check-ins, not just project tracking calls.

Building Strong Collaborative Partnerships
Best Practices

- **Honest Weekly Syncs**: Surface tension early instead of glossing over it.

- **Collaborative Documentation**: Shared Confluence spaces for briefs, definitions and production notes.

- **Leadership Engagement**: Do not isolate vendor relationships to producers only – have Directors or Leads engage periodically.

If you are not meeting regularly to discuss risks with your vendor or co-dev, your RAID log is not going to be effective.

Example: One AAA studio required quarterly joint retrospectives with each vendor. This not only improved delivery reliability but also uncovered skill gaps that the vendor was later funded to resolve. A similar approach was presented by Bungie at GDC 2020, where the Destiny team ran regular review sessions with external development partners to proactively address coordination and communication challenges (GDC Vault, 2020).

Studio	Practice	Outcome
Bungie	Joint quarterly retros with vendors	Improved delivery reliability, uncovered skill gaps
Double Fine	Asynchronous triage for QA feedback	Reduced noise, improved dev velocity
EA/Bioware	RACI-based coordination on ME: Andromeda	Reduced asset approval bottlenecks

REFERENCES

GDC Vault. (2017). Mass effect: Andromeda – The ups and downs of large scale asset production. Retrieved from: https://www.gdcvault.com/play/1024357/Mass-Effect-Andromeda-The-Ups

GDC Vault. (2019). Kipnis, A. QA at double fine: Adventures in Agile and Chaos. Retrieved from: https://www.gdcvault.com/play/1025683/QA-at-Double-Fine-Adventures

GDC Vault. (2020). *Working effectively with external development partners.* Retrieved from: https://www.gdcvault.com/play/1027046/Working-Effectively-with-External

IGDA. (2021). *Developer satisfaction survey: External partnerships in game dev.* Retrieved from: https://igda.org/dss

Wikipedia contributors. (2024). *RACI matrix.* Wikipedia. Retrieved from: https://en.wikipedia.org/wiki/Responsibility_assignment_matrix

CHAPTER 23

Communication Gaps Risks

INTRODUCTION

Poor communication is one of the most pervasive causes of risk in game development. It contributes to misunderstandings, duplicated effort, missed dependencies and delays – particularly in fast-moving or distributed teams.

Communication failure is not a fringe problem – in my experience it is the mechanism by which most other risks escalate. A hidden delay becomes a missed milestone. A change no one logs becomes a feature no one finishes. For many, it is difficult to realise that the bubble of people, work and conversations that they live within does not encompass everyone who needs to know. They are simply too busy, or relying on producers to convey messages, or they think the person they told a decision to will automatically convey that to the correct audience.

SIDEBAR: MISUNDERSTANDING WHAT "COMMUNICATION" MEANS

I think communication is a difficult word. When I say "it was communicated", what I really mean is: Conversations were facilitated, processes were in place to listen, decisions were made based on actual information and discussion – and *that* was communicated. If that does not happen, you have a built-in system risk.

COMMON COMMUNICATION RISK TRIGGERS

- **Top-Down Decisions Without Context**: Leadership makes major changes, e.g. to monetisation, scope or platform strategy, but fails to communicate the rationale, leaving teams confused, frustrated, directionless or misaligned.

- **Lack of Proper Documentation**: Critical decisions made in meetings are not recorded or shared, leading to multiple interpretations and execution drift. This seems to

DOI: 10.1201/9781003646082-26

happen an awful lot and is directly controlled through following risk management processes.

- **Remote Work Challenges**: In distributed teams, important discussions often happen in informal or private channels (e.g. DMs, hallway/video chats), leaving others unaware of key decisions.

Trigger	Root Cause	Example Outcome
Top-down decision without cascade	Strategic misalignment	Monetisation team builds obsolete system (Battlefield V – see below)
Lack of recorded decisions	No shared doc culture	Conflicting implementation, duplicated work
Remote work fragmentation	Slack + DMs + async tools	People unaware of critical updates

Every time someone says "I thought that was already handled", you have a communication risk.

SIDEBAR: THE THREE FACES OF COMMUNICATION RISK

- **Decision Drift** – We think we are aligned, but we are not
- **Information Fragmentation** – The info exists, but no one knows where
- **Async Failure** – The message is sent, but never lands

MITIGATION STRATEGIES

- **Establish Regular Sync Meetings**: Daily stand-ups, weekly cross-functional updates and leadership Q&A sessions ensure visibility and surface risks early.

- **Create a Decision-Tracking System**: Use a centralised tool (e.g. Confluence, Notion) to record and communicate key decisions and their rationale. Build it into the risk register or kanban tracking.

- **Encourage Two-Way Feedback**: Promote a culture where team members feel empowered to ask for clarification, raise flags and contribute to improving transparency (Wickham, 2024).

Real-World Example: Communication Failure in Monetisation Change

A well-known case occurred during the development of *Battlefield V* at DICE. Late in production, leadership decided to pivot away from a planned loot box system due to regulatory concerns and player feedback – but failed to cascade the change clearly to downstream teams. The economy designers and systems engineers continued to build mechanics that were later rendered obsolete, causing significant rework and a delay to post-launch content (GDC Vault, 2020).

KEY RISK PATTERNS IN COMMUNICATION FAILURES

Decision Drift

Decision drift refers to the gradual loss of clarity over what decisions were made, why they were made and who made them. In large teams or long-running projects, especially those without centralised decision logging, this leads to conflicting directions, duplicated work or even backtracking late in production.

Example: A comparable issue was highlighted during the development of *Halo Infinite* at 343 Industries. Internal miscommunication around evolving multiplayer mechanics – including respawn and equipment balance – led to frequent backtracking and reimplementation efforts late in development. Several systems had to be rebuilt as cross-disciplinary teams were not always aligned on changes to core gameplay loops, delaying some feature integrations until post-launch (Schreier, 2021).

Mitigation Strategies:

- Maintain a lightweight decision log visible to all team members.

- Assign a decision owner (often a lead or director) for each area.

- Review major past decisions during sprint planning or milestone preps.

Information Fragmentation

Modern game teams use a variety of tools, including Slack, Jira, Google Docs, Confluence, email – and while flexible, this fragmentation increases the risk that important context gets lost.

Risks Introduced:

- Conflicting task instructions across systems.

- Missed updates due to notifications being scattered.

- Onboarding becomes difficult when tribal knowledge is buried in chat threads.

Best Practices:

- Define a single source of truth for each domain (e.g. all design specs live in Confluence).

- Limit channels used for critical communication.

- Conduct regular housekeeping of obsolete or duplicate documentation.

Async Communication Failures

Remote and distributed teams rely heavily on asynchronous communication. However, without agreed norms, silence can be interpreted in different ways – approval, confusion or neglect.

If your async workflows depend on people "just noticing" something posted in Slack, you are placing unfair pressure on already information-overloaded knowledge workers.

Common Pitfalls:

- Blocking issues go unacknowledged because someone assumed they were being handled.

- Time zone delays are not factored into milestone buffers.

- Urgent changes posted in chat are missed entirely.

Mitigation Techniques:

- Define response time expectations (e.g. 24h rule).

- Use status indicators on tools ("Needs Review", "Blocked") instead of assuming people are watching.

- Summarise async threads weekly in shared docs to create shared visibility.

The Risk-Mitigating Power of Conversations

Too often, communication is treated like a box-tick: The update was sent, the Slack post was written, the email went out. But most risks do not show up because a message was not sent. They show up because **a proper conversation never happened**.

The uncomfortable truth is this: Most teams avoid hard conversations. They assume alignment or do not want to rock the boat. And that is exactly how misjudgements, bad calls and unspoken doubts build into real problems.

> Conversations are the original code review. A moment to step out of the 'I've already committed this' mindset, and instead ask: Do we agree? Did we build the same thing in our heads?
>
> (Author, 2020)

What Conversations Actually Do
Conversations are where:

- People challenge assumptions before it is too late to pivot

- Conflicts emerge early, when they are still fixable

- Leaders get a true sense of unease or disagreement

- Junior team members voice doubts they would never write down

If your team is relying entirely on dashboards, tools and async messages, you will miss the warning signs. You need to make space to hear them.

Common Conversational Failures

Pattern	What Actually Happens
"It was already communicated"	Nobody checks if it landed or was even read
One-way status updates	No room for people to flag confusion or doubt
Written-only feedback	Loses nuance, tone and the chance to probe
Avoiding friction	People go quiet instead of raising red flags

Simple Fixes

- Schedule regular space for open-ended discussion and not just updates

- Run retros that include the question: *What conversations are we avoiding?*

- Let juniors shadow or pair with seniors informally

- Make it clear that silence is not the same as agreement

Example: During the development of *Far Cry 6*, Ubisoft Toronto faced significant challenges due to the COVID-19 pandemic, which necessitated a shift to remote production. The team had to innovate rapidly to maintain communication and workflow efficiency. They implemented remote motion capture sessions with minimal on-site staff and utilised in-home audio recording setups for voice actors. To coordinate these efforts, they relied on multiple video streams and developed in-house tools to facilitate remote collaboration. Despite these adaptations, the transition highlighted the complexities of asynchronous communication, particularly in synchronising performances and ensuring consistent direction across dispersed teams (Khavari, 2021).

Studio	Risk	Outcome
DICE (Battlefield V)	Pivot not cascaded	Economy system wasted; post-launch delayed
343 (Halo Infinite)	Poor gameplay change tracking	Rebuild of multiplayer mechanics
Ubisoft (Far Cry 6)	Remote sync breakdown	Voice + mocap misalignment; workflow delays

REFERENCES

GDC Vault. (2020). *Working effectively with external development partners.* Retrieved from: https://www.gdcvault.com/play/1027046/Working-Effectively-with-External

Khavari, N. (2021, October 7). *How the team behind far cry 6 finished a game in lockdown.* WIRED. Retrieved from: https://www.wired.com/story/how-ubisoft-finished-far-cry-6-lockdown

Schreier, J. (2021, August 12). *Halo infinite's troubled past offers a glimpse into the next generation of Xbox games.* Bloomberg. Retrieved from: https://www.bloomberg.com/news/articles/2021-08-12/-halo-infinite-s-troubled-past-offers-a-glimpse-into-the-next-generation-of-xbox-games

Wickham, L. (2024). *The mindset of success: The final set.* Game Production Academy. Retrieved from: https://www.game-production.com/post/1-5-the-mindset-of-success-the-final-set

CHAPTER 24

Staffing Risks

INTRODUCTION

Staffing risks in game development are some of the most overlooked yet critical challenges that studios face. Unlike industries with standardised workflows, game development relies heavily on specialised knowledge, creative expertise and team cohesion – all of which can be disrupted by unexpected staffing changes.

In other industries, you can often plug in a new team member and pick up the slack. Not so in games. A senior designer who has shaped your combat loop or a tools engineer who knows your proprietary pipeline – these are not easily replaced. And worse, you often do not have three months for onboarding. That person needs to start making decisions on the fly, in a chaotic and creative environment, with tacit knowledge scattered across Slack, Notion and department heads.

If you are a producer, one of your core responsibilities is to notice when systems are fragile, incomplete or operating on the goodwill of overstretched veterans. Staffing risks are often treated as HR's problem, but they are just as critical to delivery cadence, team velocity and milestone stability.

COMMON RISK TRIGGERS

Staffing risks in game development do not stem from a single root cause. Instead, they emerge from a complex network of systemic issues which are often interlinked and probably hidden. The following are six recurring patterns that heighten fragility, stall delivery or cause ongoing morale damage.

Over-Reliance on Key Personnel

Losing key team members, such as senior designers, lead engineers or producers, creates immediate knowledge gaps and disrupts workflow. Game development often depends on tacit knowledge: Iinsights that are not easily transferable, especially in bespoke pipelines or experimental mechanics.

DOI: 10.1201/9781003646082-27

A frequent but unspoken trigger is when the same few seniors are pulled into every high-priority initiative. This begins to snowball: They onboard new hires, maintain legacy tools, unblock others and their own deliverables fall behind. This shadow bottleneck often precedes attrition.

The risk compounds further when those individuals are also responsible for non-transferable architecture, tools or decision histories. When they leave, even temporarily, entire workflows stall.

Risk of Knowledge Loss and Tacit Expertise

When senior team members exit – voluntarily or otherwise – years of undocumented decisions, informal workflows and personal technical insight may vanish with them.

Do not underestimate the sheer volume of unwritten knowledge embedded in a few people's heads. These are not just veterans; they are system owners, lore guardians and architecture builders. They hold the "why" behind your tools, your pipeline, your game logic. When they disengage or leave, you do not just lose productivity; you lose coherence. You may even lose the thread of what game you were building.

Tacit knowledge is the connective tissue of your project. In one studio, our AI tuning system had no formal documentation – just a custom spreadsheet and the memory of one engineer. When he left, we spent three sprints just understanding how to reset sliders. That was not a handover issue. That was a production failure.

Disruptions in Workflow

Key departures can leave projects without a clear direction, especially if replacements are unfamiliar with the game's history, the rationale behind decisions or the dependencies between tools and features. The cost is not just onboarding time; it is the delay caused by lack of confidence and second-guessing.

When velocity drops, teams often compensate by reducing scope or compromising polish, not realising the root issue is structural memory loss. Replacements can inherit Jira boards and Slack archives, but not judgement or intuition. That must be built or transferred.

Firefighter Fatigue

Another under-recognised trigger is the repetitive use of the same senior developers as crisis responders. They are constantly pulled into urgent onboarding, critical bug resolution or production fire drills. These "rotating firefighters" absorb short-term shocks but are sacrificed in the long term.

Their own feature work falls behind. Their engagement drops. And when they burn out or leave, the organisation loses both resilience and output.

This is not a resource issue, but rather a failure to distribute knowledge, rotate responsibilities and mentor backups early enough.

Fragile or Absent Succession Planning

Even predictable transitions, like contract end dates, secondments or promotions, cause disruption if no succession planning has taken place. In most teams, transition planning is deferred until the last few weeks. This leads to frantic knowledge transfer, partial documentation and often an expensive external hire who lacks critical context.

Good succession planning is not naming a backup. It is a deliberate, ongoing act: Rotating ownership, building living documentation and allowing junior staff to shadow senior systems early enough to gain trust.

Team Morale Collapse and Emotional Contagion

The impact of a sudden exit is rarely contained to logistics. It affects team morale, confidence and cohesion. If the person leaving was seen as a mentor, protector or cultural anchor, their departure can destabilise teams emotionally, especially if the cause is burnout or frustration.

Emotional contagion is real. A demotivated senior figure can quietly undermine energy across multiple pods. They still attend meetings but stop giving context, push back less in reviews or defer decisions. That demoralises others and slows down momentum.

MITIGATION STRATEGIES

- **Knowledge Retention Practices**:

  - Maintain living documentation of systems, pipelines and design rationales.

  - Regularly record architecture walkthroughs and technical demonstrations.

I once worked on a project where a senior backend engineer had cornered so much technical knowledge that no one could touch the pipeline. When they left, we were blocked for months.

- **Succession Planning Frameworks**:

  - Identify backup candidates for all senior positions.

  - Provide ongoing leadership and communication training to high-potential team members.

- **Staffing Forecasts and Exit Contingency Plans**:

  - Create heat maps of skill coverage to identify critical gaps.

  - Prepare contract staffing options or secondment arrangements for rapid onboarding.

- **Cross-Team Mentorship Programmes**:

  - Encourage mentoring relationships across departments to transfer both technical and cultural knowledge.

- **Documentation Cadence and Ownership:**

  - Schedule regular reviews of onboarding guides, system documents or design bibles.

  - Use Confluence plugins or Notion trackers to assign ownership and track updates.

  - Encourage teams to treat documentation as live and iterative, not a one-time dump.

  - Update documentation *while* you are using it. If a lead is onboarding someone into a system and says, "Oh, that doc's a bit out of date", that is the moment to fix it. Not two weeks later in a retro. Build a culture where updates happen live: In walkthroughs, design reviews, onboarding calls. No separate ticket in **Jira** is needed – just fix it immediately.

  - Asking someone to "go review documentation" is usually a dead ticket. It sounds optional. But "update doc while presenting feature X" is embedded. You are turning transient spoken knowledge into retained value. That shift matters.

- **Tool Rationalisation and Version Control:**

  - **Reduce tool sprawl:** Avoid maintaining parallel systems like OneNote, Google Docs and SharePoint.

  - Choose a single system of record for core documentation.

  - Use versioning workflows (e.g. drafts, review deadlines, approval stages) to ensure accountability.

- **Knowledge Champions and Internal Talks:**

  - Host monthly internal knowledge sharing sessions.

  - Record walkthroughs of recent technical decisions or tools.

  - Nominate domain experts who can answer questions without becoming a bottleneck.

- **Use of Technical Authors:**

  - A professional tech writer can extract, structure and maintain documentation.

  - Even one embedded writer can unblock teams from chasing context.

  - Many tech writers are creative writers who hope to move into narrative roles – offering mutual career benefit.

  - If you can afford even one part-time tech author, they will pay for themselves in recovered velocity. I have hired several and I have been one myself.

- Tech authors do not just write things down. They observe, structure and create coherence. I have hired several – some became game writers later on. If you are a producer, you can use that as a draw. Offer narrative exposure in exchange for documentation structure. Everyone wins.

Example: 343 Industries and Halo Infinite (2020)
In 2020, *Halo Infinite* saw a leadership shake-up when Creative Director Tim Longo left mid-development, followed by Mary Olson shortly after. These changes reportedly led to confusion about the game's direction and multiple production resets. The game's eventual release was delayed by over a year, in part due to the instability caused by these key staff departures (Robinson, 2021).

Replaceability, Fear and the Real Work of Succession

Some roles are difficult to replace. In game teams, you may be dealing with systems no one else fully understands, tools built in-house or workflows based on habit rather than shared documentation. Bringing someone new into that mix is rarely straightforward.

Teams often avoid proper handovers because of misplaced fear. "If I write this down, I will be replaced". In reality, that mindset creates fragility. The project ends up depending on one person who cannot step away without everything stalling. They cannot even go on holiday without a sense of guilt, in my experience.

Succession planning works best when it is embedded gradually. This means rotating responsibilities, documenting as you go, pairing people on systems and reducing the dependency on any one individual.

Example: Respawn Entertainment's Succession Pipeline
Respawn has spoken at multiple GDCs about its leadership cultivation efforts. During the development of *Apex Legends*, team leads maintained succession documents for all key disciplines. When two department leads left unexpectedly during post-launch support, the studio was able to promote internal candidates without major disruption (GDC Vault, 2020).

Psychological Safety and Silent Disengagement

Psychological safety is often discussed in vague terms, but it has a direct impact on how teams function. When people do not feel comfortable raising concerns, they usually stop trying. You lose visibility.

Teams without it tend to look productive. Meetings are attended, updates are given, but hesitation creeps in. People stop asking questions, avoid disagreements and quietly disconnect from decision-making.

This kind of disengagement does not show up in task trackers, but it affects everything from planning quality to team morale.

Rehiring Trusted Alumni

You might lose someone, but you do not have to lose them forever. Developers who leave on good terms often remain open to returning, especially for short-term help, onboarding support or advisory roles during a crisis.

Most studios do nothing to maintain these relationships. That is a mistake.

A simple alumni list and occasional outreach can save months of lost time. Someone who knows your systems, your team and your culture is worth ten generic CVs. Some of the best contractors I have brought in were former staff who were happy to drop in, clear a backlog and move on. I have been that contractor on a number of occasions.

The games industry still seems to be a "small world" and keeping on good terms with those who worked with you is respectful and common sense.

Team Morale and Retention

Team morale is a hidden but critical factor in game development success. High turnover rates don't just affect staffing numbers – they impact productivity, studio culture and overall risk management (Schreier, 2021).

- **Burnout and Crunch Culture**: Long periods of unsustainable working hours lead to high attrition rates, with senior talent leaving for better conditions at competitor studios (Weststar & Legault, 2021).

- **Lack of Transparency**: Poor communication about project delays, leadership changes or layoffs increases anxiety and reduces trust.

- **Inconsistent Vision**: If leadership constantly shifts priorities, teams become disengaged, leading to reduced motivation and work quality.

- **Communication Breakdown**: Poor communication between cross-functional teams (design, engineering, art, etc.) can lead to misalignment on project goals, delays or quality issues. These often damage morale.

- **Cultural Fit with External Partners**: Collaborating with external vendors or partners who have different cultures or work ethics can lead to miscommunications and quality concerns. This can often increase stress.

You can sign the cleanest outsourcing contract in the world – but if your external partners do not share communication norms, time zone availability or delivery expectations, things fall apart fast. Cultural fit is not a soft metric. It affects morale, rework and trust.

SIDEBAR: THE HUMAN COST OF UNRELENTING PACE

Developers who couldn't or wouldn't sustain the pace often churned, resulting in frequent backfilling and loss of experienced talent... The team culture had normalised repeated last-minute crunches... Early burndown charts may appear overly optimistic; that's intentional. They should absorb the impact when, not if, additional work emerges.

- LEAD GAME PRODUCER

Practical Solutions to Mitigate Morale Risks

- **Open Communication**: Regular town halls, AMAs and one-on-one check-ins ensure transparency.

- **Recognition and Growth Opportunities**: Career progression and skills development reduce retention risks.

- **Healthy Work Culture**: Managing crunch periods and respecting work-life balance prevent long-term attrition (GDC Vault, 2018).

- **Tactical Moves That Signal Care**: We sometimes feel powerless to influence morale, but even small moves make a difference. Record a short welcome video. Hold informal Friday demos. Run "what surprised you this week?" check-ins. These tactics do not fix crunch, but they show that someone sees the humans behind the hours.

Example: Bungie's Culture Reboot Post-Destiny Crunch
Following heavy criticism of crunch during *Destiny's* early development, Bungie restructured its work culture, introduced "no-meeting Fridays", and promoted internal career mobility. These changes helped stabilise attrition and improved morale ahead of *Destiny 2's* major expansions (Tassi, 2018).

Example: Rockstar Games and Crunch Culture Fallout (2018–2020)
After reports surfaced of 100-hour work weeks during the development of *Red Dead Redemption 2*, Rockstar faced significant backlash. In response, leadership implemented changes including more flexible working hours and restructured production pipelines. However, reports suggest that morale issues and attrition remained a challenge into the next development cycle (Schreier, 2020).

Example: Naughty Dog and Developer Turnover
During the development of *The Last of Us Part II*, reports emerged of high developer turnover caused by extended crunch and creative tension. While the final game received critical acclaim, the studio's long-term staffing stability was impacted. The studio has since taken steps to better manage scope and support developers' well-being (Klepek, 2020).

A studio with low morale will struggle to retain talent, causing an ongoing cycle of turnover and delays. Addressing team sentiment early prevents larger staffing risks later.

Morale does not only decline after crunch. It degrades when people feel unheard, directionless or disconnected from outcomes. Producers must treat team sentiment as a real-time signal and not postmortem feedback to place into a report.

KEY RISK PATTERNS

Single Point of Failure Roles

A specialist or lead owns a critical function and no backup is trained.

- **Impact**: Workflow halts when they leave.

- **Mitigation**: Cross-training and dual ownership of key systems.

Invisible Knowledge Hoarding

Key decisions are stored in heads or Slack DMs instead of accessible systems.

- **Impact**: New hires or collaborators waste time re-discovering solutions.

- **Mitigation**: Maintain living documentation and cultural incentives for knowledge sharing.

Emotional Contagion

One demotivated senior figure influences the wider team negatively.

- **Impact**: Loss of morale, slowdowns and possible attrition.

- **Mitigation**: Encourage honest retrospectives, leadership coaching and transparent escalation routes.

Succession Gaps Dismissed as Low Urgency

Delaying documentation or role transition planning creates fragile dependencies that become critical only after staff departures.

- **Impact**: Emergency handovers, system lockouts, expensive contractor stopgaps and timeline slippage.

- **Mitigation**: Build succession planning into team objectives; tie documentation outputs to sprint completion or review cycles.

Rotating Firefighter Syndrome

The same senior devs are repeatedly pulled into urgent tasks, onboarding or system triage.

- **Impact**: Their own work stalls, delivery slows and burnout risk increases.

- **Mitigation**: Cap unplanned work. Distribute onboarding. Empower mid-levels earlier.

Silent Walkout Risk

A senior developer disengages quietly. They still attend meetings – but stop contributing critical context or decisions.

- **Impact**: Loss of velocity with no obvious trigger. Passive slowdowns.

- **Mitigation**: Build psychological safety. Track contribution deltas, not just attendance.

STAFFING RISKS AS A SYSTEM DESIGN PROBLEM

Staffing risks can sometimes be seen as a system design problem. If your game would fall apart because one person gets sick or leaves, there is so much more wrong than a simple resource problem. We must embed succession planning, documentation and culture that allows change without collapse.

You cannot force engineers to write documentation. You cannot compel senior devs to mentor. But you *can* surface the production risk of not doing so: Make the invisible visible, translate silence into delivery consequences.

Treat staffing like infrastructure. You do not panic when a database goes down if you have redundancy and monitoring. But we still panic when a lead resigns – because we never built coverage. Fixing that requires cultural buy-in, not just process changes. Build teams where everyone documents, mentors and rotates – not as a task, but as part of how you work.

REFERENCES

GDC Vault. (2018). Managing talent: Retaining developers through culture and clarity. Retrieved from: https://www.gdcvault.com/play/1025472

GDC Vault. (2020). Building apex legends: A culture of ownership and trust. Retrieved from: https://www.gdcvault.com/play/1026636

Klepek, P. (2020). the human cost of the last of us part II. *VICE*. Retrieved from: https://www.vice.com/en/article/epg47k/the-human-cost-of-the-last-of-us-part-ii-naughty-dog-crunch

Robinson, A. (2021). The turbulent story behind Halo Infinite. *VGC*. Retrieved from: https://www.videogameschronicle.com/feature/the-turbulent-story-behind-halo-infinite/

Schreier, J. (2020). Inside rockstar games' culture of crunch. *Kotaku*. Retrieved from: https://kotaku.com/inside-rockstar-games-culture-of-crunch-1834981160

Schreier, J. (2021). *Press reset: Ruin and recovery in the video game industry*. Grand Central Publishing.

Tassi, P. (2018). Bungie explains how it's fixing destiny 2 and avoiding crunch. *Forbes*. Retrieved from: https://www.forbes.com/sites/insertcoin/2018/10/03/bungie-explains-how-its-fixing-destiny-2-and-avoiding-crunch/

Weststar, J., & Legault, M. (2021). *Developer satisfaction survey summary report*. IGDA. Retrieved from: https://igda.org/dss

CHAPTER 25

Agile, Lean and Kanban Risk Management

AGILE IS NOT A RISK MANAGEMENT FRAMEWORK

Agile empowers teams to iterate rapidly, test features early and respond to change. However, without boundaries, iteration can become a trap, leading to scope creep, deadline drift and confusion. Agile is not a risk management framework; it is a delivery model. However, risk management within Agile is entirely possible when teams treat risk like a living system.

This chapter explores how production leads, product owners and studio execs can embed visibility, mitigation and escalation into sprints, stand-ups and boards, without killing autonomy.

Kanban, in particular, is often misunderstood. It is not just "a board with columns" in Jira or Trello. It is a structured, data-driven approach that thrives on visualising flow, applying queuing theory and enforcing work-in-progress limits. Therefore, that makes it perfect for those moments in game production where the chaos is less exploratory and more like a relentless conveyor belt of known tasks, such as during content pipelines or live service production. Especially for artists and animators, Kanban often represents a blessed relief.

Kanban is not just for maintenance teams. It is a quiet revolution, especially in game production. When a lighting artist, localisation tester or UI engineer says, "Please just let me pull the next task", what they are asking for is Kanban. When a producer is stuck juggling daily chaos, urgent fix requests and moving deadlines, Kanban's expedite lanes and WIP limits provide breathing room and focus.

I cover Agile, Lean, Scaled Agile and more in a series of teaching videos on my YouTube channel. Much of the content from this chapter is gleaned from those. You can visit them here: https://www.youtube.com/@game-production-academy

DOI: 10.1201/9781003646082-28

STRIKE TEAMS, EXPEDITE SWIMLANES AND KANBAN DISCOVERY SUPPORT

In Discovery (so Concept and much of Pre-Production), when a high-risk question needs urgent exploration, such as testing a new mechanic or resolving a "pillar-level" unknown, some studios spin up short-lived Strike Teams. These teams operate in Scrum-like fashion: One-week sprints, a discovery backlog and a focused product owner (often the design lead). The goal is fast information delivery, not perfect implementation.

Meanwhile, the rest of the organisation may continue with Kanban. Here, the board gains an Expedite lane for urgent requests and discovery support. These expedite items reflect temporary help needed from an artist, engineer or tech designer who otherwise works in a Kanban flow. This blending allows structured chaos: Discovery sprints feed into stable pipelines, and pipelines flex to support learning.

Meanwhile, Scrum is often invoked by teams who have forgotten where it came from. The Agile Manifesto, and the principles that followed it, emerged as a rebellion against the bloated, process-heavy software culture of the 1990s. In game development, we need to revisit those founding ideas and understand them, rather than follow them slavishly. We need to remember that Agile was never meant to inspire a fanatical cult. It was meant to restore common sense, human contact and focus.

AGILE AND LEAN RISKS

Common Risk Triggers

- **Shifting Goalposts**: Features evolve mid-sprint without stakeholder alignment.

- **Perpetual Iteration/Polish Trap**: No clear point to stop refining or improving; time is spent polishing low-value features.

- **Deadline Misalignment**: Iterative loops stretch timelines unexpectedly.

- **Team Silos**: Integration problems arise when teams iterate in isolation.

- **Under-Documented Decisions/Iteration Debt**: Repeated discussions, unclear ownership and iteration cycles caused by missing intent.

- **Over-Flexibility**: Teams continually revise features or mechanics without locking scope.

- **Short-Term Fixes**: Tactical solutions create long-term technical debt.

- **Waste Blind Spots**: Inefficiencies persist without structured review.

- **Approval Loops**: Excessive or unclear approvals slow down progress.

Agile struggles are often misdiagnosed as "bad scrum" when in fact the root cause is misalignment between delivery model and development phase. Agile thrives in Discovery.

However, in full Production, the emphasis shifts to efficiency, quality and repeatable pipelines. This is where pretending everything is still "exploratory" can backfire.

WHEN AGILE BECOMES AN EXCUSE

In many studios, the word "Agile" becomes a fig leaf. Endless iteration is justified with a shrug: "Well, we're Agile". However, without clear boundaries, such as locking scope, sequencing decisions or committing to delivery milestones, Agile becomes the enemy of progress. Since we are talking about Risk Management, you need to ask: "What are we not talking about because we are afraid of looking un-Agile?"

Scrum Reality in Game Teams

Scrum theory assumes cross-functional teams solving complex problems. However, what if you are an environment artist in late production, just working through a 200-asset backlog? Or a UI engineer reviewing bugs and compliance tasks? Scrum is ill-suited here – not because of failure, but because of a mismatch.

Common breakdowns include:

- Daily stand-ups that devolve into status updates with no real team coordination.
- "Sprint Planning" performed by a lead alone, with no team buy-in.
- Retrospectives skipped because "nothing would change anyway."
- Scrum Masters who are actually Producers, juggling everything and expected to serve the team, the PO and the execs simultaneously.

The reality is a fragmented, overburdened role juggling across inconsistent backlogs, shifting team compositions and remote or hybrid constraints. It is no wonder many producers turn to hybrid or Kanban by necessity, not design.

KEY RISK PATTERNS

Velocity Theatre

Velocity hides scope creep. Teams appear productive, but progress is illusory. As I have said elsewhere: Most teams who say they use Scrum are lying to themselves. Nobody commits to a full sprint and executes it perfectly.

Mitigation: Track risk metrics, not just story points. Ensure deliverables are functional, not just counted.

Feedback Fuzz Loop

Multiple stakeholders provide conflicting input.

Mitigation: Centralise feedback through a single Product Owner or Review Lead. Use written design intent and structured reviews.

Decision Drift

Decisions are made ad hoc and never recorded.

Mitigation: Use lightweight decision logs and assign responsibility for recording major pivots.

Siloed Excellence

Teams optimise their own work but create integration risk.

Mitigation: Conduct cross-team reviews and joint integration rehearsals.

Iteration Debt Spiral

Unclear goals and documentation cause endless cycles of redo.

Mitigation: Establish clear intent before iteration. Use structured briefings and review gates.

Approval Drift

Too many or ambiguous approvers delay progress.

Mitigation: Define approval paths and reduce gatekeepers to the minimum viable reviewers.

Polish Trap

Time spent refining features that offer negligible value.

Mitigation: Regularly ask "Are we polishing value or just polishing?" Conduct value-focused waste audits.

WHEN TO USE SCRUM, WHEN TO USE KANBAN: A GAME CONTEXT MATRIX

Scrum is well-suited to exploration and experimentation. When teams face complex unknowns – like finding the fun, testing new mechanics or prototyping systems – Scrum provides a cadence for learning. It gives structure to the unstructured. One- or two-week sprints allow for rapid feedback loops, working demos and fast failure.

However, as confidence grows and the path becomes clearer, Scrum's constraints can chafe. The no-changes-within-a-sprint rule, the need to commit to blocks of work and the emphasis on velocity start to feel brittle. This is when many teams shift towards Kanban. Kanban thrives on flow, flexibility and visualising work in progress. It suits live environments, heavy asset pipelines or late production when teams are executing known work repeatedly.

Kanban can also provide breathing room for disciplines prone to chaos, such as DevOps, UI/UX, localisation or platform compliance. It enables a pull-based system where work enters the lane when capacity allows – ideal for teams supporting others or reacting to change.

Recommendation Matrix:

Context	Use Scrum	Use Kanban
Prototyping/Discovery	✅ Yes	❌ No
Systems Design (New Feature)	✅ Yes	❌ No
Asset Production (Art/Audio)	❌ No	✅ Yes
Localisation/QA	❌ No	✅ Yes
LiveOps Event Deployment	❌ No	✅ Yes
Compliance and Submissions	❌ No	✅ Yes
Final Production Polish	❌ No	✅ Yes
Multiplayer Launch Firefighting	❌ No	✅ Yes

Of course, hybrid approaches emerge too. A Strike Team might spin up a dedicated scrum cadence to explore a specific mechanic, then disband. Its members return to their Kanban-based pipelines. The key is knowing when to switch gears and having a production culture that allows it.

> **WHY KANBAN MATTERS MORE THAN YOU THINK**
>
> Kanban is not just for maintenance teams. It is a quiet revolution – especially in game production. When a lighting artist, localisation tester or UI engineer says, "Please just let me pull the next task", what they are asking for is Kanban. When a producer is stuck juggling daily chaos, urgent fix requests and moving deadlines, Kanban's expedite lanes and WIP limits provide breathing room and focus. I adore Kanban and use it whenever and wherever appropriate. A stressor here is that so few people understand it or have training in it, that they fall into an unofficial "scrumban". That too has its own merits, but you need to understand why you are using each.

Meanwhile, the rest of the organisation may continue with Kanban. Here, the board gains an Expedite lane for urgent requests and discovery support. These expedite items reflect temporary help needed from an artist, engineer or tech designer who otherwise works in a Kanban flow. This blending allows structured chaos: Discovery sprints feed into stable pipelines and pipelines flex to support learning.

DELIVERY MODELS ARE NOT A SAFETY NET

There is nothing magical about being Agile. Risk shows up wherever it is not discussed. Delivery models only help if they surface risk, not obscure it.

Scrum works brilliantly when you have a small team, a complex problem and the support to maintain cadence and continuity. However, as many producers discover, the ideal conditions rarely last. Teams get reshuffled. Ceremonies degrade. Tools become more about tracking than learning. The result? Zombie scrum – undead rituals going through the motions.

ZOMBIE SCRUM CHECKLIST

- Are your stand-ups silent?
- Do retrospectives get skipped, or turn into "status therapy"?
- Is your backlog just a dumping ground with no roadmap?
- Are you using story points without ever tracking velocity?

If yes, you are not doing Agile. You are enacting the rituals of a dead process.

This is why so many game teams describe themselves as "hybrid". They borrow from Scrum but ditch the pieces that do not fit. That is fine – but only if the hybridisation is deliberate. Too often it is accidental and the problems remain.

To stay risk-aware, you need more than rituals. You need:

- Clear agreement on when Discovery ends and Delivery begins.

- Willingness to evolve your delivery model, not just your backlog.

- Support for technical investments like CI/CD that make rapid delivery sustainable.

- Clear tracking of vertical dependencies between features, content and tooling.

- A realistic understanding of team maturity and composition: Not every squad is truly cross-functional.

If your model is not surfacing risk, it is failing you. If your stand-ups are silent, your retros skipped and your Jira board is just a conveyor belt of assumed tasks – then you are not managing risk, only motion.

SUGGESTED READING

Anderson, D. J. (2010). *Kanban: Successful evolutionary change for your technology business*. Blue Hole Press. The original foundational text on Kanban systems, including WIP limits, flow metrics and evolutionary change management. David has started releasing a new series of books in the last year, with his Kanban Maturity Model already published.

Kniberg, H. (2007). *Scrum and XP from the trenches*. InfoQ. A practical guide to real-world Scrum implementation. Good for context on Scrum team dynamics and pitfalls.

Leffingwell, D. (2019). *SAFe 5.0 distilled: Achieving business agility with the scaled agile framework*. Addison-Wesley. Authoritative book on SAFe for scaled Agile. Personally I do not recommend SaFe, but it may work for you.

Reinertsen, D. G. (2009). *The principles of product development flow: Second generation lean product development*. Celeritas Publishing. Donald's books changed my life. This one introduces concepts like Cost of Delay, queueing theory and batch size risks. I consider them all essential reading.

Walker, J., & Deemer, P. (2020). *Zombie scrum survival guide: A journey to recovery*. Addison-Wesley. This book identifies symptoms of dysfunctional Agile and offers ways to recover.

CHAPTER 26

Governance Risks and Organisational Debt

INTRODUCTION: THE GOVERNANCE RISK YOU CANNOT SEE

In most postmortems, we name the symptom: Missed milestones, scope creep, misaligned execution. However, we rarely name the system that allowed it to happen. Governance risk is what happens when decision-making lacks visibility, consistency or ownership. It is the invisible enabler of chaos.

In game development, where creativity meets shifting scope and tight timelines, governance must be flexible – but it cannot be absent. When people do not know who owns the decision, or how to escalate a change, or whether something was approved or just assumed, risk flourishes.

Governance does not mean formality for formality's sake. It means clarity. It means you know who owns a decision, what the escalation path is and where to find the record. Good governance makes less work, not more. It reduces meetings, firefighting and redundant work by making the invisible visible.

I have spent probably a decade of my life attempting to unpick governance risks from organisations. This stuff can bring down studios.

COMMON ORGANISATIONAL TRAPS

Ghost Processes

No clear workflow for approving design changes, production shifts or feature cuts. People assume approvals happened because no one said otherwise.

Unowned Change

Major roadmap shifts occur without an audit trail or impact review. Teams adapt based on hallway conversations or Slack assumptions.

DOI: 10.1201/9781003646082-29

Passive Leadership Approval

Decisions are floated, but not formally accepted. Approval is interpreted from silence, leading to misalignment.

The Leadership Literacy Gap

One major contributor to governance risk is the lack of structured training for leadership roles. While creative and technical staff often receive formal development, producers, project leads and executives are left to self-navigate risk ownership, change control and cross-discipline coordination.

The 2025 IGDA and GDC surveys revealed that formal training in risk and programme management is still rare. As a result, even senior staff may struggle to maintain governance hygiene under pressure. This training deficit compounds organisational debt, as governance systems degrade or remain informal.

Studios should treat leadership development as a governance investment. Without it, decision ownership defaults to personality, memory or convenience.

WHAT IS ORGANISATIONAL DEBT?

Organisational debt refers to the accumulation of broken, missing or poorly understood processes that make effective execution harder over time. Like technical debt, it builds interest – the longer you wait to address it, the more it costs.

SIDEBAR: SIGNS YOUR STUDIO HAS GOVERNANCE DEBT

- Important decisions are made in private DMs
- You are waiting for approval, but do not know from whom
- You realise too late that multiple teams worked on the same thing
- People keep saying, "Was that actually agreed?"
- Risk owners exist – but only on paper

Examples from games:

- No consistent method for onboarding new staff, leading to missed documentation, tool access delays and duplicated effort.

- Absence of change control process means last-minute pivots are introduced without planning for QA, marketing or engine implications.

- One engineer hoards system knowledge, blocking cross-functional collaboration and delaying vertical slices when absent.

MITIGATION STRATEGIES

Define and Visualise Governance Paths

- Who signs off on what?

- What triggers a re-evaluation of a roadmap decision?
- Who owns risk evaluation for scope, budget or team changes?

Audit Escalation Culture

- Is it safe to challenge or escalate unclear decisions?
- Are there formal moments to surface concerns?
- Do producers or leads act as functional risk routers?

Make Ownership Observable

- Publicly tag risk owners on Confluence/Jira/Notion.
- Summarise key directional decisions in sprint demos.
- Maintain a Decision Log with rationale and impact review.

GOVERNANCE HYGIENE QUESTIONS
- What was the last major decision made in your studio?
- Where is that decision documented?
- Who owns the outcome of that decision?
- Who was informed – and who was not?

If you cannot answer all four easily, governance debt is growing.

Governance in Shared Toolchains

As publishers consolidate development environments into shared platforms (e.g. internal engines, build systems), governance clarity becomes essential. Who approves tool changes? Who maintains documentation? When bugs are platform-wide, who prioritises them?

Governance risks are amplified when no single team owns platform decision-making. Studios should define governance paths not only for features, but also for pipelines and infrastructure.

CASE STUDIES

Case Study: Bungie's Governance Reset During LiveOps

In 2022, Bungie described its internal restructuring of production governance in response to live operations misfires on *Destiny 2*. After community blowback around delayed updates and unclear messaging, Bungie shifted to a governance model with visible decision ownership across live, design and community teams. Weekly cross-discipline syncs were implemented, change logs were shared internally across departments and high-risk live decisions (like economy tuning or event scheduling) were assigned explicit owners. This restructuring restored community trust and smoothed the update pipeline.

Bungie is not alone. In 2024, Arrowhead Game Studios struggled to maintain decision coherence during Helldivers II's runaway success. Patch cadence, server scaling and policy reversals (e.g. the PSN account requirement) revealed weaknesses in cross-functional governance. CEO Johan Pilestedt later admitted the team was not prepared for the level of complexity and scrutiny. Governance systems that work during stable times often collapse under live pressure.

Source: Bungie Developer Insights, 2022

Case Study: Ubisoft's Cross-Team Restructure to Address Governance Drift

In 2020, Ubisoft initiated structural reforms following internal misconduct scandals and leadership churn. One outcome was the creation of multidisciplinary editorial hubs across studios – explicitly designed to decentralise control and clarify who had sign-off authority on design and vision. These changes followed postmortems showing that governance ambiguity had delayed several major projects, including *Skull & Bones* and *Beyond Good and Evil 2*. By re-establishing ownership chains and transparency protocols, Ubisoft aimed to reduce invisible friction and re-empower delivery teams.

Source: Schreier, Bloomberg, 2020

Case Study: CD Projekt Red – Audit Failure and Governance Collapse

CDPR's launch of *Cyberpunk 2077* in 2020 exposed deep governance issues, including missed escalation of critical bugs, undocumented build processes and unrealistic executive oversight of console QA. Despite warnings from staff and external testers, leadership maintained a December release date. Lack of transparent decision paths meant no one could effectively intervene. The result was a catastrophic launch, lawsuits, store takedowns and years of reputational damage.

Source: Bloomberg, 2021; Jason Schreier

Key Risk Patterns
Governance Drift
Decision-making loses rigour as project pressure increases. Ownership is assumed rather than confirmed.
   Example: Producer assumes feature is cut; team continues building it.
   Mitigation Checklist:

- Run governance reviews every sprint
- Define minimum info needed for decisions
- Clarify sign-off chains with senior leads

Hero Culture

One individual becomes central to delivery due to speed or clarity, creating systemic dependency.

Example: Lead programmer writes 80% of core systems but resists code sharing.

Mitigation Checklist:

- Require walkthroughs for all critical systems

- Rotate technical leads or pair reviews

- Incentivise mentoring and documentation

No Escalation Path

Team members spot issues but have no clear path to raise them safely.

Example: QA team repeatedly flags regression, but issue never reaches production leadership.

Mitigation Checklist:

- Establish escalation routes with psychological safety

- Use RAID log escalations in milestone reviews

- Ensure risk owners are accountable across functions

The rise of unionisation across the industry – from the Overwatch and World of Warcraft teams to the United Videogame Workers-CWA – shows how developers are responding to environments with insufficient governance and risk routing. In many cases, unionisation emerges not just from labour conditions, but from the lack of reliable escalation systems.

REFERENCES

Bungie. (2022). *Developer update: Building better processes*. Retrieved from: https://www.bungie.net

Game Developers Conference. (2025, February). GDC 2025 state of the industry: Devs weigh in on layoffs, AI and more. Retrieved from: https://gdconf.com/news/gdc-2025-state-game-industry-devs-weigh-layoffs-ai-and-more

GamesRadar. (2024, May). Helldivers 2 will "slow down patch cadence" to maintain quality and stability. Retrieved from: https://www.gamesradar.com/games/third-person-shooter/helldivers-2-is-slowing-down-the-release-of-new-patches-to-maintain-the-quality-standard-we-want-and-you-deserve

IGDA. (2023). *Developer satisfaction survey: Training, education and career growth*. International Game Developers Association. Retrieved from: https://igda.org/resources/research-reports/

Massively Overpowered. (2024, April). Helldivers 2 CEO talks live service pressure and leadership under fire. Retrieved from: https://massivelyop.com/2025/04/07/helldivers-2-ceo-talks-live-service-sudden-popularity-and-business-leaders-who-have-taken-stupid-risks

PC Gamer. (2024, May). Helldivers 2 delisted in 177 countries as PSN login policy sours commu-nity. Retrieved from: https://www.pcgamer.com/games/third-person-shooter/with-over-84 -thousand-negative-helldivers-2-steam-reviews-in-two-days-developer-arrowhead-seems-to -be-grappling-with-sony-over-its-controversial-psn-sign-in-requirement

PC Gamer. (2025, May). *Nearly 200 Overwatch developers at Blizzard form a new union: The Overwatch Gamemakers Guild*. Retrieved from: https://www.pcgamer.com/gaming-industry /nearly-200-overwatch-developers-at-blizzard-form-a-new-union-the-overwatch-gamemak-ers-guild

Schreier, J. (2020). *Ubisoft employees demand change after abuse allegations*. Bloomberg. Retrieved from: https://www.bloomberg.com

Schreier, J. (2021). *Inside cyberpunk 2077's disastrous rollout*. Bloomberg. Retrieved from: https:// www.bloomberg.com/news/articles/2021-01-16/cyberpunk-2077-what-caused-the-video -game-s-disastrous-rollout

The Verge. (2025, March). *Nearly 200 Overwatch developers form a new union at Blizzard*. Retrieved from: https://www.theverge.com/news/664873/overwatch-union-microsoft-activision -blizzard

Weststar, J., & Legault, M.-J. (2022). Video game developers' experiences of project management training and team leadership. *Game Studies, 22*(3). Retrieved from: https://gamestudies.org /2203/articles/weststar_legault_training

PART IV

Major Risks in the Common Stages of Game Development

UNDERSTANDING THE LIFECYCLE OF VIDEO GAME PROJECTS

Game development is not a single process, but a complex and evolving journey through a set of semi-standardised stages. These stages (Concept, Pre-Production, Production, Post-Production and Live Operations) are widely used throughout the industry. Yet, the degree to which they are followed, and how cleanly a project transitions between them, varies drastically depending on the type of game, team size, funding structure and business model.

Understanding risk in the context of this lifecycle requires a flexible mindset. Some of you reading this may be right in the thick of development – grappling with real dependencies, schedules and teams. Others may operate at a strategic or oversight level, only touching part of the lifecycle or reviewing builds and milestones at a distance. Some may work in support roles or on titles that clone existing games, launching rapidly and bypassing some of the traditional steps altogether. Still others are managing live products, wondering how on earth they got landed with two years of updates after shipping what they thought was the final release.

In reality, very few teams follow a pure, linear path through the game development lifecycle. Agile and Lean methodologies encourage iteration, responsiveness and ongoing discovery. And yet most studios, especially when beholden to external funders, still use classic stage gates: Clear milestones that unlock funding or approval to proceed. These stage gates are not inherently bad. In fact, they are one of the few formal mechanisms available to embed risk management into development, by ensuring teams meet key criteria before investing more time and money.

Historically, stage gates emerged not just as planning tools but as risk mitigation strategies. They originated to serve a financial function – assuring stakeholders, publishers or platform holders like Sony or Meta that a game was progressing in a controlled and verifiable way. If a studio failed to demonstrate progress or quality at a gate, they could be cut off. In many ways, this contractual relationship enforces risk management whether a team likes it or not.

However, these stage gates can also distort development. They can interrupt Agile cycles, force "hardening" sprints to polish builds for demos, and push studios into premature commitments just to meet billing requirements. These risks must be managed explicitly – not just accepted as part of the process. If stage gates are to be useful, they should serve the development team as well as the funder/sponsor, offering a genuine checkpoint for pivoting, validating the original vision or choosing to cancel.

Beyond funding considerations, stage gates can act as key risk checkpoints. They provide a structured moment for evaluating whether the foundations are strong enough to proceed. Have we proven our concept? Is the vertical slice functional and engaging? Do we have confidence in our tech stack, our market understanding and our team? It is in answering these questions that stage gates become true tools of de-risking. They transform uncertainty into commitment.

Moreover, these lifecycle stages offer a common language. Even if your own studio uses different terminology, or works in overlapping rather than sequential phases, there is value in mapping your work to these stages. Doing so allows for clearer communication across teams, alignment with partners and more effective risk identification at every step.

It is also important to recognise that risk profiles shift significantly depending on the scale and nature of development. Indie developers may sprint from concept to launch in weeks, with risks concentrated around funding, overwork and market visibility. In contrast, multi-studio AAA projects face coordination risks, contract risks and deeply embedded technical debt. Live service teams must manage community sentiment, content cadence and long-term engagement metrics.

In this section, we will explore each major stage of the game development lifecycle, outlining the most common risks and risk triggers associated with that phase. These will not be exhaustive, nor will they apply to every project, but they will offer a framework for better understanding and managing risk as it evolves across a project timeline. Each stage will be addressed in full in its own dedicated chapter.

Let us now look at each phase briefly, beginning with the Concept stage.

Concept Phase

The Concept Phase is where the creative vision is born and where high-level risks are at their most theoretical, but no less important. The core question here is: *Should* this game be made at all?

- **Vision Definition**: What is the game about? What is its core hook? How will it stand out creatively and commercially? Teams often skip this clarity and jump into asset creation without validating the game's core purpose.

- **Technical Feasibility**: Is the core gameplay achievable with available technology, tools and platforms? Are we entering into risky R&D territory without a plan?

- **Market and Competitor Fit**: Does this concept meet an unmet market need? Are we chasing trends or creating something genuinely valuable?

- **Funding Model**: Is this an internally funded idea or are we reliant on external pitch acceptance? Do we have the right materials – pitch decks, prototypes, financials – to gain approval?

- **IP Ownership and Partnerships**: Are we building our own IP or entering work-for-hire or co-development deals? Each path alters the risk profile significantly.

This phase often gets bypassed or compressed under pressure, but it is one of the cheapest and most powerful places to eliminate failure. Teams that conduct thoughtful risk identification and scenario planning early save months – if not years-of downstream pain.

Let us now briefly examine the common risk concerns during the remaining phases, each of which will receive a dedicated chapter later in this book.

Pre-Production Phase

The Pre-Production Phase turns vision into viable execution. It is where workflows, tools, team structures and production pipelines are locked in. Here, early missteps can lead to months of downstream pain.

- **Pipeline Definition**: Are development pipelines for design, art, engineering and QA clearly defined and integrated?

- **Tech Stack Commitment**: Have we chosen the right engine, middleware and toolchain for our needs and scope?

- **Platform Risks**: Are we targeting the right platforms, and have we considered certification requirements and limitations?

- **Resourcing and Budgeting**: Do we have the right team in place, and are our headcount and skills aligned with the roadmap?

- **Scheduling Foundations**: Are milestone definitions realistic, and have we accounted for buffers and interdependencies?

- **Workflow Clarity**: Have we aligned on definitions of done, handoff expectations and communication cadences across disciplines?

Many studios enter production without truly finishing pre-production, skipping decisions that later re-emerge as blockers. Pre-production is the first major opportunity to treat process design as risk prevention.

Please reread that last paragraph – in my experience, this phase is rushed due to pressures from above. Protect yourself using risk management to highlight why proper time needs to be invested here.

Production Phase

Production is where the bulk of the work takes place and where risks are at their most numerous. Execution pressure increases, visibility to stakeholders ramps up and any flaws in earlier planning become painfully apparent.

- **Milestone Risk**: Are internal and external deliverables truly achievable, or is the team heading for a crunch spiral?

- **Scope Volatility**: Are new features or polish demands being introduced without proper impact assessment?

- **Cross-Team Alignment**: Is coordination working across departments and locations, or are key dependencies breaking down?

- **Bug Volume and Tech Debt**: Are QA and code hygiene practices sufficient to manage defects and maintain iteration speed?

- **Tooling and Build Stability**: Is the build pipeline reliable? Are developers losing time due to instability or bad tooling?

At this stage, communication risk often outweighs technical risk. Many projects fail not because they are technically impossible, but because coordination fails at scale.

Post-Production Phase

Post-production often includes Alpha, Beta and Final QA. It is often characterised by panic, polish and the painful realisation of what was missed earlier.

- **Stability and Optimisation**: Can we meet performance targets and prevent game-breaking bugs from slipping through?

- **Certification**: Are we on track to pass first-party checks with Sony, Microsoft, Nintendo, Apple or Google?

- **Marketing Delivery**: Do we have final assets for trailers, screenshots and store listings? Are we synchronised with marketing beats?

- **Day-One Preparedness**: Are hotfix and patch teams in place, and do we have a realistic server launch plan (if online)?

This phase often exposes the consequences of overly optimistic production plans. Risk management here is about triage, messaging and damage control.

In the most severe cases, it may also expose a worrying negative response to your game as you pass it on to gamers to actually try out, as part of Alpha and Beta.

Live Operations and GaaS Phase

LiveOps transforms a shipped game into a product that lives and evolves. But it also means inheriting a persistent risk surface.

- **Content Cadence**: Can we ship new content fast enough to retain players without burning out the team?

- **Community Management**: Are we listening and responding to feedback constructively, or feeding outrage cycles?

- **Revenue vs Player Trust**: Are monetisation strategies sustainable and ethical, or short-term revenue traps?

- **Security and Cheating**: Are we investing in protecting the game from bots, hacks, exploits and toxicity?

Many teams underestimate the operational cost of success. Shipping is not the end – it is often the beginning of an entirely new risk landscape.

Each of these phases presents opportunities to reduce uncertainty, validate direction and strengthen delivery confidence. The chapters that follow will examine each stage in detail.

CHAPTER 27

Concept Stage Risks in Game Development

INTRODUCTION

The concept stage may appear deceptively calm, but it is foundational. It is during this phase that the vision, market positioning and business model of the game are established. Decisions made now will reverberate across every later stage. Failure to identify and manage risks here can lead to wasted resources, misaligned teams and projects that collapse under their own weight.

Mobile, PC, and console games will experience concept risk differently. In mobile, speed and market agility may dominate. In console, the risks often centre on over-investment, IP ownership or platform expectations.

A clear, validated and resilient concept sets the stage for successful development. Missteps at this phase are often unrecoverable.

MAJOR RISKS IN THE CONCEPT STAGE

Unclear Vision

Without a precise, well-communicated vision, teams drift. Misalignment across leadership, design and production leads to wasted development effort and fractured products.

If your vision is not clear, then over time everyone is making a game you did not ask for.

Mitigation:

- Create and maintain a *living* Game Design Document (GDD) accessible to all disciplines

- Align early with stakeholders and conduct regular vision alignment sessions

- Treat the GDD as a collaborative source of truth, updating it responsively

DOI: 10.1201/9781003646082-31

SIDEBAR: THE LIVING GDD

Replace static GDDs with shared, cloud-accessible documents that evolve with feedback. Tools like Notion, Miro or Confluence can help teams continuously align. Include commentary, links and real-time updates rather than locking vision in a vault.

Market Misalignment

Building a game without understanding player needs or market timing results in products that miss their window or fail to find an audience. **This a HUGE RISK!** Forgive me, but everyone I spoke to regarding this topic emphasised that you must never make a game that is simply one you like, or worse, the studio boss likes. You can waste years of development and people's lives only to find out nobody cares about your game.

You need data. You need to be objective.

Trend chasing is particularly risky when your dev cycle is long. Just because extraction shooters are big today does not mean the market will be receptive in 24 months. This is especially true in mobile, where the velocity of trend change is brutal. You can spend years making something that was trending when you started, but irrelevant by the time you finish. This book is already filled with such examples.

Mitigation:

- Conduct early market validation exercises such as player surveys, competitor analyses and concept testing

- Monitor trends with caution – differentiate between fads and lasting shifts

- Design flexibility into the concept to pivot if necessary

MARKET FIT AND AUDIENCE CLARITY ARE NOT OPTIONAL

Game concepts often begin with passion, but passion alone does not guarantee success. One of the most consistent failure points in modern game development is weak market fit, where teams chase trends, build for themselves, or assume an audience exists without evidence.

Defining your target audience early, validating that there is a real unmet need and building community touchpoints long before launch are critical safeguards against wasted development effort. Just as importantly, studios must retain the flexibility to pivot if data, trends or audience expectations shift mid-production.

Growing a fanbase early does not mean locking in every feature, but it does mean building in an effective feedback loop with your fans. Market awareness, community listening and the courage to course-correct are now foundational to commercial and creative viability.

Scope Creep

Uncontrolled ambition at the concept stage results in unwieldy projects that are impossible to deliver on time or on budget. It is a time for dreaming, but try and place a bubble around the dreams to rein them in.

Mitigation:

- Define a Minimum Viable Product (MVP) or Minimum Lovable Product (MLP)
- Use user story mapping and feature prioritisation techniques early
- Set the expectation that additions must be offset by cuts. Everyone has to work within constraints. Every decision is a sacrifice of something else

Tip: Introduce a story mapping tool suggestion:
User story mapping workshops are powerful at this stage. Physically mapping gameplay loops with cards or sticky notes – digital or physical – can show how bloated your vision actually is, and where the "must-haves" live. If you have not already, read Patton's brilliant book (Patton & Economy, 2014).

Unclear Monetisation Strategy

Monetisation design that is an afterthought often leads to player backlash, broken game economies or commercial failure. It is well established that many companies go live and have an "oops, how do we make money now?" moment then try and force a monetisation loop into the game. Please do not be like them.

Mitigation:

- Define monetisation and economic systems during concept
- Engage monetisation designers and product managers from day one
- Validate monetisation models against player expectations and market norms

Good monetisation is not an add-on. It must shape content loops, progression and economy systems. Think of it as part of the ecosystem, not an aftermarket bolt-on. For live-service or F2P games, early involvement of product designers and economists is essential.

Ignoring Systemic Interdependencies

Viewing design, tech and business considerations in isolation causes misalignment that destabilises games later.

Mitigation:

- Promote systems thinking within the team
- Map out how decisions in one area (e.g. monetisation) affect others (e.g. progression, balance)
- Conduct "ripple effect" reviews before finalising major design choices

Tip: Introduce a "Ripple Effect" exercise:
Before signing off key design or economic decisions, teams should run a short ripple-mapping exercise. Ask: "If we do X, what breaks in Y?" Who needs to adjust for this to succeed? This systems lens is vital before technical debt or design debt locks in. Design debt is a real thing.

KEY RISK PATTERNS IN CONCEPT
Vision Drift
Definition: Initial clarity of the game concept erodes over time due to inconsistent leadership or stakeholder interference.

Impact:

- Wasted development effort
- Bloated or incoherent gameplay experiences

Mitigation:

- Establish a single point of vision ownership (Creative Director or equivalent)
- Hold quarterly vision reviews involving cross-discipline leads

Case Study: *Anthem* (Schreier, 2020) suffered from severe vision drift. Jason Schreier's reporting revealed leadership turnover and internal confusion over the game's direction, resulting in major last-minute changes and a critically poor launch (Schreier, 2020).

Why does this matter? It shows how high-profile vision drift can derail even the best-funded projects.

Trend Chasing
Definition: Designing a game primarily to emulate the success of an external hit without unique value propositions.

Impact:

- Saturated markets
- Audience fatigue
- Weak brand differentiation

Mitigation:

- Anchor game concepts in core competencies and unique experiences
- Validate audience appetite through testing rather than assumptions

Case Study: *LawBreakers* (Polygon, 2018) was positioned against trending hero shooters but failed to distinguish itself sufficiently, resulting in low player counts and eventual studio closure (Polygon, 2018).

Why does this matter? It illustrates that trend-chasing without differentiation is a death sentence.

Premature Scaling

Definition: Expanding team size or production investments before the core concept has been validated.

Impact:

- High burn rates
- Sunk cost fallacies
- Difficult pivots when problems are discovered

Mitigation:

- Stage team growth based on concept validation milestones
- Fund early work as "discovery" phases, not guaranteed productions

Case Study: *Paragon* (Epic Games, 2018) expanded significantly before confirming player engagement. After Fortnite's success, Epic redirected resources and Paragon was cancelled despite substantial investment (IGN, 2018).

Why does this matter? Highlights the risk of scaling before validation, even within a successful studio.

Risk Management as a Pivot Enabler

Studios often think of risk management as a constraint. In reality, it is a form of creative insurance. When you do the work early – validating assumptions, mapping dependencies, stress-testing your vision – you create options. You know what the risks are, where the dependencies lie, and how decisions connect. When the market inevitably shifts, the audience reacts poorly or new data emerges, you are not locked in. You are equipped to pivot fast and with confidence.

True agility is not just about process. It is about knowing what you can safely change as well as what you cannot afford to ignore. Change can be our friend if we have established risk management fundamentals.

Concept is where the seeds of both success and failure are sown. Rigorous validation, disciplined scope control and systemic thinking transform promising ideas into solid foundations.

Without this discipline, games drift, bloat or collapse before they ever have a chance. Treat the concept as seriously as any later milestone – because in reality, it is the most critical risk juncture of all.

Concept risk is quiet but deadly. What you lock in, or ignore, during this phase echoes for years. You can pivot on mechanics, platforms, even business models, but vision, alignment and structural blind spots are almost always rooted here. Investing rigour at this stage is essential.

Doing the work at this stage actually empowers future pivots, as investigations reveal where the ideas that came up here need to change, or better ideas are revealed. A firm foundation at this point enables you to much more accurately predict the value and cost of such changes.

REFERENCES

IGN. (2018). *Epic games pulls the plug on Paragon*. IGN.

Patton, J., & Economy, P. (2014). *User story mapping: Discover the whole story, build the right product*. O'Reilly Media.

Polygon. (2018). The rise and fall of LawBreakers. Polygon. https://www.polygon.com/features/2018/9/14/17859010/lawbreakers-closure-boss-key-productionhttps://www.polygon.com/features/2018/9/14/17859010/lawbreakers-closure-boss-key-production

Schreier, J. (2020). *Anthem: The shocking story behind bioware's big failure*. Bloomberg.

CHAPTER 28

Major Risks in the Pre-Production Stage of Game Development

INTRODUCTION

Pre-production is the phase where ideas must become structured, testable plans. It marks the transition from conceptual dreaming to operational reality. However, this is also where enthusiasm often blinds teams to fundamental gaps. Pre-production errors, if uncorrected, propagate through production and magnify, leading to costly failures later.

It is very normal, in my experience, for pre-production to be the stage where a few of the biggest unknowns are explored and tested, but time pressures force a bucketload more to be relegated to the production phase. These are risks and need to be transparently logged and communicated and dealt with.

Pre-production success demands rigorous validation, flexibility and a ruthless focus on de-risking the project while it is still feasible to pivot.

At this stage, the project needs to shift from enthusiasm to structure. You are building the operational base that will either support production or cause it to unravel later.

MAJOR RISKS IN THE PRE-PRODUCTION STAGE

Inadequate Planning

Premature confidence in early estimates often results in brittle schedules, unrealistic budgets and false expectations.

DOI: 10.1201/9781003646082-32

Mitigation:

- Treat all plans as provisional until validated by prototypes and proofs of concept
- Focus early schedules on milestone validation, not feature delivery
- Clearly communicate plan uncertainty to all stakeholders

Most of what is planned at this stage will change. That does not make planning point-less, but it does mean expectations must be managed. Early schedules should be treated as working drafts. Where you are unsure, say so.

Label early milestones with confidence levels and ranges. Use this to explain why some plans are firmer than others, rather than pretending all of them are fixed.

Technical Uncertainty

Critical technical risks ignored during pre-production become crippling production delays.

Mitigation:

- Prioritise high-risk technical areas for early prototyping
- Define "technical validation milestones" separate from feature milestones; these may grow into fully fledged vertical slices
- Challenge assumptions about third-party tools and middleware integrations

Just because the tools are familiar does not mean the configuration is safe. Risks often come not from the tools themselves, but from how they are combined, or from what is assumed about third-party support. Perhaps you have never put them together in that way before.

List key tech systems and highlight anything unproven, untested or dependent on partners.

Team Skill Gaps

Misaligned or incomplete team capabilities create hidden risks that only surface under production pressure.

Mitigation:

- Conduct skill gap analyses aligned to project requirements
- Begin upskilling programmes or external recruiting early
- Assign shadowing roles for areas where expertise is thin

Map skills to the roadmap. If a capability will be needed later, build a plan for how it will be covered – either through training, recruitment or outsourcing. It is better to address this now than to discover the shortfall mid-production. You could bring people in early and train them, even if they are not needed yet.

Inadequate Platform-Specific Planning

Ignoring platform compliance, performance requirements or hardware constraints sets up future crises. This is often overlooked when teams assume platform parity. Even minor differences between console versions, or between mobile and tablet, can introduce rework or certification problems that take weeks to resolve.

Mitigation:

- Research and integrate platform TRCs (Technical Requirement Checklists) into pre-production deliverables; ignoring this will land you in a whole heap of trouble when the phased TRC submission deadlines loom

- Engage with platform representatives early

- Prototype platform-specific challenges (e.g. performance on target hardware)

Stakeholder Assumption Traps

Inherited promises about dates, budgets or features can destroy realistic planning if not surfaced and challenged.

Mitigation:

- Document and review all stakeholders' expectations formally

- Conduct assumption mapping workshops

- Negotiate reality-based resets early rather than deferring conflict

It is not unusual for stakeholders to make promises that have not been stress-tested with the development team. Pre-production is the best time to push back and clarify what is actually feasible. When you see what has been promised, it is not necessarily what you would like to have promised!

Tip:
Ask: *Who made this promise? On what basis? What happens if we cannot deliver it?*

KEY RISK PATTERNS IN PRE-PRODUCTION

Illusion of Certainty

Definition: Early schedules and budgets are treated as binding commitments rather than informed guesses.

Impact:

- Locked-in unrealistic milestones

- Chronic schedule pressure

- Erosion of trust when targets are missed

Mitigation:

- Present plans with risk ranges and confidence levels

- Build contingency buffers explicitly into schedules

Case Study: *Mass Effect: Andromeda* (Schreier, 2017) suffered from overoptimistic pre-production planning, with late technical pivots and overambitious scope decisions that led to compressed production timelines and a troubled release (Schreier, 2017).

Why does this matter? Planning assumptions made early in pre-production caused serious pressure later, once technical pivots were needed.

Prototype Neglect

Definition: Prototypes are rushed or skipped entirely, leaving core technical and design risks untested.

Impact:

- False sense of readiness

- Hidden integration failures

- Costly rework late in production

Mitigation:

- Treat prototyping as a mandatory pre-production deliverable

- Define clear success criteria for each prototype

Case Study: *Agents of Mayhem* (Kotaku, 2017) struggled partly due to unvalidated design assumptions. Core gameplay loops were not adequately stress-tested during pre-production, leading to disappointing engagement metrics at launch (Kotaku, 2017).

Why does this matter? Core gameplay assumptions went untested, which left the game exposed at launch.

Invisible Scope Creep

Definition: Expansion of expectations during pre-production without formal review or resource adjustment.

Impact:

- Underestimated production demands
- Team burnout
- Quality sacrifices to meet unchanged timelines

Mitigation:

- Implement formal change review processes even during pre-production
- Update scope and resourcing plans visibly with each accepted change

Case Study: *Crackdown 3* expanded dramatically during early phases, particularly around cloud-based destructibility, without proportional team scaling. This contributed to multiple delays and a muted reception (The Verge, 2019). I was involved indirectly near launch and saw what inflated promises that could not be delivered resulted in. Be careful how expectations can lead to external as well as internal disappointment.

Why does this matter? The scope increased, but resourcing did not keep up. Teams were set up to fail.

CERTAINTY IS A DECISION, NOT A FEELING

Pre-production is not about certainty. It is about making well-informed decisions, knowing full well that some unknowns remain. The job is not to eliminate risk entirely, but to reduce it to a level where progress is safe and justifiable.

Some teams treat this phase as a formality. That is a mistake. This is the last realistic chance to check your assumptions before money and headcount scale up. Once production begins, the cost of change increases sharply.

Pre-production is your best opportunity to ask: Are we ready? Are the gaps known? Have we done enough to proceed responsibly? If you can answer those questions with honesty and the right structures in place, then you are ready to move forward. It does not need to be with 100% confidence, but close enough to have mitigated most known risks.

REFERENCES

Schreier, J. (2017). *The troubled development of mass effect: Andromeda*. Kotaku. https://kotaku.com/the-troubled-development-of-mass-effect-andromeda-1795886428

Totilo. (2017). *What happened to agents of Mayhem?* Kotaku. https://kotaku.com/what-happened-to-agents-of-mayhem-1798584485

Webster A. (2019). *The long, troubled history of crackdown 3*. The Verge. https://www.theverge.com/2019/2/13/18222964/crackdown-3-history-xbox-one-delays-development

CHAPTER 29

Major Risks in the Production Stage of Game Development

INTRODUCTION

Production is where real delivery pressure begins. Teams expand, systems integrate, content creation accelerates and deadlines loom. At this point, you are no longer testing whether the game can exist – you are committing people, time and resources to building it at scale. The margin for error narrows, and the cost of mistakes increases. This is where projects can either maintain momentum or implode under the combined pressures of scale, complexity and unpredictability.

Risks multiply dramatically in production. Without strong risk management, production descends into chaos, scope bloats, technical debt balloons and morale collapses.

MAJOR RISKS IN THE PRODUCTION STAGE

Feature Creep

Unchecked addition of features destabilises scope, erodes testing time and weakens product focus.

Mitigation:

- Enforce strict change control processes for any new features

- Demand impact assessments and trade-off discussions for every change request

- Anchor all teams to the agreed MVP or MLP scope

DOI: 10.1201/9781003646082-33

Not all late-stage features are bad, but they must be planned. When a new system is introduced without thinking through how it interacts with the rest of the game, it usually causes more harm than good. Even small changes can unbalance a carefully tuned ecosystem.

Adding melee weapons six months before launch sounds exciting, but it will touch a hundred systems you did not plan for.

Tip:
Ask: Did we plan for this? If not, what breaks when it is added?

Lack of Change Management

Undocumented or poorly communicated changes cause cascading system failures, bugs and resource waste.

Mitigation:

- Assign change gatekeepers for critical systems
- Document and circulate all change approvals
- Conduct regular change impact reviews

Creative enthusiasm is not the problem. Uncontrolled implementation is. Passionate individuals may tweak a stat, improve a mechanic or introduce a clever fix, without realising the impact on others. Someone makes a change because they are excited, not realising they have just broken everything downstream. Left unchecked, this creates invisible divergence across systems.

Tip: Make it clear who owns the system, and who is allowed to change it.

Integration Issues

Incompatible systems, divergent pipelines and isolated teams create invisible technical risks until late builds.

Mitigation:

- Schedule regular full integration builds
- Implement continuous integration practices where feasible
- Allocate dedicated integration triage teams

It is common to find that what worked in small teams or prototypes does not scale. Tools clash. Formats drift. Third-party SDKs stop playing nicely. Integration problems often sit unnoticed until late builds reveal them all at once.

A typical example I have come across countless times: You find two different teams using two different tools that do not talk to each other, but need to. You only realise it once you scale.

Quality Problems/Bug Overload

Accelerated production without embedded QA leads to exponential bug growth and falling confidence in builds.

Mitigation:

- Embed QA within all feature teams

- Treat bugs as risks, not just defects

- Track bug velocity and severity visually across sprints

Bugs can be treated as a risk category in their own right. Not all bugs are equal. Prioritise them with the same methods used for risk: By impact, by probability and by visibility. Use heatmaps or dashboards to stop the list from becoming overwhelming.

Otherwise, the all too common scenario of launching with 1,000 bugs and no time left manifests – and it is all avoidable if you prioritise and treat them with the same respect you would features and core engine work.

Tip: Encourage teams to include bug-fix time in sprint planning, not just velocity estimates.

Poor Prioritisation of Backlog Features

Focusing on low-impact or low-risk features wastes time needed for critical, complex deliverables.

Mitigation:

- Prioritise based on player value, technical risk and effort estimates

- Review and revalidate priorities at every milestone exit

- Kill or defer non-critical features **ruthlessly. Please do this**. Archive backlog items without fear – you can always drag them back later. Make a note of why, and they will show up in searches. Nothing is lost, but your backlog becomes cleaner and more manageable

Many teams struggle to let go of earlier ideas. But if a feature is still waiting near the end of production, it is probably either unproven or low priority. One side-effect of allowing your backlog to grow and grow is that the leads will end up spending days at a time sitting together trying to work out what should or should not be there at all. Prioritisation sessions will take multiple days and become a death march of covering 10% of the items before time runs out. Even now I am having flashbacks to three-day workshops where we literally had 20,000 items in our backlog and covered perhaps 100 in three days.

Please do a favour to the whole team and archive whole swathes of backlog items that are clearly part of the old Living Design Document, not the current one. Be ruthless and you will be a Champion, and your name will be called out with reverence and awe. Do not be that project manager who is so tied up in their own rules and regulations that you kill valuable days for busy senior people just because you "shouldn't" and you "have to" go through every one of the 20,000 items in order. I will find you, and I will delete your backlog.

Seriously, I *will* find you.

Tip:

Ask: What does the player actually need? What will break if we leave this out? Or use my technique of "You wanted this back when life was great and you were young. Is it just on the list now because it was there six months ago and nobody had the time to remove it?"

After I have had a chance to have a lay-down and calm myself, we can move on to the next major risk.

Performance Issues

Optimisation left too late results in final builds that fail certification, frustrate players or miss performance KPIs. Everything is fine until someone checks frame rate and suddenly the whole asset pipeline is in trouble.

Mitigation:

- Include target hardware performance validation in Definition of Done

- Run regular optimisation sprints focused on high-risk areas

- Build scalable asset pipelines, not one-off fixes

Performance risk is cumulative. It comes not from one decision, but from hundreds of small oversights that stack up. You need to test regularly, not just hope for a miracle fix at the end.

KEY RISK PATTERNS IN PRODUCTION

Production Paralysis

Definition: Teams become overwhelmed by technical debt, QA failures or process bottlenecks, leading to stagnation.

Impact:

- Missed milestones
- Declining team morale
- Quality decline

Mitigation:

- Break work into smaller, testable slices
- Use feature flags to decouple incomplete systems
- Run targeted "stabilisation sprints" when velocity dips

Case Study: *Star Wars Battlefront II* (EA DICE, 2017) faced significant internal pressures due to last-minute feature additions and balancing issues. Production stagnation contributed to controversial launch problems (Gamasutra, 2018).

Why This Matters: Shows how last-minute scope changes create production stalls that spiral into launch problems.

Death by a Thousand Cuts
Definition: Accumulation of uncoordinated minor changes destabilises systems and overwhelms QA.

Impact:

- Regression bugs proliferate
- Testing coverage gaps widen
- Final builds become brittle

Mitigation:

- Institute micro-change reviews for even minor tweaks
- Tie all change approvals to end-to-end test validation

Case Study: *Assassin's Creed Unity* suffered from numerous minor technical problems at launch that combined into a reputational disaster, driven by rushed final months and insufficient holistic testing (Eurogamer, 2014).

Why This Matters: Demonstrates how small issues, if uncoordinated, combine into serious technical failure.

Burnout Cascade

Definition: Sustained high production pressure without sufficient recovery periods leads to wide-scale burnout.

Impact:

- Talent attrition

- Falling productivity

- Rising error rates

Mitigation:

- Build mandatory cooldown periods into milestone plans

- Monitor team health metrics and intervene early

- Normalise sustainable delivery culture over "heroics"

Case Study: *Telltale Games'* production culture of tight episodic delivery without sufficient downtime was a major contributor to burnout and eventual collapse, as documented in extensive postmortems (Polygon, 2018).

Why This Matters: Burnout is not just cultural; it is structural. Without time to recover, quality and morale collapse.

SUSTAINABLE PRODUCTION IS A LEADERSHIP DISCIPLINE

By the time production is underway, it is easy to assume the project will now run on momentum. Everyone is busy. Work is visible. Systems are in motion. But that is exactly when small problems start to build.

Production risk is rarely dramatic. It usually comes from things being assumed, delayed or quietly dropped. Bugs accumulate. Priorities drift. Coordination falters. None of it breaks the project immediately, but it adds up.

This is where production leadership matters. The role is not just to keep things moving, but to spot early signs of strain, surface risks and hold scope and quality together under pressure.

You do not need heroics. You need consistency, visibility and calm decision-making. A well-run production phase does not need to be exciting; it just needs to deliver what was agreed, in the right order, with the right people. That is more than enough.

REFERENCES

Alexander, J. (2018). *Inside the collapse of Telltale games.* Polygon.

Frazier, D. (2018). *Postmortem: Star Wars Battlefront II's development challenges.* Gamasutra.

Whitehead, D. (2014). *What went wrong with Assassin's Creed Unity?* Eurogamer.

CHAPTER 30

Alpha Stage Risks in Game Development

T HE ALPHA STAGE IS one of the most misunderstood yet pivotal moments in the game development lifecycle. It marks the first time your game is exposed outside the internal development bubble. Alpha isn't just about polishing features, but is the chance to start looking at feedback from the gamers. Quality expectations increase, features should be functionally complete and external feedback begins to shape future development. This stage can make or break a game's momentum.

There is no consistent industry definition of what "alpha" means. It varies across studios and projects. In practical terms, alpha is when you find out whether the game works at all outside the comfort of the development team. It is the point where pressure rises, issues surface and quality is no longer optional.

MAJOR RISKS IN THE ALPHA STAGE

Incomplete Features and Core Loops

Arriving at Alpha with unfinished core features is more common than anyone likes to admit. Sometimes your monetisation loop is not plugged in. Sometimes critical UI flows are still a Figma dream. Often, major features are still being desperately worked on or entirely replaced. The impact of all of this is that it can make testing ineffective and feedback shallow – you are not testing the final game.

Mitigation:

- Set a firm cut-off before alpha for core loop completion.

- Ruthlessly prioritise what needs to make it in – and cut the rest.

- Use risk meetings to pressure test "must-have" features against the timeline.

DOI: 10.1201/9781003646082-34

There is a point where trying to squeeze in every planned feature becomes counterproductive. If something is not in yet and it is not essential to core gameplay, drop it. You will not be able to get meaningful feedback if the systems being tested are half-baked.

Stop and think. It's not about going fast. It's about doing the right work.

Bugs and Stability Issues

Alpha is where your tech debt shows up with a megaphone. Stability problems that got deferred suddenly become unignorable. Showstopper bugs lurk everywhere and they do not always affect every player in the same way. On mobile, one device might be flawless while another is unplayable.

Mitigation:

- Swarm bug fixing in the lead-up to alpha. Make it a team priority.

- Embed QA fully and do not treat it as a bolt-on.

- Allocate proper time in sprints to both find and fix bugs.

- Use a real variety of devices and environments to test edge cases.

Bugs at Alpha are not a surprise, but pretending they are not there, or hoping to deal with them later, is where teams lose control. Treat Alpha as a systems stress test. That includes devices, platforms, connections, input methods and anything else players might use.

Team Fatigue

Alpha is not the end. If your team is flatlining now, you are in trouble. If you are not careful, alpha becomes the start of a death march. You have been pushing hard through production; now you are at alpha and it turns out there is no break before beta and none before release either. Even worse, live support is looming. I find that teams rarely can look that far ahead and will be in need of a break and holidays just when the gamers are playing the game – just when you need the team specialists in place to fix those emerging bugs. It is brutal.

The best people often leave quietly during or just after alpha – not because of the work, but because it has not stopped. Sustainable delivery culture starts here. If you do not reset the pace, you carry burnout straight into beta and release.

Mitigation:

- Design your schedules with headroom. Don't run at 100% capacity all the time.

- Build in downtime – actual, restorative time off. Seriously, do this.

- Reinforce a culture of sustainable delivery: People do their best work when they're allowed to breathe.

Burnout is not just bad for morale – it is bad for quality and retention. And guess what, when people leave, it is your best ones who go first. The best people find their next jobs the fastest after all.

Limited Test Coverage

Still relying on a tiny QA team or last-minute outsourced testing? Still thinking, "we'll catch it in beta"? That is a recipe for public embarrassment.

Mitigation:

- Build in proper test planning – starting in pre-production.

- Treat QA as quality assurance, not just bug hunting.

- Use automated testing where possible and run tests constantly.

- Plan for scale testing well before launch – mock the conditions your players will experience.

QA pros know your game inside out. They will play it more than anyone. They are the best players of your game, even if they grow to hate it after the 100th playthrough. Treat them as core contributors.

This is where testing gaps become real. QA should be embedded by now, not brought in after the fact. You also need to test in conditions that reflect actual player use: Platforms, devices, accounts, behaviours, exploits. Your players will find the bugs you missed, and they will post them publicly.

SIDEBAR: WHAT IS QA?

QA does not stand for "testing", but for "quality assurance". Treat it as part of your development cycle and team, not as an outsourced checkpoint. Agile QA requires a separate book (we gave it a special chapter in Part V), but rest assured that QA team members must be sat alongside cross-departmental product and feature teams from the start. The more you listen and act, the higher the quality of the work and the less you are mired in technical debt and accumulating problems. See *Phantom QA* below!

KEY RISK PATTERNS IN ALPHA

The False Alpha

Definition: Alpha in name only. Core systems are missing, so feedback is shallow or misleading.

- **Impact**: Feedback is limited or misleading. Confidence in the schedule is misplaced.

- **Mitigation**: Set a formal milestone review to assess readiness for alpha. Delay if core loops aren't working.

Case Study: *The Stomping Land* launched in Early Access with incomplete core features and numerous glitches. Despite raising $114,000 on Kickstarter, development ceased shortly after release, leading to community backlash and eventual removal from Steam.

Bug Avalanche

Definition: Tech debt shows up all at once. QA is overwhelmed and the team is pulled into unplanned firefighting.

- **Impact**: Lost velocity, morale crashes, QA overwhelmed.
- **Mitigation**: Lock a pre-alpha bug sprint. Use priority labels and swarming techniques.

Case Study: During *Halo 2*'s development, a gameplay demo showcased features that were not game-ready. The graphics engine used had to be discarded and the trailer's environment never appeared in the final game. This led to significant restructuring, with much of the team's work over two years being scrapped, causing delays and resource bottlenecks.

Fatigue Cascade

Definition: Alpha crunch rolls straight into beta. No recovery time, no stability, no perspective.

- **Impact**: Burnout, rising attrition, quality degradation.
- **Mitigation**: Build rest periods into the roadmap. Communicate the post-alpha decompression plan early.

Case Study: Jon Shafer's *At the Gates* experienced a protracted development cycle, with Shafer working solo for extended periods. The lack of structured breaks and overextension led to personal burnout, communication breakdowns and significant delays, with the game releasing five years later than planned.

Phantom QA

Definition: If QA are not embedded, you are flying blind. Bugs are missed, coverage is patchy and the player becomes your test team.

- **Impact**: Missed issues, underdeveloped coverage plans, brittle releases.
- **Mitigation**: Integrate QA into sprint planning. Include them in stand-ups and retrospectives.

Case Study: *Spacebase DF-9* entered Early Access with minimal QA involvement. The game suffered from numerous bugs and incomplete features, leading to negative reviews. Development was eventually halted and the game's source code was released to the community, which attempted to address the shortcomings.

Alpha Is Where the Game Grows Up

Alpha is the moment the game moves from internal belief to external reality. That makes it uncomfortable, but necessary. Features that looked promising suddenly feel incomplete. Systems creak under scale. Feedback comes in fast, and it is not always what you hoped.

This is where real progress happens. If you have done the work to prepare – core loops stable, bugs managed, QA involved – then alpha gives you the information you need to move forward with clarity. If you have not, it exposes that too.

Alpha does not need to be perfect. It needs to be honest. Honest with players, with systems, with your own team. It is not the finish line but rather the first real checkpoint. Be warned though, this is not a relay, where the baton is handed on to others and the majority of the team can relax – quite the opposite is true. There needs to be a sense of "ready to respond" across all teams, as the triages start happening and the fixes and requests start coming in. There will be very busy people trying to not only finish the game, but improve the quality sufficiently to be ready for Beta.

REFERENCES

Adams, E. (2014). *Fundamentals of game design* (3rd ed.). New Riders.

Double Fine. (2014). *Spacebase DF-9 update.* Retrieved from: https://blog.doublefine.com/post/spacebase-df9-final-update

Barwood, H., & Falstein, N. (2017). *The 400 project: Common pitfalls in game development.*

GDC Vault. (2020). *Pre-alpha to alpha: Reality checks and milestone planning in modern game production.* Retrieved from: https://www.gdcvault.com

IGDA. (2021). *Developer satisfaction survey: Trends in studio practices and workforce challenges.* Retrieved from: https://igda.org/dss

Kickstarter. (2014). *The stomping land.* Retrieved from: https://www.kickstarter.com/projects/535191245/the-stomping-land

Schreier, J. (2017). *Blood, sweat and pixels: The triumphant, turbulent stories behind how video games are made.* Harper Paperbacks.

Shafer, J. (2019). *Postmortem: At the gates.* Gamasutra. Retrieved from: https://www.gamedeveloper.com/design/postmortem-jon-shafer-s-at-the-gates

Valve. (2013). *Postmortem: Dota 2's alpha and beta infrastructure.* Valve Developer Community (archived).

CHAPTER 31

Major Risks in the Beta Stage of Game Development

INTRODUCTION

Reaching beta is a significant achievement, but it is not a time for complacency. Beta is where your game faces real user feedback at scale and the difference between manageable problems and disasters comes down to how well you manage risks. By beta, features should be locked, but bug fixing, balancing, optimisation and certification preparation are in full swing. Every decision made at this stage has the potential to significantly impact launch quality, player reception and commercial success.

Beta is often described as the "polishing phase," but that framing hides the reality. Underneath the polish, teams are fixing critical bugs, responding to live feedback, rewriting systems and trying to hold the game production together under increasing scrutiny. For many, this is the most stressful part of the entire development cycle.

The game is no longer protected by internal teams or friendly early adopters. Beta exposes it to harsher realities: Real-world device performance, genuine player behaviour and external validation processes. Mishandling beta risks can undermine years of effort just when success is within reach.

MAJOR RISKS IN THE BETA STAGE

Unresolved Major Bugs

By beta, it is common to carry a backlog of serious issues in gameplay, performance or UX. These unresolved bugs can spiral if not triaged and managed aggressively.

By this point, you are typically dealing with the bugs that were either deferred or not visible at smaller scale. The challenge is less about technical fixes and more about triage. It is common for multiple teams to disagree on which issues to prioritise. This is where structured bug review processes and agreed prioritisation criteria are essential.

DOI: 10.1201/9781003646082-35

There is often much noise: Everyone says their bug is the one to fix first. You really need daily focused prioritisation sessions and calmness around those sessions, with a decent balance between communicating decisions outwards vs the need for urgency.

Mitigation:

- Conduct daily triage sessions with a cross-disciplinary team

- Prioritise bugs based on player impact, not internal inconvenience

- Deploy rapid bug-fixing sprints focused solely on critical issues

- Use clear ownership models to avoid duplicated effort or missed priorities

Gameplay Balancing Failures

Beta provides the first large-scale stress test of your game's economy, difficulty curves and progression systems. Unexpected exploits, difficulty spikes or player abandonment rates can appear rapidly.

Gameplay balancing at beta is rarely just a matter of tuning numbers. It often involves larger structural questions around progression, pacing or the economy. Balancing discussions can become strategic and political, with different departments pushing for different fixes based on their priorities. Often, discipline directors and the exec producer (if you have one) need to sit down and decide what can and cannot change.

Mitigation:

- Instrument the game thoroughly with telemetry to capture real player behaviour

- Run focused beta playtests segmented by player type (newcomers, veterans)

- Set up balance strike teams to rapidly iterate on problem areas

- Use a "fail fast" philosophy: Small, quick tuning passes over big sweeping changes

Tip: Create a balance category risk register: Which systems are still being debated? What can be changed safely at this stage? You have an example and more explanation in the toolkit for this chapter.

Platform Certification Failures

Failure to pass the first submission can derail launch plans, marketing campaigns and revenue forecasts. Certification issues are often minor but blocking.

The biggest risk with certification is not the technical failure, but rather underestimating how long the process takes, or failing to escalate issues early enough. It is worth having someone on the team whose only job is to track cert criteria, liaise with platform partners, and chase development tasks that support submission.

Mitigation:

- Assign a dedicated compliance lead responsible for monitoring all certification requirements

- Perform internal mock submissions, treating them as real deadlines

- Engage with platform representatives early to resolve ambiguities

- Budget time for multiple submission attempts, not just one

Weak Retention Metrics

Poor Day 1, Day 3 or Day 7 retention in beta is an early warning of launch struggles. Retention failures often reflect deeper issues in onboarding, early game pacing or first-session experience.

Poor retention numbers in beta are rarely caused by one issue. They reflect broader systemic problems in onboarding, pacing or player motivation. Treat retention as a shared concern across disciplines. Use player journey tracking to understand where and why people are dropping off.

Beta is where you start to really see where people are quitting and hopefully why. This is where you see enough players coming through the game to make it worth using annotated heatmaps and clickstream data to support player journey analysis. It seems still far more prevalent in mobile games, where ensuring hooks are in place and big data is harnessed has been supported from the start. I believe that many PC and console games still lag behind with the knowledge and do not build into their production plans the need to include those same hooks and data points that will give so much powerful data at this stage onwards.

Data-driven or data-empowered decision making is much easier when you have some data.

Mitigation:

- Run closed beta rounds focused specifically on onboarding and early progression

- Analyse player journeys to identify early abandonment triggers

- A/B test different onboarding flows to optimise engagement

- Invest time in tutorials and first-session delight features

Beta Feedback Overload

At beta, feedback floods in from players, QA, external partners and internal teams. Without disciplined filtering, teams can become overwhelmed and lose focus.

Beta feedback tends to arrive from multiple sources at once, including players, QA, marketing, external partners and internal staff. Without clear triage, teams quickly lose focus. It helps to assign someone to own this feedback stream, summarise inputs and keep the team focused on priorities.

In other words, everything is coming in at once. Without structure, you drown.

Mitigation:

- Use structured priority frameworks (e.g. severity x frequency grids)
- Appoint a feedback coordinator to triage and summarise input
- Re-anchor teams to the milestone roadmap weekly
- Say "no!" firmly but respectfully to late feature suggestions

KEY RISK PATTERNS IN BETA

Certification Crisis

Definition: Failing first submission to major platform holders (Sony, Microsoft, Nintendo) or app stores.

Impact:

- Delayed launch
- Increased marketing costs
- Damage to platform relationships

Mitigation:

- Pre-certification checklists integrated into regular QA sprints
- Dedicated compliance review gates at Alpha exit and Beta mid-point

Case Study: *No Man's Sky* faced severe certification challenges before its 2016 release. Sean Murray of Hello Games revealed in interviews that they had to work intensively with Sony to pass certification hurdles, leading to last-minute crunch periods (Eurogamer, 2016).

Why This Matters: Shows how seemingly minor compliance issues can disrupt launch timelines and team morale.

Telemetry Blindness

Definition: Launching beta tests without sufficient data collection, leaving teams to rely on anecdotal feedback.

Impact:

- Misinterpreted player behaviour
- Wrong prioritisation of fixes
- Hidden systemic issues

Mitigation:

- Mandatory telemetry and player journey analytics before any public beta
- Cross-check feedback against quantitative behavioural data

Case Study: *Destiny* (Bungie, 2014) used an extensive closed beta with heavy telemetry instrumentation to uncover progression blockers and engagement gaps. Their data-led approach led to significant reworks of early game experiences before launch (GDC Vault, 2015).

Why This Matters: Demonstrates the danger of acting on anecdotal feedback instead of real player behaviour.

Beta Crunch Spiral

Definition: Teams burn out due to unrealistic bug-fix targets and open-ended feedback cycles during beta.

Impact:

- Declining quality of bug fixes
- Rising attrition
- Morale collapse before launch

Mitigation:

- Time-box bug sprints with hard stop reviews
- Prioritise "must fix" over "nice to have"
- Build decompression days into the beta schedule

Case Study: *Telltale Games*' later seasons were marked by crunch fatigue, exacerbated by tight episodic release cycles and minimal breathing room between betas and launches. Postmortems revealed how lack of sustainable pacing contributed to eventual studio closure (Polygon, 2018).

Why This Matters:
Highlights how unclear boundaries and endless triage loops can burn out teams before release.

BETA IS POLISHING IN PUBLIC

Beta is often described as a polishing phase, but the reality is more complex. Teams are still fixing core systems, responding to live feedback, and trying to hold the project together as external visibility increases. It is a fragile phase where momentum can just as easily falter as carry you to release.

By this point, every change must be discussed, negotiated and prioritised. Production leads, QA, design, engineering and leadership all have competing perspectives. Some systems are still being rewritten. Others are being held together until they can be removed, replaced or patched later. The pressure to improve the product is real, but so is the risk of overreaching.

This is not where everything quietens down. It is often the busiest phase of all, especially for discipline leads and producers who must make rapid decisions with limited time. There is no safety net now. The game is being played, judged and dissected in real time.

Beta is not where the work ends. It is where decisions matter most. If your risk management practices are solid, you will stay focused. If not, you will chase too many fixes, burn out your team and compromise the release.

This is polishing in public. Prioritise well. Stay calm. Eight hours sleep a night.

REFERENCES

Eurogamer. (2016). No Man's Sky postmortem: Launch challenges and certification. Retrieved from: https://www.eurogamer.net

GDC Vault. (2015). Building destiny: How Bungie created their beta analytics system. Retrieved from: https://www.gdcvault.com

Polygon. (2018). The fall of Telltale games: Crunch and collapse. Retrieved from: https://www.polygon.com

CHAPTER 32

Major Risks in the Release Stage of Game Development

INTRODUCTION

The release stage often represents the culmination of years of work but also the most visible and vulnerable moment for a project. The gap between private readiness and public perception can be brutal. Release risks are often technical, operational, reputational and commercial. Even small issues become magnified under the spotlight of launch.

A successful release calls for the ability to respond with speed, clarity and credibility.

Release is not just about the deployment of your game, but it is of course a visibility shift. Issues that used to be internal are now exposed. Minor problems can escalate because players, press, partners and platform holders are all watching at once. You are no longer managing just delivery; you are adding managing perception and momentum.

MAJOR RISKS IN THE RELEASE STAGE

Server, Network and Launch Failures

Load-related crashes, login failures, or matchmaking breakdowns can immediately alienate players.

Mitigation:

- Conduct large-scale stress testing well before launch
- Establish dynamic scaling architectures with cloud providers
- Prepare crisis communication and response plans for server incidents

DOI: 10.1201/9781003646082-36

Load failures are no longer just a technical problem. They immediately turn into a customer service issue, a community narrative and potentially a platform credibility concern. This is where calm handling and good incident response planning matter more than heroics.

As a colleague once said: "Everyone loves your game so much they crash your servers, and then they hate you."

Tip: Include a launch-day crisis plan that outlines who leads comms, who triages and who gives the all-clear. In other industries, there is commonly a Go Live or Cutover Plan, where everything that needs to be accomplished for a few weeks before the day itself and directly afterwards is listed and owners assigned. I recommend this model.

Negative Player Feedback

Unaddressed bugs, missing features, or mismatched expectations generate waves of negative reviews and community backlash.

Mitigation:

- Prioritise launch stability and completeness over marginal features

- Communicate transparently about known issues and patch plans

- Deploy Day 1 patches with prepared triage teams for live feedback

Not all negative feedback is a surprise. Some of it is predictable and planned for. The problem arises when there is no agreed response, or when community teams are promising things the dev team cannot realistically deliver in time.

Remember too, the worst thing for players is when community people say something is going to happen and it never does.

As we have seen in previous chapters, it is best to include pre-written holding statements and realistic FAQs. Release day is not the time to draft messaging from scratch.

Marketing and PR Failures

Mismatched marketing narratives, underpowered campaigns, or false expectations sabotage even strong launches.

Mitigation:

- Align marketing and product teams closely in the final months

- Refine messaging based on late-stage player feedback and perception

- Plan agile post-launch marketing adjustments to counter unexpected narratives

Sometimes the problem is not marketing failure, but rather marketing mismatch. If the message players received before launch does not line up with the actual experience, trust collapses quickly. Your marketing team might not have understood the game or could not explain it clearly. Perhaps they did not listen; perhaps they listened to a misguided version of what the game would be.

Tip: Align marketing sprints with dev milestones. Make sure late-stage builds are shown and understood before final messaging goes out.

Low Player Acquisition and Launch Momentum

If initial player numbers underperform, retention strategies and post-launch content become irrelevant.

Mitigation:

- Launch targeted UA (user acquisition) campaigns with flexible spend allocation
- Prepare influencer engagement and community growth strategies pre-launch
- Analyse and pivot UA targeting rapidly based on real player behaviour

Lack of early players does not just affect revenue; it also undermines team morale and the justification for ongoing support. Calm leadership is essential here. Early results can be misleading, but only if there is a plan to react, not just panic. Unfortunately, this tends to be exactly when people start to panic. Teams start to shrink as they move on to other projects or games. Priorities shift fast, and bad decisions can be made that have a huge impact on the success of the game.

Tip: Run some workshops before launch to try and think through some post-launch pivot plans. You will not have time to build them from scratch when panic sets in.

KEY RISK PATTERNS IN RELEASE

Launch Day Collapse

Definition: Critical online infrastructure failures during the first hours of release.

Impact:

- Mass refunds
- Negative press amplification
- Loss of early adoption momentum

Mitigation:

- Overprovision server capacity by safe margins
- Schedule rolling regional launches where feasible
- Monitor social sentiment live and respond immediately

Case Study: *Diablo III* (Blizzard, 2012) faced massive login server failures on launch day ("Error 37"), leading to intense community backlash and negative press coverage (PC Gamer, 2012).

Why This Matters: Highlights how infrastructure issues instantly become public narratives and trust problems.

Review Bombing

Definition: Coordinated or organic negative review waves based on launch issues or controversies.

Impact:

- Damaged store page visibility
- Lowered player trust
- Compromised sales projections

Mitigation:

- Proactively monitor sentiment and identify root causes
- Communicate transparently and offer goodwill gestures where justified
- Work with platform holders to contest bad-faith reviews where appropriate

Case Study: *Metro Exodus* (4A Games, 2019) faced review bombing on Steam following the decision to move to Epic Games Store exclusivity. Proactive communication and visible post-launch support helped regain player trust over time (PCGamesN, 2019).

Why This Matters: A reminder that community frustration can have platform-level impact if it is not acknowledged properly.

Patch Panic

Definition: Rushed emergency patches introduce new bugs or destabilise builds post-launch.

Impact:

- New waves of negative feedback
- Diminished technical credibility

Mitigation:

- Maintain a separate hotfix branch with strict testing gates
- Timebox patch QA even under urgent conditions

Case Study: *Cyberpunk 2077* (CD Projekt Red, 2020) suffered cascading patch issues post-launch, where rushed hotfixes sometimes worsened stability on various platforms, exacerbating public dissatisfaction (The Verge, 2020).

Why This Matters: Demonstrates how rushed fixes without testing can make everything worse, not better.

RELEASE IS EVERYONE'S PROBLEM NOW

Release is not the end. It is a shift in pressure, visibility and accountability. Problems are not theoretical anymore but become only too real, public and interconnected. A platform outage is no longer just an engineering concern. A late patch is no longer just "QA's fault". The way your team handles these moments reflects the strength of your whole studio.

This is where years of planning, culture and risk management are either visible or exposed. The spotlight is on. Your comms, your decisions, your follow-through all matter more now than they did last month.

That said, there is also something deeply collaborative about launch. It is one of the many heartening and uplifting moments where you see teams come together quickly to fix problems, support each other and hold the line. Heroes are made. Pizzas are consumed. Buckets fill with salty tears.

It is intense. It is messy. It is shared. And it works best when it has been prepared for.

As I said at the top of this chapter, the Release phase is not a test of perfection. Be patient, be calm, remember to continue attempting to remain objective and keep those risk management principles in mind. We are all in it together.

REFERENCES

PC Gamer. (2012). *Diablo 3's launch day disaster: A timeline*. PC Gamer.
PCGamesN. (2019). *How metro exodus recovered after steam review bombing*. PCGamesN.
The Verge. (2020). *The fallout from Cyberpunk 2077's botched launch*. The Verge.

CHAPTER 33

Major Risks in the Post-Release Stage of Game Development

INTRODUCTION

Post-release is not a "maintenance mode" – it is an operationally intense, player-visible phase that determines the long-term viability of a game. At this stage, the game's performance, reputation and revenue curve are either consolidated or degraded based on LiveOps execution, community management and commercial adaptability.

This chapter **does not attempt to fully cover the LiveOps or continuous content pipeline** – that deserves its own chapter – and it follows in Part V. Instead, this chapter focuses on the transitional risks: the critical early weeks and months after release, when teams shift from launch mode to sustaining the game as a product.

Post-release risks are often underestimated during development. Success here demands as much proactive risk management as any earlier phase.

MAJOR RISKS IN THE POST-RELEASE STAGE

Insufficient Post-Launch Support

Neglecting the player base after release leads to declining engagement, negative sentiment and reputational damage.

Mitigation:

- Plan post-launch patch schedules and resource allocations pre-release

- Maintain a LiveOps roadmap visible to players and internal stakeholders

DOI: 10.1201/9781003646082-37

- Prioritise bug fixes, quality-of-life improvements and community requests

Most teams want to do the right thing for players post-launch. But the risk is not laziness; it is resourcing. If the game underperforms, headcount drops quickly. If it overperforms, the team is overwhelmed. Planning for both is essential.

I remember a game launch in which I was told by marketing, "We don't think it's going to be a huge hit… but we're not ready if it is." Slightly disheartening, but this is a classic risk situation with uncertainty and limited resources. What was more heartening was that the marketing team was ready to pivot if they were proven wrong.

Tip: Plan support for three trajectories: Slow burn, viral hit and modest growth. Your resourcing should scale accordingly.

Revenue Model Failures

Failure to adjust monetisation strategies based on live data results in declining revenue and community distrust.

Mitigation:

- Monitor purchasing behaviour continuously
- Adjust offers, pricing and content cadence based on real player trends
- Involve economy designers and LiveOps managers in all revenue decisions

Monetisation that worked in development may not hold up in the wild. Live player behaviour, platform changes and community expectations all shift quickly. The goal is not just revenue, but trust. Desperation pricing almost always backfires. Why? Because you need the money, so you start squeezing people, and that breaks the ecosystem.

Player Churn

Players will naturally leave, but unmanaged churn can lead to catastrophic population collapse.

Mitigation:

- Launch regular new content, events and engagement initiatives
- Create player progression paths that extend well beyond launch
- Leverage community-driven content and initiatives

You cannot stop churn, but you can prepare for it. The risk is not that players leave, because they will; it is that you do not know why. Churn should be tracked, analysed and anticipated with the same rigour as bugs or performance issues.

Churn will happen, but proper analysis of the data and metrics will reveal a world of possible improvements and opportunities.

Tip: Build player retention data into your risk review cycles, not just marketing dashboards.

LiveOps Failures

LiveOps is often handed off with little preparation. The people running events, balancing offers and pushing content are often undertrained or unsupported. This is not a team problem; it is a structural one. Poor tooling, under-resourced teams or lack of integrated support cripples post-release content delivery.

Mitigation:

- Build LiveOps systems and pipelines during core development

- Ensure LiveOps teams have autonomy, tools and escalation paths

- Train LiveOps operators properly rather than relying on ad hoc learning

For more detail on LiveOps tooling, event design and operational cadence, see the Chapter 34 "LiveOps and the Content Pipeline".

KEY RISK PATTERNS IN POST-RELEASE

Content Drought

Definition: Insufficient new content or meaningful updates post-launch. A predictable risk that is often deprioritised during development. Content must be queued before launch rather than hoped for later.

Impact:

- Player base erosion

- Declining revenue

- Community disengagement

Mitigation:

- Prepare a backlog of live content before launch

- Timebox content updates to predictable cadences

Case Study: *The Division* (Ubisoft, 2016) suffered a steep post-launch player decline partly due to a long gap between launch and the first meaningful updates. Ubisoft's later Year 1 expansions helped recover momentum (Polygon, 2017).

I well remember a game being developed in one of my studios where there was a very real fear before launch that the content would all be used up during Beta and none would be left for the actual launch or post-launch. Fortunately, this was discussed and addressed far in advance of launch!

Monetisation Backlash

Definition: Player rejection of perceived exploitative, unfair or poorly communicated monetisation strategies. A reminder that revenue models are part of player trust. Overreaching post-launch undoes years of goodwill.

Impact:

- Revenue contraction
- Reputation damage
- Increased churn

Mitigation:

- Communicate monetisation transparently
- Focus on fair value exchange and avoid pay-to-win perceptions

Case Study: *Star Wars Battlefront II* (EA DICE, 2017) initially launched with a loot box system perceived as pay-to-win, triggering widespread backlash and regulatory scrutiny. EA restructured the monetisation system post-launch but sustained reputation damage (BBC, 2017).

LiveOps Technical Debt

Definition: Legacy tools and brittle workflows collapse under the strain of real-time demands. This is where you pay for not planning earlier.

Impact:

- Slow content delivery
- Increased risk of live errors
- Operator burnout

Mitigation:

- Integrate LiveOps tooling requirements into core tech planning
- Establish technical debt payment plans specifically for LiveOps

Case Study: *Destiny* (Bungie, 2014) faced initial LiveOps challenges due to the fragility of their early content update pipelines. Bungie invested heavily in new tools and processes between Year 1 and Year 2 to improve LiveOps agility (GDC Vault, 2016).

POST-RELEASE IS A TRANSITION, NOT A WIND-DOWN

Post-release is not where things settle; it is where they start again. What changes is not the pressure but the shape of it. Bugs are now service tickets. Patch timing is now player-facing. Internal debates are now public threads.

The risk is assuming the hard part is over. In truth, if you are lucky, the game has only just entered the most sustained and unforgiving phase of its life. If you are not so lucky, the game could already be facing a shut-down or a rapidly dwindling support plan if player numbers disappoint.

LiveOps, content delivery, player support, community and moderation comms are now front-line systems. That is why we dedicate an entire chapter to what happens next.

REFERENCES

BBC News. (2017, November 21). *Star wars Battlefront II: Loot box controversy explained*. Retrieved from: https://www.bbc.co.uk/news/technology-42041704

Lambert, J. (2016, March). *Destiny's LiveOps evolution: Building an agile content pipeline* [Conference presentation]. Game Developers Conference (GDC), San Francisco, CA. GDC Vault. Retrieved from: https://www.gdcvault.com/play/1023658/Destiny-s-Live-Ops-Evolution

Tassi, P. (2017, March 9). *How The Division rebuilt its player base*. Polygon. Retrieved from: https://www.polygon.com/2017/3/9/14866200/the-division-year-two-ubisoft-massive-update

PART V

Special Topics and Emerging Risk Frontiers

THIS SECTION EXPLORES COMPLEX and evolving risk domains that extend beyond the core production lifecycle, highlighting areas where traditional game development practices face new pressures. From the operational intensity of LiveOps and the strategic dependencies of mobile ecosystems to the cultural volatility of social media and the structural implications of studio scale, these chapters examine how modern risk manifests across diverse contexts.

Each topic challenges the assumption that risk management can be confined to project planning or QA pipelines. Instead, they demonstrate how risk must be understood as a function of ongoing relationships between players, platforms, teams and technologies.

What unites these chapters is their strategic relevance. Whether navigating the trust economy of live services or surviving the compliance gauntlet of mobile platforms, these special topics reveal how risk is now as much about culture, communication and coordination as it is about features or schedules. I encourage you to view these domains not as edge cases, but as increasingly central to sustainable game development.

Studios that succeed in the next decade will be those that engage with these frontiers deliberately, structurally and early.

DOI: 10.1201/9781003646082-38

CHAPTER 34

LiveOps and Content Pipeline Risks

INTRODUCTION

This chapter picks up where the post-release stage leaves off. Now that the game is live, the challenge shifts from responding to launch issues to running the game as a service. LiveOps is not just maintenance, but rather a new kind of production cycle, with its own pressures, tooling needs, and long-term risks. What follows is not an afterthought, but a new operational phase in its own right. Even only a few years ago, LiveOps was almost a niche, but nowadays it is more and more essential and even commonplace.

I was fortunate, as my first opportunity within the games industry was on PlayStation Home – a free virtual world on PS3. I experienced the world of LiveOps and all its challenges before most PC/console game companies were exposed to it. Mobile games were far more quick to commit to LiveOps and the need to measure retention and stickiness, staring into the new player funnel and making data-informed changes to the games.

Before "LiveOps" became an industry term, PlayStation Home offered a glimpse of what always-on game operations could become. As a free-to-access virtual world on PlayStation 3, it combined real-time events, content publishing, avatar customisation and persistent social spaces – well ahead of its time.

During my tenure at Sony PlayStation, I oversaw operations and production for Home, managing infrastructure that delivered over 80,000 unique items, supporting weekly publishing cadences across multiple territories. We served half a billion server requests per month, managed concurrent users in dynamic shared spaces, and routinely coordinated content drops, promotions and live events. What we were running was, effectively, a LiveOps platform – just before the industry had a term or shared language for it.

Working on PS Home taught me foundational lessons in stakeholder alignment, server-side risk, cross-team coordination and resilience under pressure. Many of the risks in this chapter (tooling fragility, event timing, monetisation misfires, player trust) were already visible

DOI: 10.1201/9781003646082-39

then. They remain today. What has changed is that now, we finally understand that *LiveOps is production*. And it needs to be resourced and respected as such (Kuchera, 2015).

Live-service games run like online services: Their infrastructure and content pipeline must handle continuous updates and events. This creates many failure points. Common risks (as highlighted in the Post-Release chapter) include:

- Prolonged server or network outages (hardware/network failures or bot attacks causing downtime)

- Broken or rushed content updates (bugs or balance issues in new features)

- Depleted engagement due to weak content pipelines (slow release cadence or "content drought")

Aggressive monetisation or unpopular changes can provoke player backlash – in a 2024 survey, 31% of developers were "very" concerned about live-service monetisation models.

Platform-specific limits also matter: Console patches require costly certification cycles, and mobile store reviews can delay fixes.

Finally, security exploits or data loss (e.g. corrupted player data or unpatched vulnerabilities) can break trust.

These issues can knock players offline or alienate fans (as when Fortnite's 2019 "black hole" downtime had players waiting hours in queues and venting on social media).

This chapter is therefore not just about operational stability, but also the structures and practices that keep a live game healthy, playable, and commercially viable over time. This needs to be achieved without burning out the team or alienating the players.

COMMON RISK TRIGGERS

- **Server/Infrastructure Failures**: Crashes or capacity overloads (e.g. DDoS or scale limits) can take the game offline, losing engagement and revenue. These are often caused by success. Load spikes during seasonal events, influencer streams, or surprise PR wins can all overwhelm capacity. Make sure you are planning for success, not just failure.

Niantic's 2017 Pokémon GO Fest suffered a full-day outage due to unexpected load, forcing Niantic to compensate players.

- **Pipeline Bottlenecks and Quality Issues**: Content production overruns or flawed releases (e.g. hotfixes that introduce new bugs) can stall game updates or break gameplay. It is not just about how fast content gets made; it is about how stable that content is when it arrives. An aggressive release cadence without proper tooling or testing ends up backfiring.

I remember chasing LiveOps to ask why a series of broken pieces of content had passed through a much vaunted quality testing tool into live only to hear, "They said they'd write that tool during beta. It never happened".

If your team is spending more time fixing last month's patch than preparing the next one, your content pipeline is not ready. Content pipelines are enormous ventures for larger games and should not be approached lightly.

- **Unintended Gameplay Imbalance**: New content (characters, items, economy changes) can create overpowered builds or inflation if not tuned, damaging fairness.

Balance fixes in live environments need more than intuition. Remember to track when balance changes affect more than one core system, especially when they are player-facing.

Use data to detect power creep or inflation, but make sure changes are reviewed across disciplines. Economic tweaks affect trust and progression and require careful communication to players once agreed.

- **Monetisation and Policy Backlash**: Aggressive price points, pay-to-win content or unpopular changes (e.g. surprise nerfs) often trigger community outrage and distrust.

Most monetisation controversy is not about the pricing – it is about communication. Surprises, stealth changes, or shifting value without warning cause more damage than high prices. Always give players a reason before you give them a change. Silence is way more expensive than the extra revenue expected from any tweak you made.

- **Compliance/Platform Constraints**: Console/mobile platforms enforce certification or store approval, adding delays and complexities to patches. Console certification, mobile store reviews, and platform freezes (e.g. during holidays) all create real bottlenecks. If your LiveOps plan does not account for these windows, you will miss them and be stuck waiting.

- **Security and Cheating**: Live games face cheating, hacking or data breaches; failure to secure servers or timely patch exploits can erode player confidence. Once you are live, you are a target. Cheating is not just a gameplay issue; it is a reputational risk. Players will not wait for a fix if they think the game is compromised.

If you do not have a plan to handle your first cheating scandal, you are already behind. Please refer to the Crisis Management chapter for pragmatic advice and templates you can use to build up your anti-cheat plan.

WHAT IF THE BUSINESS KEEPS CHANGING ITS MIND?

Imagine your LiveOps team has spent months preparing a stable roadmap of seasonal events, minigame updates, and avatar content. Suddenly, your regional leadership pivots:

- **One division wants LiveOps to pivot towards structured gameplay**, demanding mission systems and progression loops.

- **Another prioritises monetisation**, pushing for exclusive branded content and IP-driven experiences.

- **A third wants culturally tailored features**, such as new animations, localisation variants, or social norms that differ by territory.

Each regional ask cascades through the LiveOps pipeline – affecting infrastructure, content tooling, QA schedules, certification windows, and third-party partners. Your feature prioritisation collapses under the weight of competing agendas. Internal teams are caught between appeasing stakeholders and protecting developer velocity. Players, meanwhile, experience inconsistency: Missing features, broken promises, or events that feel half-finished.

This was not a hypothetical for those of us working on PlayStation Home. It was the daily reality. Competing business priorities across Sony's regional divisions regularly redirected focus. Teams pivoted repeatedly, often abandoning partially built systems or reprioritising requests that served short-term commercial targets over long-term player value.

LiveOps does not survive frequent top-down redirection. Unlike a boxed product, it is a continuous system: Interdependent, timed, and fragile. I always like to call this the Fragile Ecosystem. The real risk is not a missed patch. It is organisational misalignment becoming operational entropy. The slow descent into the lowest common denominator as you try and strike a middle route to keep everyone happy.

Mitigation Tactic: If your LiveOps roadmap serves multiple business units, enforce a **single prioritisation channel** – ideally through a cross-functional steering group. Without one, you are running three games with one team.

MITIGATION STRATEGIES

- **Development Process**: Adopt DevOps/CI-CD pipelines for builds and deployments and use feature flags or dark-launches to roll out content gradually. Integrate game analytics early to "test in prod" (use these analytics and a controlled rollout to monitor live impact before full deployment) and measure the impact of tweaks. Maintain a content calendar so updates are synchronised across dev, ops and marketing teams.

- **Automated Testing and QA**: Build a dedicated LiveOps QA team and automated test suites (smoke tests, regression tests) to vet patches. Leverage automation tools to simulate user flows and stress-test servers. Maintain a dedicated test server or beta channel (e.g. closed Android build, Steam Beta) for new features.

- **Monitoring and Alerting**: Instrument the game with real-time telemetry (crash reports, performance metrics, usage stats) and set up alerting (e.g. via Grafana/Datadog) to detect anomalies immediately. Regularly run game-day drills or simulate outages to test incident response.

- **Communication and Feedback**: Keep players informed through in-game notices, social media and patch notes. Have a customer support channel ready to collect bug reports. Quickly analyse player feedback and triage bugs. If an update fails, communicate an apology and ETA for fixes.

- **Contingency Planning**: Maintain reserve capacity (cloud scaling) to handle event surges. Use managed backend services (e.g. AWS GameLift, Azure PlayFab) to offload server scaling (Amazon Web Services, 2023) (Microsoft, 2023). Plan for content backups and data redundancy. Have kill switches or emergency hotfix builds ready.

SIDEBAR: WHAT ARE FEATURE FLAGS?

(LaunchDarkly, 2024) Feature flags (also called toggles) are switches in the code that allow developers to enable or disable specific features without changing the entire build. They are commonly used to:

- **Gradually roll out new content** to a subset of users
- **Test features in live environments** before a full release
- **Turn off problematic systems quickly** without a patch
- **Manage regional or platform-specific differences** (e.g. showing a feature only on iOS)

They are incredibly useful in LiveOps because they allow for safe experimentation and fast responses. But they also come with risk.

If no one outside engineering knows what is toggled on or off, confusion follows. QA may report a "bug" in a feature that was never meant to be live. Community teams may reference something players cannot see.

Keep feature flags documented and shared. Treat them as part of the product roadmap, not just internal tooling.

CRISIS MANAGEMENT AND TRUST RECOVERY

- **Technical Response**: Mobilise an on-call team immediately. Use logs and monitoring to diagnose the issue, then deploy hotfixes or rollbacks as needed. Maintain communication between engineers, ops and community managers.

- **Public Communication**: Issue clear, honest updates on Twitter/Discord/forums. Acknowledge the problem, outline steps being taken and set realistic timelines for fixes. Over-communication (frequent updates) is usually better than silence.

- **Player Compensation**: Offer in-game makeup for affected players – free currency, items, experience boosts, or account credit. Refunds or credit can also be issued for paid features if the issue is severe.

- **Postmortem and Follow-up**: Once fixed, publish a retrospective (if possible) on what went wrong and how it's prevented in future. Update players on what was learned and what permanent changes will be made.

- **PR Strategy**: Coordinate with marketing/PR to manage media narrative. A genuine apology (blog post or video from leadership) can soften anger. Highlight positive action (e.g. "we learned X and now are doing Y").

- **Economic Rebalancing**: If the incident caused economic imbalance (free items or skipped challenges), plan how to re-sync. For example, some games may temporarily disable competitive modes or adjust reward curves to prevent exploitation of freebies.

These practices are not just useful in a crisis. They are part of your ongoing reputation. Players do not remember the outage as much as how you handled it.

KEY RISK PATTERNS

Content Drought Spiral

- **Definition:** Slow or inconsistent content delivery causes players to disengage.

- **Trigger:** Pipeline bottlenecks, LiveOps team burnout, or failure to plan a long-term content cadence.

- **Outcome:** Churn increases, monetisation drops, and community sentiment erodes. Players assume the game is "abandoned" even if work continues in the background.

- **Mitigation:** Maintain a content calendar with visible releases, staggered events, and fallback content. Build in buffer capacity to protect creative teams from burnout. Use telemetry to identify engagement drop-offs and target content accordingly.

Stealth Nerf Backlash

- **Definition:** Changes to balance, monetisation, or rewards are made without adequate communication to players.

- **Trigger:** Silent pricing updates, hidden nerfs to character abilities, or stealth changes to progression speed.

- **Outcome:** Reddit blowups, influencer criticism, and long-term erosion of trust in patch notes and LiveOps communication.

- **Mitigation:** Document and disclose all major gameplay and economy changes in public-facing patch notes. Use "before/after" framing and explain rationale. Invite player feedback on contentious changes and adjust if justified.

Unscalable Tooling Trap

- **Definition:** Tooling promised during development never materialises or is abandoned post-launch, leaving the LiveOps pipeline fragile or overly manual.

- **Trigger:** Tech debt deprioritised during launch crunch, unfinished tools handed over to LiveOps teams, or over-reliance on one engineer.

- **Outcome:** Broken updates, hotfix chaos, high friction between dev, QA, and LiveOps teams. Pipeline velocity declines, and errors multiply.

- **Mitigation:** Protect post-launch tooling budget during pre-launch planning. Include QA and LiveOps in tooling design. Assign ownership and maintain tool documentation. If necessary, prioritise tooling fixes over new content.

Cert Deadline Collapse

- **Definition:** A patch or event misses its console certification window or mobile store approval, causing delays or forced triage.

- **Trigger:** Last-minute bugs, overlooked platform constraints, or missed pre-flight checks (e.g. file size, save compatibility).

- **Outcome:** Scheduled events or offers are delayed, marketing coordination is broken, and players face outages or mismatches. The team scrambles to recover.

- **Mitigation:** Include platform-specific "cert buffers" in all release timelines. Maintain a detailed pre-cert checklist. Rehearse submission processes. Ensure marketing and support are looped in when timelines shift.

Patch-Apology Loop

- **Definition:** Updates introduce new bugs or regressions, triggering rollbacks, hotfixes, and repeated public apologies.

- **Trigger:** Incomplete testing, automation gaps, rushed approvals, or unstable builds deployed under time pressure.

- **Outcome:** Player frustration, QA burnout, and support ticket spikes. Studio reputation suffers as LiveOps cadence becomes synonymous with failure.

- **Mitigation:** Enforce minimum QA gates before go-live. Use staggered rollouts and telemetry to catch issues early. Maintain rollback infrastructure. Publicly own mistakes and show visible improvement over time.

Roadmap Fracture

- **Definition:** Conflicting business directives or regional leadership demands cause LiveOps priorities to shift repeatedly, undermining delivery stability and eroding developer trust.

- **Trigger:** Business units push competing agendas – e.g. one region wants gameplay systems, another prioritises monetisation, and another demands localisation or cultural features – without central alignment.

- **Outcome:** Teams pivot midstream, cancel or rework half-built features, and overload third-party partners with shifting briefs. Developer morale suffers, delivery timelines slide, and players experience inconsistency and dropped expectations.

- **Mitigation:** Appoint a single roadmap owner with authority to align stakeholder input into a unified backlog. Establish a steering group to negotiate strategic direction, but freeze delivery windows (e.g. 6–8 weeks) to protect production. Track context-switch cost and defend developer focus as a risk mitigation priority.

REAL-WORLD EXAMPLES: WHAT LIVEOPS RISK LOOKS LIKE IN PRACTICE

These case studies go beyond outages – they show how LiveOps success or failure is defined by preparedness, communication, and trust recovery. In each case, we examine the incident, the studio's response, and the embedded risk pattern it exposed.

Pokémon GO Fest (2017)

Studio: Niantic

Issue: Full-scale outage at a major live event due to server overload.

Trigger: Underestimating concurrent load during the first Pokémon GO Fest in Chicago.

Response: Niantic issued widespread refunds, travel reimbursements, and released rare Pokémon to all attendees' local areas as compensation (Niantic, 2017).

Outcome: Negative press was balanced by visible recovery actions and sincere community-facing communication. Trust was strained, but the game survived.

Risk Pattern: *Server Overload as Reputational Risk, Crisis Management as Player Retention*

Takeaway: A single LiveOps failure in public view can dominate your reputation for months. What matters most is how fast, generous, and human your response is.

Fortnite's "Black Hole" Event (2019)

Studio: Epic Games

Issue: Game taken fully offline as part of a narrative reset.

Trigger: Deliberate "black hole" used as a marketing and narrative transition between Fortnite Chapters.

Response: Players were kept in suspense with no official statement for 36 hours. The game relaunched into Chapter 2 with massive fanfare.

Outcome: Mixed. Many players loved the stunt, but others reported frustration and confusion. It worked because Epic controlled the narrative fully (Epic Games, 2019).

Risk Pattern: *Controlled Downtime for Maximum Impact, Trust as Spectacle*

Takeaway: Only attempt intentional downtime if you can control the context, message, and timing. Any technical wobble will be interpreted as failure.

Gigantic: Rampage Edition (2024)

Studio: Abstraction Games

Issue: Day-one server issues prevented logins and gameplay.

Trigger: Server-side misconfiguration during launch window.

Response: Abstraction issued a public apology and granted all players in-game rewards (Abstraction Games, 2024).

Outcome: The issue was contained within the first 24 hours and sentiment recovered quickly.

Risk Pattern: *Patch-Apology Loop, Server Misfire with Fast Compensation*

Takeaway: Mistakes happen. Players will forgive almost anything if the fix is fast, the apology sincere, and the make-good generous.

Marvel Rivals (2025)

Studio: NetEase

Issue: One-hour server outage during open beta.

Trigger: Load balancing issue during high demand window.

Response: NetEase proactively gave 200 premium currency to all players (NetEase, 2025).

Outcome: The community widely praised the speed and generosity of the response.

Risk Pattern: *Micro-Outage, Macro-Compensation*

Takeaway: Even short incidents can become goodwill moments. Player trust is built on consistency but bonded through generosity.

SCALING AND INNOVATING IN LIVEOPS

Failure recovery and outage disruption reflect only one dimension of LiveOps. LiveOps is also about:

- Retention and re-engagement design
- Content pacing and seasonal architecture
- Operational innovation (tooling, infrastructure)

- Player-driven economy or governance systems

- Ethical risk in monetisation and event design

Here are four additional case studies that reflect positive or complex LiveOps systems, not just crises.

Baldur's Gate 3: Community-Led Balance and Hotfix Strategy (2023)

Studio: Larian Studios

Focus: LiveOps feedback loop and transparency

Insight: Larian maintained a high-frequency patch cadence post-launch, with over a dozen hotfixes in the first six weeks. What set them apart was their transparent and human patch notes, frequent acknowledgements of community issues, and deliberate pacing: delaying changes to avoid player disorientation.

Lesson: Not every LiveOps moment is about uptime: Tone, pacing, and trust are operational levers. Their patch communication style became a model in itself (Rock Paper Shotgun, 2023).

Relevant Risk Pattern: *Patch-Apology Loop (Prevented)*

Genshin Impact: Seasonal Cadence and LiveOps Architecture

Studio: miHoYo

Focus: LiveOps content pacing and tooling

Insight: Genshin Impact runs a tightly structured six-week seasonal cadence, with built-in systems for narrative beats, progression resets, and economy rotations. Their team pre-loads future patches to minimise risk and designs seasonal events a full year ahead. Tooling, calendar coordination, and QA prep are all centralised (Game Developer, 2022).

Lesson: This is LiveOps as an industrial content machine – an example of how LiveOps can become sustainable, even at enormous scale, with planning and pre-production.

Relevant Risk Pattern: *Content Drought Spiral (Mitigated)*

Warframe: Community as Operational Partner

Studio: Digital Extremes

Focus: Transparency, livestreaming, community interaction

Insight: Through Devstreams, forums, and TennoCon, Warframe treats its player base not as consumers but co-stakeholders in LiveOps. Roadmap discussions are often public (Eggplante, 2019). Players are invited into prioritisation decisions.

Lesson: Community dynamics can be part of your LiveOps tooling – but only if you are ready to treat feedback as input, not noise.

Relevant Risk Pattern: *Roadmap Fracture (Prevented through Transparency)*

FIFA Ultimate Team (EA): LiveOps as Economic Engine

Studio: Electronic Arts

Focus: Content-driven monetisation and economy shaping

Insight: FIFA's Ultimate Team mode uses LiveOps to manage rotating inventory, dynamic pricing, and seasonal promotions, all driven by real-world football events. Each patch or event has economic consequences – intended and not so much. This is LiveOps as financial governance (Eurogamer, 2023).

Lesson: If your LiveOps team lacks economic oversight, monetisation becomes fragile. FIFA shows the power and peril of managing live economies.

Relevant Risk Pattern: *Stealth Nerf Backlash*

TOOLS AND PLATFORMS

The right tools will not prevent failure, but they will make recovery faster and less painful.

Tool	Purpose
Microsoft PlayFab	Backend, analytics, A/B testing, economy control
AWS GameLift	Scalable servers, matchmaker, game session metrics
Unity Multiplay and Analytics	Hosting, cross-platform data tracking
Firebase, Datadog, Sentry	Real-time monitoring and logging
Jenkins, GitHub Actions	CI/CD pipelines and rollback support
LaunchDarkly, ConfigCat	Feature flagging and incremental rollout

LIVEOPS IS NOT MAINTENANCE

LiveOps is not about keeping the lights on. It is a continuation of production, with the same need for clarity, tooling, prioritisation, and trust. It runs under more pressure, in public, with higher expectations and fewer excuses.

It is tempting to treat post-release work as secondary, or to assume that whoever is left can "keep it going". That assumption leads to burnout, content slips, player churn, and loss of credibility.

The best LiveOps teams are treated like product teams. They are given runway, context, support, and input. They are also trusted to say "NO" – to kill ideas that are not ready, or to delay content that will cause more harm than good.

The difference between a game that fades after launch and one that thrives is rarely about the release itself. It is about what happens afterwards and how prepared the team is to keep going.

REFERENCES

Abstraction Games. (2024, April 5). *Gigantic: Rampage Edition launch statement.* Steam Community. Retrieved from: https://store.steampowered.com/news

Amazon Web Services. (2023). *GameLift and LiveOps infrastructure: Game Tech solutions overview.* AWS Game Tech Documentation. Retrieved from: https://aws.amazon.com/gametech

Eggplante. (2019). *Warframe's dev-first transparency model.* Retrieved from: https://www.eggplante.com

Epic Games. (2019, October 13). *Fortnite chapter 2: Black Hole event recap.* Retrieved from: https://www.epicgames.com/fortnite/en-US/news

Eurogamer. (2023). *How EA balances Ultimate Team events.* Retrieved from: https://www.eurogamer.net

Game Developer. (2022). *Inside Genshin's content delivery engine.* Retrieved from: https://www.gamedeveloper.com

Kuchera, B. (2015, March 31). *PlayStation Home closes its doors: A social experiment ahead of its time.* Polygon. Retrieved from: https://www.polygon.com/2015/3/31/8319927/playstation-home-closed

LaunchDarkly. (2024). *Feature flags for games: Minimising risk in LiveOps.* Retrieved from: https://launchdarkly.com/solutions/gaming

Microsoft. (2023). *LiveOps best practices with PlayFab.* Microsoft Game Dev Resources. Retrieved from: https://learn.microsoft.com/en-us/gaming/playfab

NetEase. (2025, June 15). *Marvel Rivals server outage compensation notice.* Marvel Rivals Discord (Archived Announcement). Retrieved from: https://discord.gg/marvelrivals

Niantic. (2017, July 24). *Pokémon GO Fest: A learning experience.* Niantic Labs Blog. Retrieved from: https://nianticlabs.com/blog/pokemongofest2017

Rock Paper Shotgun. (2023). *Larian's post-launch hotfix philosophy.* Retrieved from: https://www.rockpapershotgun.com

CHAPTER 35

Unique Risks in Mobile Game Development

INTRODUCTION

This chapter focuses on structural risks specific to the mobile games market; those that emerge from platforms, privacy law, monetisation models and external volatility. It complements, but does not repeat, our chapters on Product Management and LiveOps, which focus on internal team structure and continuous delivery.

Mobile game development presents a distinctive and rapidly evolving risk environment that differs fundamentally from traditional PC and console game development. The mobile ecosystem is shaped by unique factors such as global device fragmentation, reliance on app store distribution channels, short product lifecycles, liveops-driven content and aggressive monetisation strategies. The rise of free-to-play models, combined with opaque platform regulations and increasing user acquisition costs, makes mobile game development both highly scalable and uniquely volatile.

Unlike traditional game projects, which often operate in a premium model with fixed pricing and a focus on single-platform optimisation, mobile games must be designed to run seamlessly across thousands of devices, navigate ever-changing app store policies and sustain user engagement through continuous content and monetisation updates.

In recent years – especially following Apple's App Tracking Transparency (ATT) policy in 2021 – the mobile games industry has been reshaped by privacy restrictions, rising acquisition costs and platform power consolidation. Developers have faced declining efficiency in digital advertising, increased dependency on Apple and Google, more scrutiny of monetisation methods and greater operational pressures across both user acquisition and liveops. These shifts have fundamentally changed the way mobile teams manage risk.

DOI: 10.1201/9781003646082-40

This chapter explores these risks, how they differ from those in traditional PC/console game development and how production leaders can respond effectively through strategic and operational risk management.

MOBILE VS TRADITIONAL DEVELOPMENT – KEY DIFFERENCES

Mobile game development differs from traditional (PC/console) development in several ways that significantly alter the risk landscape:

Area	Mobile Game Development	Traditional Development
Monetisation Model	Free-to-play with IAPs, ads, subscriptions	One-time purchase, DLC or subscription
Device Environment	Highly fragmented across OS versions, screen sizes and hardware	Fixed specs (e.g. consoles, high-end PCs)
Development Cycle	Rapid cycles, soft launches, ongoing updates (liveops)	Multi-year projects with large launches and limited post-launch changes
User Acquisition	Paid UA (ads, influencer marketing), ASO dependent	Brand marketing, reviews, launch campaigns
Platform Dependency	Full reliance on Apple/Google for distribution, monetisation and rules	Distribution across Steam, consoles; slightly more control
Regulatory Pressure	High: GDPR, ATT, COPPA, ad restrictions, loot box scrutiny	Moderate: Primarily ESRB/PEGI, IP/ licensing, online features regulation

In short, mobile game development introduces more continuous, data-driven and externally influenced risk factors than traditional game development. Risks are not just front-loaded in pre-production and launch, but persist daily through live operations, platform compliance and monetisation balancing.

EVOLUTION OF MOBILE RISK (2019–2025): A STRATEGIC SHIFT

Over the last five years and especially since 2021, mobile game development has become more commercially competitive, operationally complex and strategically constrained.

These are not abstract commercial trends. Each of these changes has introduced new risk categories, especially around user acquisition volatility, regulatory fragility and content sustainability.

The following section highlights how these risks have emerged and how they now shape everyday decision-making for mobile production teams.

Platform Policy Risks: Apple's App Tracking Transparency (ATT) policy (AppsFlyer, 2022) dramatically reduced the ability to track and target users, leading to increased acquisition costs and reduced campaign efficiency. Developers now rely more heavily on Apple's ad network, increasing dependency and cost.

WHY ATT WAS A RISK EVENT, NOT JUST A POLICY CHANGE

Apple's App Tracking Transparency (ATT) reduced how much user data third-party apps could access. But the real risk was strategic: teams that relied heavily on targeted advertising lost their ability to scale profitably overnight. User acquisition became a creative guessing game. CPMs rose. LTV projections got noisier. ATT erupted from a privacy regulation to a game-changing asteroid event for many F2P mobile teams.

Marketing and UA Risks: With targeted advertising losing precision, UA costs have risen. Studios must now focus on creative optimisation, influencer partnerships and community building to acquire users, often with less predictability (Business of Apps, 2024).

Monetisation Design Risks: Pressure to monetise effectively while retaining players has grown. Aggressive monetisation is now a reputational and regulatory risk. Studios are shifting towards hybrid models (Ads + IAP + Subscriptions), often regionally tuned to match legal and cultural expectations (Sensor Tower, 2023).

Live Operations and Content Pressure: Successful mobile games are live services requiring constant content delivery. Failure to maintain cadence leads to churn. This places intense pressure on teams to maintain quality while scaling quickly.

Data Privacy and Compliance Risks: GDPR, COPPA and similar laws demand careful tracking of data use and consent flows. Failure to comply can result in fines or app store rejection. Even compliant games may suffer user backlash if perceived as exploitative.

Small Studio Vulnerability: Without scale, user base or marketing budgets, small studios are more exposed to UA inefficiencies, revenue volatility and platform restrictions. Many now rely on publishers or subscription service partnerships (e.g. Apple Arcade, Netflix Games) for support (Deconstructor of Fun, 2023a).

The Mobile Middle Is Disappearing: Mobile gaming is dividing. At the top, we see massive studios spending $500M on UA, while at the bottom we have hyper-casual teams burning through prototypes. The middle ground sees those trying to grow a premium-feel game with modest monetisation – and they are being squeezed out. Many cannot afford modern UA strategies, but cannot survive on organic reach alone. Again and again, we see the top 10 list of mobile games firmly linked to the top 5 or so mobile game companies (see below).

Risk Mitigation Shifts: Studios have responded by churn building first-party data systems, diversifying revenue streams and planning more adaptable feature pipelines. Risk management could become a strategic differentiator, especially in market forecasting, budget control and liveops infrastructure planning.

These trends mean mobile risk must be viewed holistically – incorporating market, platform, operational and compliance perspectives into daily production decision-making.

Who Really Owns the Global Top 10?

In global mobile games, as we noted above, the biggest hits are rarely indie successes. Instead, they come from a tight circle of highly resourced, globally integrated companies

– many based in China, Southeast Asia and non-Western regions. The May 2025 global top 10 (by revenue and/or downloads) looked like this:

Game	Publisher	HQ Country
Honor of Kings	Tencent	China
PUBG Mobile/Game for Peace	Tencent	China
Monopoly GO!	Scopely	US (owned by Saudi Arabia's Savvy Games Group)
Roblox	Roblox Corporation	US
Candy Crush Saga	King (Activision Blizzard)	UK/US
Royal Match	Dream Games	Turkey
Garena Free Fire	Garena (Sea Group)	Singapore
Block Blast!	Hungry Studio	China
Ludo King	Gametion	India
Subway Surfers	SYBO/Miniclip	Denmark/Switzerland

As you can see, at least five of the top 10 are published by companies outside the US or Europe. Tencent alone owns or operates three of the top five globally and also holds stakes in Supercell, Riot, Epic and more. Regional giants like Sea Group (Singapore) and Dream Games (Turkey) show how global the mobile market truly is and how hard it is to compete without deep infrastructure and local adaptation.

In mobile, the winners have massive distribution platforms, real-time data teams and multi-country liveops capacity.

COMMON MOBILE GAME RISK TRIGGERS

Category	Risk Trigger
Technical Limitations	Device fragmentation, performance variance, overheating and battery drain
Network Dependency	Unstable or unavailable internet in target markets impacting gameplay and monetisation
Platform Gatekeeping	Policy updates from Apple/Google can deprecate core features or monetisation strategies overnight
Monetisation Pressure	Monetisation practices backfiring due to poor design or regulatory scrutiny
Acquisition Costs	High CPI, declining ROAS and difficulty scaling user acquisition campaigns
Retention Fragility	Players churning due to lack of compelling content or frustration with monetisation
Compliance and Data Privacy	Violations of GDPR, COPPA, CCPA or ATT; fines, user trust erosion
App Store Rejection	Non-compliance with unclear or evolving rules causing launch delays or delisting

These risk triggers may seem like operational annoyances in isolation, but their combined effects shape studio strategy. What follows are several examples where these risks materialised and how different teams responded.

CASE STUDIES: ANALYSING MOBILE GAME CHALLENGES

Case Study: *Pokémon GO* – Real-World Integration and Technical Fragility

Studio Type: Large-scale mobile-first developer (Niantic, backed by Google)
Primary Risks: Device fragmentation, real-world gameplay volatility, scaling infrastructure

What Happened: *Pokémon GO* launched with unprecedented viral success in 2016 but was plagued by GPS spoofing, inconsistent device location services and early server crashes due to underestimated global demand (GDC Vault, 2017) (TechCrunch, 2016). Real-world integration exposed players to public safety incidents and compliance complexity in different jurisdictions.

Mitigation Strategy: Niantic scaled gradually using staggered regional rollouts, increased backend resilience and refined location logic. Over time, they added features to promote safe play and refined their event scheduling to prevent systemic overload.

Lesson: Games that rely on real-world data or behaviour must account for device variance, geographic legal differences and unpredictable demand surges.

Case Study: *Clash of Clans* – LiveOps Longevity and Portfolio Discipline

Studio Type: Mid-size studio under a global publisher (Supercell, owned by Tencent)
Primary Risks: Monetisation fatigue, retention volatility, content cadence management

What Happened: *Clash of Clans* saw sustained success through the 2010s, but maintaining engagement became harder as content aged and player expectations rose (Deconstructor of Fun, 2022). Supercell faced risks in both player churn and cannibalising monetisation by over-rewarding.

Mitigation Strategy: They introduced battle passes, seasonal events and segmented offers tailored to whale, mid-tier and free players. Supercell also applied rigorous soft launch evaluation to cut underperforming titles, preserving focus on scalable hits (Supercell, 2020).

Lesson: Long-term success in mobile requires dynamic liveops and ruthless portfolio curation. Managing churn and LTV across cohorts is a leadership-level risk responsibility.

Case Study: *Monopoly GO!* – Scaling Under Acquisition Cost Pressure

Studio Type: Large-scale mobile studio with deep UA funding (Scopely, owned by Savvy Games Group)
Primary Risks: User acquisition cost exposure, platform dependency, creative testing risk

What Happened: Scopely launched *Monopoly GO!* in 2023 with massive investment (reportedly over $500M in UA spend) amid rising ATT-related ad inefficiencies (PocketGamer.biz, 2023). Reliance on Apple's ad ecosystem made them vulnerable to cost spikes and data opacity.

Mitigation Strategy: Scopely countered with aggressive creative iteration, hybrid monetisation (ads + IAP) and expanded brand licensing and partnerships to increase organic LTV. Internal risk forecasting helped steer spend and content decisions.

Lesson: Mobile scale is not just a monetisation problem. You need to keep a tight data, spend and creative testing discipline. Teams must model break-even thresholds, not just chase volume.

Case Study: *Temple Run* – Viral Spike and Monetisation Pivot

Studio Type: Small Indie Studio With Breakout Hit (Imangi Studios)
Primary Risks: Infrastructure scaling, missed monetisation windows, backend fragility

What Happened: *Temple Run* went viral shortly after launch but lacked the backend and monetisation systems to capitalise (PocketGamer.biz, 2018). Initial revenue was ad-only, leaving significant value on the table.

Mitigation Strategy: In later versions and spin-offs, Imangi introduced IAP and more flexible monetisation mechanics. Infrastructure investments came too late for peak monetisation but helped future titles.

Lesson: Sudden success is a risk if you cannot scale tech or monetisation in time. Even small teams need contingency planning for traffic surges.

Diablo Immortal – Regional Rejection and Political Risk

Studio Type: AAA mobile spin-off by global publisher (Blizzard + NetEase)
Primary Risks: Content regulation, monetisation legality, geopolitical risk

What Happened:
Diablo Immortal was delayed in China and suspended in Belgium due to regional backlash over loot mechanics and data handling (Reuters, 2021). It also faced reputational damage from regulatory commentary on "predatory monetisation".

Mitigation Strategy:
Blizzard and NetEase reworked mechanics to meet local expectations and adjusted monetisation for new markets. The political fallout led to re-evaluation of global rollout strategies.

Lesson:
Global mobile games face geopolitical risk just as much as technical or design risk. Publishing infrastructure must include localisation, regulatory pre-emption and scenario planning for compliance failure.

KEY RISK PATTERNS

Platform Policy Whiplash

Definition: Dependency on third-party platforms results in sudden operational and commercial disruption when policies change (The Verge, 2021).
Example: Apple's 2021 App Tracking Transparency (ATT) policy significantly reduced access to IDFA, breaking UA pipelines for many free-to-play games. CPMs rose sharply and ROAS tracking became unreliable, forcing studios to rework acquisition models and attribution frameworks.

Mitigation Checklist:

- Track policy changes across Apple, Google, EU and global regulators (European Commission, 2023).

- Build modular monetisation systems and avoid hardcoded ad dependencies.

- Maintain multiple UA attribution pathways and consent-gated analytics flows.

UA Trapdoor Effect

Definition: Paid user acquisition campaigns fail to scale or maintain profitability, leading to budget waste and retention drops.
Example: Hypercasual studios saw CPI spike post-ATT while monetisation via ads remained flat (GameAnalytics, 2023). Many teams scaled too fast and were forced to cancel promising titles mid-cycle due to poor CAC:LTV ratios.

Mitigation Checklist:

- Model breakeven points using segmented LTV projections.
- Diversify UA with influencer outreach, community-building and ASO.
- Run creative A/B tests with real-time cost/reward feedback loops.

Churn-Content Spiral

Definition: Retention loss increases pressure to ship updates, which decreases content quality and accelerates further churn.

Example: A mid-tier mobile RPG lost players after a delayed event cadence caused negative reviews (Deconstructor of Fun, 2023b). The team rushed new content with reduced QA, triggering more bugs and frustration. Review scores and D30 retention declined month over month.

Mitigation Checklist:

- Build sustainable LiveOps roadmaps with flexible pacing.
- Reuse systems where possible to avoid fresh tech debt.
- Set hard caps on release frequency during churn spikes.

Monetisation-Compliance Clash

Definition: Revenue mechanics trigger regulatory, platform or player backlash due to legal breaches or ethical concerns.

Example: *Diablo Immortal* was delayed in China over political and loot box-related concerns and restricted in Belgium due to gambling regulation. Global rollout was complicated by localisation of monetisation mechanics (Bloomberg, 2022).

Mitigation Checklist:

- Track monetisation regulations in target regions (e.g. loot box laws).
- Review monetisation with platform policy and age rating in mind.
- Include compliance sign-off before A/B testing monetisation variants.

SDK Risk Drift

Definition: Use of untracked or outdated SDKs introduces silent compliance, data privacy or security vulnerabilities.

Example: Several popular SDKs were flagged for covert data sharing after the enforcement of GDPR and COPPA. Apps with no malicious intent were still delisted due to inherited behaviour from third-party analytics or ad services (Usercentrics, 2023).

Mitigation Checklist:

- Maintain a full SDK inventory with update and vendor ownership status.
- Audit SDKs for data flows and consent model alignment.
- Include SDK review in build pipelines and submission checklists.

MOBILE IS A HIGH-SPEED, HIGH-RISK OPERATING ENVIRONMENT

What defines mobile is not that it is easy, but that it is fast and fragile. Visibility can spike or disappear in a day. Monetisation can be flagged or blocked. App store rules can break your update cadence overnight.

Mobile game production must combine engineering reliability with market alertness. Production leaders must think in platform dependencies, regulatory optics and player churn cycles, not just velocity or milestone burn.

More and more PC/Console releases are encountering the same world that Mobile game development and publishing has been exposed to for years. This is the perfect opportunity to learn from them and add this arsenal of knowledge and advice to our risk management framework.

REFERENCES

AppsFlyer. (2022). *The ATT impact: Cost increases and targeting challenges post-IDFA*. Retrieved from: https://www.appsflyer.com/resources/reports/att-impact/

Bloomberg. (2022, June 21). *Diablo Immortal postponed in China, delayed in Europe over regulation*. Retrieved from: https://www.bloomberg.com/news/articles/2022-06-21/diablo-immortal-postponed-in-china-delayed-in-europe-over-regulation

Business of Apps. (2024). *Mobile advertising post-ATT: Trends and response strategies*. Retrieved from: https://www.businessofapps.com

Deconstructor of Fun. (2022). *Clash of Clans turns 10: A live ops masterclass*. Retrieved from: https://www.deconstructoroffun.com/blog/clash-of-clans-turns-10

Deconstructor of Fun. (2023a). *Arcade vs. ad-driven monetization: Netflix, Apple Arcade, and the new middle*. Retrieved from: https://www.deconstructoroffun.com/blog

Deconstructor of Fun. (2023b). *When LiveOps turns toxic: Managing event fatigue in puzzle and match-3 games*. Retrieved from: https://www.deconstructoroffun.com/blog

European Commission. (2023). *Digital Markets Act (DMA) overview*. Retrieved from: https://ec.europa.eu

GameAnalytics. (2023). *Hypercasual trends post-IDFA*. Retrieved from: https://gameanalytics.com/blog

GDC Vault. (2017). *Pokémon GO: A postmortem*. Retrieved from: https://www.gdcvault.com/play/1024262

PocketGamer.biz. (2018). *How Temple Run grew: An early mobile success story*. Retrieved from: https://www.pocketgamer.biz/feature/65997/how-temple-run-grew/

PocketGamer.biz. (2023). *Monopoly GO! hits $2B in revenue in under a year*. Retrieved from: https://www.pocketgamer.biz/news/82167/monopoly-go-hits-2-billion/

Reuters. (2021). *Diablo Immortal delayed in China amid social media backlash*. Retrieved from: https://www.reuters.com/business/media-telecom/diablo-immortal-release-delayed-china-2022-06-20/

Sensor Tower. (2023). *State of mobile gaming monetization.* Retrieved from: https://www.sensor-tower.com

Supercell. (2020). *Clash of Clans turns 10.* Retrieved from: https://supercell.com/en/blog/

TechCrunch. (2016). *Why Pokémon GO keeps crashing: Infrastructure and scaling risks.* Retrieved from: https://techcrunch.com/2016/07/14/why-pokemon-go-keeps-crashing/

The Verge. (2021). *Epic v. Apple trial guide: Platform policies on trial.* Retrieved from: https://www.theverge.com/2021/5/3/22417393/epic-v-apple-trial-guide-fortnite-app-store-antitrust

Usercentrics. (2023). *Privacy compliance in mobile games: Consent, SDKs and risk.* Retrieved from: https://www.usercentrics.com/resources

CHAPTER 36

The Missing Discipline

Product Management for Risk Reduction

Tʜɪs ᴄʜᴀᴘᴛᴇʀ ᴇxᴘʟᴏʀᴇs ʜᴏw the role of Product Management, particularly as practised in mobile game development, can significantly mitigate risks in PC and console game projects. By examining the strategies and responsibilities of mobile Product Managers (PMs), we identify practices that, if adopted in traditional development, could lead to more successful and sustainable outcomes.

THE OVERLOOKED ROLE IN TRADITIONAL GAME DEVELOPMENT

SIDEBAR: PRODUCT MANAGER VS PRODUCER – A FUNCTIONAL COMPARISON

Area of Responsibility	Product Manager	Producer
Primary Focus	Player outcomes, retention, revenue	Team velocity, delivery, timeline
Metrics Used	Retention curves, ARPU, churn, DAU	Sprint burndown, velocity, milestone status
Team Integration	Close collaboration with design, analytics, LiveOps	Close collaboration with design, tech, art, QA
Decision Authority	Roadmap input, feature prioritisation based on data	Milestone planning, scope execution
Risk Ownership	Feature performance, monetisation perception	Production delays, scope creep
Typical Background	Analytics, business, systems design	QA, production, project management

DOI: 10.1201/9781003646082-41

Most PC and console developers have no idea what a Product Manager does. And if they do, they often do not respect it. Product Management is seen – when seen at all – as something to do with monetisation or maybe app store optimisation. In mobile game studios, however, the Product Manager is a central figure. Not an analyst or support role, but someone who directly shapes feature priorities, design direction, business outcomes and player retention strategy.

This lack of understanding leads to risk. If no one owns the player outcome, no one owns retention, monetisation coherence, feature prioritisation or live event tuning. All of that ends up done ad hoc, if at all.

By contrast, mobile development teams typically place a PM at the heart of decision making from day one. They start with the player type, not the idea. They monitor key behaviours post-release and shape the roadmap around the response. They run experiments, make rapid changes and constantly test whether players are engaging the way the team intended. It is rigorous, iterative and player-focused.

As Anil Das-Gupta puts it, "Product Managers should be in the room during concept, not just after soft launch. If you're only bringing them in at monetisation, you've already missed most of the player risk".

UNDERSTANDING THE MOBILE PRODUCT MANAGER

A good mobile Product Manager is not just a data person. They are a creative partner with the authority and mandate to shape decisions based on how players actually behave.

A mobile game product manager is almost like a mini-CEO of the game. They wake up thinking about data: Day 1 retention, monetisation loops, user acquisition and behavioural drop-offs.

Core Responsibilities:

- Defining and targeting specific player personas during concept and prototyping

- Designing monetisation strategy in tandem with feature roadmap

- Monitoring and reacting to real-time KPIs (Day 1/Day 7 retention, session length, ARPU)

- Running structured experiments through A/B testing or segmented rollouts

- Working closely with designers, developers, LiveOps and marketing to coordinate updates

In the mobile space, this is a well-established discipline. At companies like Wooga and King, product managers are part of the core team. Every major feature goes through a validation pipeline. If it does not improve the target KPIs, it is cut or reworked. It is not personal. It is structural.

Contrast that with many PC/console workflows, where once a feature is in the milestone plan, it tends to stay, even when the data suggests it is unnecessary.

As Callum Godfrey put it, "Product Managers obsess about outcomes. Producers obsess about throughput".

Case Studies: Successes from Mobile Gaming
Wooga: A/B Testing Onboarding
Wooga ran iterative A/B tests on onboarding tutorials across several games to see which combinations improved retention and conversion. Small changes like reordering tasks or highlighting a reward had a measurable impact. The goal was not perfect UX. It was better retention by reducing early player drop-off. (Wired, 2024)

Nintendo's Animal Crossing: Pocket Camp
Nintendo kept Pocket Camp alive through a data-informed LiveOps strategy. Events were tuned based on participation rates, cosmetic drops were prioritised using usage tracking, and churn triggers were analysed to revise early-game flow. The result was an extended commercial life far beyond expectations. (The Guardian, 2024)

RISKS MITIGATED BY EFFECTIVE PRODUCT MANAGEMENT
Player Churn
PMs flag drop-off points early and focus updates on keeping players engaged. They treat churn like a design issue, not just a marketing problem.

Monetisation Pitfalls
Without a PM, monetisation is often bolted on too late or executed without balance. PMs ensure offers feel fair and are tested before going wide.

Feature Creep
Mobile PMs push back on features that cannot be justified by data. They force teams to ask: Who is this for, and what does it do for the player? Apparently, roughly 80% of features never get used. Product Managers look for value, not just velocity. They ask: "what is the outcome we want", not "how many things can we ship?".

There is a well-known phrase in Product Management: **Outcome over output**. In other words, only add something if you can justify that it adds value. Do not add something just because you think you should be busy building more stuff.

Misaligned Marketing
PMs help align marketing promises with what is actually in the game. They help avoid the classic "trailer vs real game" mismatch by owning the roadmap.

Bridging the Gap: Applying Mobile PM Practices to PC/Console Development
PMs may not be standard in console and PC pipelines (yet), but their techniques are useful to everyone.

Adapt A/B Testing for Core Systems

Start with tutorial flow or reward delivery. Run structured tests internally or through closed betas. Use what works.

Use KPIs in Production

Set targets for Day 1 retention or first-session completion. Track player flow. It will reveal design issues before release. It will also help ensure the Vision is mapped all the way to the KPIs – this will keep developers focused through a very useful lens.

Empower Someone to Own the Player Perspective

It does not need to be a PM, but someone needs to ask: Is this working for the player? Are we spending time where it matters?

Promote Cross-Functional Decision Making

Include designers, analysts, producers and marketing in feature reviews. Let the data speak, but interpret it together.

> **SIDEBAR: WHAT WOULD A PM ASK AT CONCEPT STAGE?**
>
> This is from my Agile Product Management training material:
>
> - Why are we making this?
> - Who is it for?
> - *Will this still be a good idea in three years?*
> - Where is the data?
> - *What problem are we solving for the player?*

Embracing Product Management for Sustainable Game Development

Adding Product Management does not mean turning every studio into a mobile clone. It means learning from a discipline that has already spent years solving the very problems PC and console teams now face: Player churn, feature bloat, shallow engagement and update failure.

This is not about changing your genre or business model. It is about reducing the number of bad decisions made because no one had the time, structure or data to say, "Let us check that first".

FURTHER READING

Are you keen to learn more? Great! I can personally recommend the following:

Me – My Agile Product Management summary as a YouTube video https://www.game-production.com/post/agile-product-management

Anil Das-Gupta – Product leadership insights via *Scopely* and conference talks (search GDC Vault) My old mate Anil is very smart.

Deconstructor of Fun – Deep dives into mobile game monetisation, retention, and product loops (deconstructoroffun.com) This is a quite famous source for deep dives and interviews.

Eric Seufert – *Mobile Dev Memo* (mobiledevmemo.com) – industry analysis on mobile product strategy

GameRefinery Blog – Market-level breakdowns of feature trends in mobile games

Marty Cagan – *Inspired: How to create tech products customers love* (Silicon Valley Product Group) Marty has written several books and has a brilliant website and newsletter. He is a Master of Product Management.

Roman Pichler – *Agile product management with Scrum* (Pichler Consulting) I really like Roman's books. Very clear and concise.

The Guardian. Pushing Buttons: Nintendo's Mobile Playbook in Pocket Camp. *TheGuardian.com*, December 4, 2024. Retrieved from: https://www.theguardian.com/games/2024/dec/04/pushing-buttons-nintendo-animal-crossing-pocket-camp-mobile-games

Wired. Test, test, test: Inside Wooga's design-driven A/B testing culture. *Wired.com*, 2024. Retrieved from: https://www.wired.com/story/test-test-test

CHAPTER 37

Risk Reduction Through User Testing and Embedded QA

INTRODUCTION: TESTING IS NOT A PHASE – IT IS A PHILOSOPHY

User testing is not something you schedule at the end of development. It is a mindset and a system. When implemented well, it becomes one of the most powerful tools for reducing production risk and raising product quality. When ignored, sidelined or bolted on too late, it becomes a liability.

This chapter is about how studios learn – and how the structures and timing of that learning shape everything from team velocity to commercial success. Strong QA and User Testing produce feedback loops – if they are shallow, delayed or overloaded, your game will not be resilient. However, if they are intentional, structured and respected, they drive better design, higher player satisfaction and fewer catastrophic failures.

After so many years of agile methodologies, lean software development and all the rest, there remains in too many studios a remarkable misunderstanding of the role of QA and User Feedback. Telemetry is underutilised, lessons come too late. Let us fix that together.

COMMON RISK TRIGGERS

The Phantom QA Problem

Too many studios still treat QA as something to bring in once the game "works". That mindset means most opportunities to shape quality are already lost. Bugs compound. Coverage is patchy. Edge cases multiply. Teams end up firefighting problems they could have prevented with earlier input. QA gets blamed for not catching issues they were never resourced to look for.

Let me put it another way: When you focus on feature work and allow the bugs to grow, not only are you ensuring that quality is lowered, but you are guaranteeing future problems and reduced velocity. If you partner with QA from the start and put time aside each sprint

DOI: 10.1201/9781003646082-42

(or whatever cadence cycle you use), you are actually developing correctly and being agile – congratulations. If you are instead giving in to the pressures and demands to deliver, what you are delivering is only survivable in the short or medium term. Tech debt is real. Avoiding all of this is wholly possible.

The truth is that if you embed QA from the start, they are not just finding problems – they are helping you design the systems that avoid them. An embedded QA team member can flag testability concerns during feature planning, write automated smoke tests for key mechanics, and pressure test assumptions about user flow. Good QA engineers are product thinkers. They see the gaps in logic, in flow, in structure. They are not a cost centre. They are a risk detection network. Stop treating them as beneath other disciplines and you might make better games. I stand by that statement. Anyone who understands why has taken the time to learn about software development and also understands why we iterate. Ignorance is no excuse for ignoring that.

Common anti-patterns include:

- Having QA "wait" until features are "ready to test"
- Using QA only as bug hunters without involving them in sprint planning
- Ignoring QA feedback because it is not tied to code or asset output
- Sidelining QA during roadmap discussions or content cuts

Studios that do this often find themselves repeatedly surprised by bugs that should not have made it through – not because QA failed, but because QA was structurally prevented from succeeding. If your QA team is seen as a cost rather than a multiplier, your project is already at risk. A QA team does not exist solely to sense and pressure-test the latest game build and tell you if it still works.

Better practice looks like this:

- QA sits alongside devs and designers *from the start*
- Test plans are part of every epic, not just the release build
- QA is given time, tooling and authority to speak on risk
- Automation and manual testing are aligned to product value, not vanity coverage

Agile QA is not about moving faster. It is about learning earlier. And that is the cheapest form of risk mitigation you will ever find. Early learning means you can make decisions earlier and have far more confidence in those decisions. Unknowns become knowns.

Shallow Feedback Loops

Design-led user testing, such as friends-and-family or guided sessions, often becomes about validation rather than discovery. If these sessions are not structured to uncover weak spots or provoke real player reactions, the feedback loop becomes shallow. No amount of sentiment can replace behavioural truth.

Overloaded Beta Feedback

Once a game hits beta or early access, feedback starts flooding in – from players, QA, community managers, executives and external partners. Without prioritisation systems and feedback ownership, the team drowns. Urgency replaces clarity. Teams chase the loudest voice, not the most urgent risk.

> **SIDEBAR: BUILD IN TIME TO RESPOND**
>
> Even if you are performing user testing well, if you are not putting aside time to respond to your findings, you may as well stop the testing. I have witnessed this multiple times and it is extremely frustrating. Build in the user testing as a phase of production and development that requires time to digest, time to present back to leadership, time to plan against the findings, time to cost out the options, time to decide what happens next, and time to plot out the new world of dependencies and changes to system designs and so much else. That is, after all, the entire point.
>
> If you expect the user testing to simply happen concurrently with normal development, you have just shut down the opportunity to change for the better and misunderstood the phase you are in, most likely all in the name of chasing dates and milestones.

Missed Telemetry and Analytics

Many studios launch public tests without adequate telemetry. They rely on forum posts and Discord channels to assess player sentiment, without structured behavioural data. That leads to wrong assumptions, misplaced priorities and missed opportunities to improve retention, onboarding or progression systems. It also leads to cherry-picking the feedback that you want to hear or falling victim to Loudest Shouter Wins.

Neglected DevOps and CI-/CD Practices

Automated testing, smoke checks, feature flagging and rollback infrastructure are common in modern LiveOps and software engineering, but rarely adopted systematically in traditional game development. As a result, each patch becomes an unstructured gamble.

MITIGATION STRATEGIES: BUILDING TESTING INTO THE HEART OF DEVELOPMENT

If risk management is the act of preventing failure before it happens, then quality assurance is the toolkit to get you there. But in too many studios, QA remains underfunded, sidelined or treated as a reactive service. The goal here is not just to outline best practice – it is to reframe the way you think about QA and user testing entirely. These are not optional extras. They are your feedback engine, your early warning system and your last line of defence. There is so much research and evidence backing this up and I have referenced it again and again throughout this book.

Embed QA as a Development Discipline

Modern risk reduction demands that QA be present from the beginning, not added when production is nearly done. QA professionals should be embedded within development teams, included in sprint planning, retrospectives and daily stand-ups. Their role is not simply to "find bugs" but to help shape testability, tooling and quality assumptions throughout development.

Give QA the mandate to:

- Define test coverage targets for major systems

- Influence production tooling decisions

- Own smoke test and regression test automation

- Flag risks related to delivery stability and scope

Agile QA and Continuous Integration (CI)

Treat QA as a continuous service, not a final gate. Automate as much as possible:

- Use smoke tests to catch critical path issues

- Build regression suites for gameplay systems, localisation, UI

- Validate builds using CI pipelines (e.g. Jenkins, GitHub Actions)

Adopt a DevOps mindset:

- Deploy quickly, test in controlled environments

- Use feature flags to release features gradually and roll them back quickly

- Set up dedicated test branches or closed testing channels

Structured Feedback Loops

As we have already intimated, not all feedback is equal. Define sources, frequency and filtering mechanisms early. Teams that fail to distinguish between noisy feedback and high-signal insight will constantly chase the wrong fixes.

USER TESTING

There are multiple different types of user testing, depending on the phase of the game and the intentions:

- Design-Led Friends and Family Testing

This is often run by the design team internally and happens around Alpha, or far earlier if sensibly handled. Sessions are typically one-on-one or small groups, observed live or through screen recordings. Players may be asked to "think aloud" while playing, narrating what they see and feel. Notes are taken on confusion points, misclicks and engagement drops. To reiterate previous points in this chapter for emphasis, if not structured carefully, this testing becomes about comfort rather than discovery – make sure sessions include pre- and post-session surveys and a facilitation guide that includes tasks to complete and areas to probe.

At Sumo Digital, early Friends and Family Testing was used on the latest Little Big Planet game. We ensured that we focused on a single level with higher polish than other levels (it was early days of development), and the design team expertly handled guiding, listening and carefully handling feedback. It was invaluable for guiding us towards a successful assessment of the controls, responses, difficulty, fun factor, level objects, etc.

- User Acceptance Testing (UAT)

This is very often outsourced to specialist firms like Keywords Studios, who recruit players based on target demographics and run structured evaluations. These may be blind tests – testers are not told what the game is trying to do, and feedback is gathered on usability, clarity, onboarding and enjoyment. Reports usually include tagged video clips, priority-ranked issues and participant quotes. UAT is expensive, but when done properly, it validates design intent against real-world perception.

- Staged Rollout Testing

Also called gradual or regional rollouts, this has become more and more popular and was first seen in mobile games. The game is released in waves: To specific territories, platforms or player cohorts. These allow the team to test infrastructure, progression, monetisation and engagement under real conditions. Common in mobile and free-to-play, but increasingly used on Steam and consoles.

I have witnessed this rollout (sometimes called a rolling launch) and it is quite appealing: You have control over the scale of your launch phases and can give yourself more time to respond to whatever comes out of it. Once sufficiently confident you can open more gates and control the scale and load. Of course, not all games can launch in this fashion and sometimes publishers will not allow it, or there will be certain marketing and promotional deadlines.

SIDEBAR: FRIENDS AND FAMILY TESTING – A QUICK PRIMER

How to run it well:

- Recruit testers who have not been exposed to the game daily
- Create a task list (e.g. "build a camp", "complete a combat encounter")
- Encourage testers to speak aloud as they play
- Observe, record and take notes unobtrusively
- Follow up with targeted questions ("what did you expect this button to do?")

Common discoveries:

- Players miss the tutorial prompt
- Inventory systems feel confusing
- Onboarding is too long or too fast
- Mission goals are unclear
- Players are entertained by elements you had not even noticed before
- Players play your game entirely differently to how you expected, based on their play styles

Friends and Family testing, when well run, can save weeks of design iteration by identifying gaps in clarity, UX or retention before you scale player access. It can also be very surprising and revealing!

How to Manage Feedback

Assign a feedback coordinator or task force:

- Collect all feedback sources (Discord, forums, surveys, test agencies, bug trackers)

- Tag and theme the input using agreed taxonomies (e.g. "UI pain point", "early drop-off", "confused onboarding"). Please do this! You will find it far more ordered, and you might use a Miro board to start ordering multiple tickets from multiple sources

- Visualise the relationship between sentiment and behaviour (e.g. heatmap confirms player complaints about a navigation bottleneck)

- Feed summaries into risk review or feature planning weekly

This approach ensures feedback is not just heard – it is acted upon, prioritised correctly and used to support roadmap decisions rather than derail them.

- Summarise and tag feedback by theme, frequency and impact

- Facilitate weekly risk review sessions based on incoming feedback

- Say no to changes that jeopardise stability

Using Publishers' Own UAT/Playtest Capabilities

Indie or independent-funded teams working with publishers may benefit from access to structured UAT pipelines, but only if:

- Their contract explicitly includes support from these teams, or

- The project is high priority within the publisher's portfolio.

Teams relying on smaller publishers (e.g. Devolver, Raw Fury, Team17) generally do not have access to this level of UAT infrastructure and must manage player feedback themselves or through third-party vendors.

Major Western Publishers with In-House UAT/Playtest Capabilities

Publisher	Has Dedicated UAT / Research Team?	Player Recruitment Capability	Notable Details
Sony Interactive Entertainment	✅ Yes – PlayStation UX Research and PlayStation Studios QA	Extensive access to registered PlayStation users and closed beta signups	Known for deep usability testing during exclusive title development (e.g. *The Last of Us, Ghost of Tsushima*)
Microsoft/Xbox Game Studios	✅ Yes – Xbox Research, Xbox Preview Program, PlayFab Telemetry	Xbox Insiders and PC game preview programs; telemetry across Game Pass	Offers developers access to structured feedback and behavioural data at scale
Nintendo	✅ Yes – Nintendo Product Evaluation and QA teams	Recruits internally and via loyalty programs and special partner networks	Extremely closed loop; mostly internal-facing and platform-specific
Ubisoft	✅ Yes – Ubisoft User Research Labs in Montreal, Paris, etc.	Has internal player pools; also runs public *Ubisoft Insider* playtest recruitment	One of the most structured global player research networks in AAA
Electronic Arts (EA)	✅ Yes – EA Research (Experience and Insights), Firemonkeys, DICE QA	Uses EA Playtesting (playtesting.ea.com) to recruit players across titles	Supports A/B testing, early feedback, UX flow and retention analysis
Activision Blizzard	✅ Yes – Blizzard UX Research, Activision QA and Player Insights	Long history of beta testing via Battle.net and structured feedback groups	Focused on telemetry, systems balance and liveops stress testing
Take-Two/2K/Private Division	✅ Yes – Limited but established QA/UAT for internal and select partner studios	Mostly closed testing for mid/late dev stage projects	Partner teams may not always access the full suite unless co-funded
Riot Games	✅ Yes – Riot Player Insights, UX Labs, Vanguard QA	Leverages live community + structured playtest groups in LA and globally	Known for iterative feedback loops and champion testing before public rollout
Epic Games	✅ Yes – Player Experience and UX Research Teams	Uses Fortnite and Epic Games Store communities for feedback	Unreal Dev Grant recipients may receive access depending on project alignment

Publisher	Has Dedicated UAT / Research Team?	Player Recruitment Capability	Notable Details
Valve	✅ Yes – Steam User Playtest Tools and internal QA	Steam Playtest feature gives structured access to real players via wishlist	Tools available to any developer using Steam, but Valve runs internal research too

Major Eastern Publishers with UAT/Player Research Teams

Publisher	Region	Has Dedicated UAT/ Player Insights?	Player Recruitment Capability	Notes
Tencent Games	China	✅ Yes – extensive in-house UX and telemetry analytics teams	Massive access to QQ, WeChat and Honor of Kings player bases	Internal testing at scale; AI-driven behaviour modelling; often runs silent test builds via TapTap or regional servers
NetEase Games	China	✅ Yes – multiple internal UXR and QA units	Taps into mobile userbase via NetEase App Store and game-specific loyalty programs	Heavy focus on monetisation sensitivity, localisation testing and live event pacing
miHoYo (HoYoverse)	China	✅ Yes – UX Research and live telemetry loops across Genshin, Honkai etc.	Enormous global reach via in-game surveys, closed betas and public events	Builds its own analytics platforms and continuously iterates on feedback, even post-launch
Bandai Namco	Japan	✅ Yes – internal QA/UX teams and external playtest centres	Uses dedicated facilities in Tokyo and Osaka; structured player pools	Highly systematised for fighting games, JRPGs and licensing-heavy titles
Capcom	Japan	✅ Yes – Capcom Dev 1 QA and player testing labs	Player feedback collected via Japanese fan events, beta tests and surveys	Playtest feedback informs early design pivots, esp. for RE and SF series
Kakao Games	South Korea	✅ Yes – player testing and QA across its liveops-heavy platforms	Community-led feedback; runs Korea-based closed test groups	Leverages PC cafés, web-based surveys and live test clusters before global release
NCSoft	South Korea	✅ Yes – player research across Lineage, Blade & Soul, etc.	Internal QA plus massive liveops data collection	Sophisticated feedback processing across Korean and SEA markets
Nexon	South Korea	✅ Yes – Nexon Intelligence Lab and Game Insight team	Structured player profiling and telemetry	Advanced churn prediction and monetisation sensitivity testing
Square Enix	Japan	✅ Yes – Structured testing teams and external partner labs	Uses fan networks, event feedback and traditional research panels	More closed-loop and slower than some peers, but robust internally

Publisher	Region	Has Dedicated UAT/ Player Insights?	Player Recruitment Capability	Notes
SEGA/Atlus	Japan	☑ Yes – QA + UX built into development flow	Regular testing sessions held in controlled labs and at publisher events	Player testing influences balancing and content tuning in RPGs and strategy titles

Key Differences in Eastern and Western UAT Culture

Eastern UAT models:

- **Player Testing Is Often Embedded in Soft Launch + Live Telemetry:** Especially in China and Korea (e.g. Tencent and NetEase).

- **Japan Prefers Controlled Environment Testing:** Lab-based, small batch and highly NDA-protected.

- **Korean Publishers:** Frequently leverage PC café telemetry, influencer loops and regional test servers as informal UAT environments.

- Many Eastern publishers are also **highly sensitive to localisation accuracy**, monetisation flow perception and first-session churn – these dominate their player research priorities.

Western UAT models are typically:

- **More formalised and opt-in**

- More focused on UX and narrative validation

- **More isolated from live telemetry than Eastern systems**

They can offer powerful insights if engaged early and often, but many indies and mid-tier studios only access them through publisher programs and even then only if the title is prioritised.

Dimension	Western UAT Culture	Eastern UAT Culture
Player Access Model	Often uses structured recruitment (e.g. Xbox Insiders, EA Playtesting, Ubisoft Insider), sometimes outsourced	Heavily integrated into platform ecosystems (e.g. QQ, TapTap), fan loyalty loops or soft-launch regions
Focus Areas	Emphasis on user experience, accessibility, narrative clarity and interface usability	Focus on monetisation flow, content cadence and first-session retention
Tooling and Infrastructure	Relies on opt-in programs, labs and controlled builds (Steam Playtest, platform betas, in-person labs)	Uses internal storefronts and real-player telemetry on early builds or test servers

Dimension	Western UAT Culture	Eastern UAT Culture
Transparency and Comms	Publishers may share UAT insights with dev teams – especially in co-dev	Insights are often centralised, not shared directly with external studios
Risk Mitigation Function	Often treated as part of pre-launch polish and player validation	Viewed as essential for ongoing LiveOps pacing and monetisation control
Playtester Demographics	Tries to recruit a cross-section of platform or genre users (via CRM or beta lists)	Tends to be regionally and demographically specific, e.g. Korean café players or Chinese mobile spenders
Scale	Mid-sized batches (20–200 users typical); larger for AAA betas	Can run thousands to millions of users through test versions silently (esp. in mobile)
Integration with QA	UAT and QA are often parallel but distinct – UAT focuses on "is it fun/ usual/clear?"	UAT more tightly blended with QA, balance and LiveOps readiness
Common Weakness	Often too late in dev cycle to meaningfully pivot; over-indexed on "feedback polish"	Over-focused on retention and monetisation, sometimes ignoring qualitative feedback

TELEMETRY AS RISK INSURANCE

At the risk of over-simplifying, if you are not tracking player journeys you are just guessing. Modern games need:

- Annotated heatmaps

- Clickstream and session analytics

- Retention and conversion funnels

- Error logs tied to user flow

Make these visible to the team. Let designers, engineers and PMs explore behaviour, not just opinions. These do not need to be secrets or jealously guarded by the design team or leadership.

Another key factor in telemetry is the choice of data visualisation tools. Popular options include Power BI, Grafana, Prometheus and Tableau. The selection should be driven by the specific use cases, scalability and integration capabilities of each tool. A critical consideration is the tool's support for scripting SQL queries to extract tailored data insights efficiently.

KNOW WHEN TO CUT

Real feedback often reveals what *not* to build. Do not waste QA or dev time on systems that players do not engage with. Kill the features, biomes, or storylines that offer no return. Obviously, in some games, a promise of minimum playtime on the golden path has been made – sometimes those biomes that would be cut need to be kept in!

Adopt product management principles:

- Track usage before expansion

- Justify systems by impact, not effort

- Ask what outcome you want, not what asset you want to ship

- Outcome over Output, remember

WHAT IS A QA FUNCTION TEST PLAN?

A QA function test plan is a document or checklist created in collaboration with developers and QA leads that outlines the expected behaviours, systems and outcomes for a specific feature, area or update.

What it typically includes:

- Feature objective and what "success" looks like
- Key flows or actions to be tested (e.g. user onboarding, item purchase)
- Preconditions and test environment setup
- Edge cases, risk flags or known weak areas
- Pass/fail criteria and links to relevant telemetry

Without a test plan, QA must guess what the system is supposed to do. With one, they become a structured layer of defence against regression, confusion and inconsistent quality.

REAL-WORLD CASE STUDIES

Case Study: Destiny (Bungie)

Context: During the closed beta of *Destiny*, Bungie noticed that players were frequently failing to complete the tutorial missions. Forum sentiment was positive, but the data told another story: Too many new users were dropping off in the first session.

Approach: Rather than rely on player feedback alone, the team used in-game telemetry to monitor where players stalled or exited the game. They then rebuilt the onboarding mission flow, clarifying objectives, surfacing guidance and smoothing out early friction.

Outcome: Retention improved significantly between the first and second beta waves. The early game was restructured before launch, helping set a foundation for player engagement that continues to this day. Bungie's internal QA and analytics teams were credited with championing the effort.

Case Study: Wooga – A/B Testing for Onboarding

Context: Wooga identified a high Day 1 churn rate in one of their puzzle games. The team suspected tutorial length and complexity might be contributing factors, but they had no clear direction.

Approach: They built multiple onboarding variations and used A/B testing to roll out these flows to segmented user cohorts. One group saw a shorter tutorial with fewer required interactions; another had delayed monetisation prompts. Metrics included time-to-first-reward, tutorial abandonment and early spend.

Outcome: One version improved Day 1 retention by over 12%. The A/B test also disproved several internal assumptions about what new players cared about. Learnings were implemented across the studio's other titles. QA and Product worked closely together to ensure test validity and data integrity.

Case Study: Supercell and Keywords Studios – Fully Integrated QA Partnership

Context: Supercell, the creators of *Clash of Clans*, sought a long-term QA and localisation partner to support their globally distributed player base. Rather than outsourcing QA as a service, they aimed to fully integrate external testers into their development structure.

Approach: Supercell worked with Keywords Studios to establish co-located QA and localisation teams that operated within Supercell's workflows. These teams handled test plans, supported feature launches across languages and regions, and operated as if they were an internal department. Supercell maintained daily communication with the embedded teams, who had access to real-time data tools, internal release notes and development builds.

Outcome: The collaboration significantly reduced Supercell's bug backlog and accelerated content update cycles. According to Silvio Clausen, Head of Localisation at Supercell: "Their ability to understand our needs and solve them with a tailored solution has led to creating dedicated teams that work as if they were part of our own organisation".

Case Study: Turtle Rock and Keywords Studios (Volta) – Art, QA and DLC Support

Context: During the production and post-launch content lifecycle of *Back 4 Blood*, Turtle Rock Studios partnered with Volta (a Keywords division) to provide both art and QA support.

Approach: Initially brought in to assist with post-launch content development, Volta's role expanded to include testing of live DLC assets, environment consistency and cosmetic functionality across different versions of the game. QA leads collaborated directly with the Turtle Rock pipeline, helping vet features ahead of community rollouts.

Outcome: The teams delivered polished content updates across multiple platforms with reduced rework. QA feedback influenced the pacing and feature roadmap of live releases. The partnership was publicly credited in postmortem reflections for its ability to deliver scalable and high-integrity support.

These cases show that QA and feedback loops are not just operational concerns – they are production-defining leverage points. When used well, they elevate the quality, reduce launch chaos and preserve morale. When neglected, they create blind spots that erode trust, delay releases and demoralise teams.

I am not promoting the use of Keyword Studios, as there are plenty of others out there – they just so happen to be the biggest and have the most case studies.

CROSS-PLATFORM INSIGHT: WHAT MOBILE QA AND TESTING CAN TEACH EVERYONE ELSE

Mobile game development has, in many respects, evolved a more sophisticated and scalable QA and testing culture than much of the PC and console space. Why? Because mobile lives or dies by data. You are not facing thousands of concurrent players; you are potentially selling to millions.

A/B Testing as the Most Basic Default

In mobile development, A/B testing is built into the release cadence. Almost every new feature – from onboarding flows to button placement – is tested across user segments. A/B testing is foundational although many more sophisticated techniques have evolved since the early days.

Example: Wooga, King and Supercell routinely run dozens of A/B tests monthly, feeding results back into design.

Tooling Suggestions

- **Firebase A/B Testing** (free for small apps)

- **Leanplum** (for multivariate testing, user segmentation)

- **SplitMetrics** (used for App Store experimentation)

Console and PC games rarely do this at scale. Why? Because the tooling is often not integrated into their engines, and the team culture does not demand it. That gap is a risk.

Moving on from Simple A/B Testing

There are issues with only considering A/B testing:

It only tests two static variants at a time

- A/B testing compares Variant A vs Variant B in isolation

- Modern user behaviour is more complex: Players enter at different times, with different cohorts, devices and monetisation patterns

It assumes a fixed outcome window

- A/B often relies on short-term metrics (e.g. Day 1 retention or ARPU after seven days)

- But many games now aim to optimise long-tail engagement, not just initial conversion

It struggles to handle feature interdependence

- Many live games have overlapping features (e.g. a tutorial revamp also affects shop engagement)

- A/B cannot disentangle multiple concurrent changes without contaminating results

MODERN APPROACHES IN MOBILE GAMES

Technique	What It Does	Why It Is More Powerful
Multivariate Testing (MVT)	Tests multiple variables (e.g. UI + pricing + timing) simultaneously	Uncovers interaction effects between features
Bayesian Optimisation	Uses probabilistic models to continually update the "best" option based on incoming data	Faster convergence with fewer users; ideal for live balancing
Bandit Algorithms (e.g. Multi-Armed Bandit)	Dynamically shifts traffic towards better-performing variants as data arrives	Maximises real-time player value rather than waiting for full test completion
Cohort-based Experimentation	Analyses long-term performance by player segments (e.g. whales, new users, lapsed users)	Reduces misleading averages and lets you optimise per user type
Real-Time Personalisation	Uses machine learning to adapt content or offers based on individual player behaviour	Goes beyond testing to deliver tailored experiences without needing fixed test groups
Sequential Testing/Adaptive Trials	Stops tests early when a clear winner emerges; refines over time	Reduces exposure to poor variants and saves time

Examples of Modern Use

- **King (Candy Crush):** Uses MVT and bandit models to test thousands of level variants and monetisation flows per week

- **Supercell**: Known for soft-launch strategies with multi-metric testing across countries, not just A/B gates

- **Zynga**: Integrates behavioural clustering into segmentation, moving beyond static A/B to dynamic performance tuning

- **Playrix/Scopely**: Combine event sequencing tests with predictive churn modelling for high-value retention tracking

Real-Time Telemetry and Analytics Dashboards

Mobile teams obsess over minute-by-minute player behaviour: Funnel conversion, daily retention, drop-off points, session length and monetisation impact.

Why it works: Because their data systems (Amplitude, GameAnalytics, DeltaDNA) are built to be queried and visualised by designers, Product Managers and QA – not just engineers.

Key Aspects of Data:

It is essential for teams to define which game analytics events should be sent to the analytics system. Careful consideration must be given to this decision, as there are costs associated with processing and storing data within the analytics ecosystem. Prioritising high-value events can help ensure both meaningful insights and cost efficiency.

Complexity in Data Querying and Insights:

The absence of a streamlined ETL (Extract, Transform, Load) process can significantly hinder the ability to generate timely and actionable insights. A well-structured ETL pipeline is critical for ensuring data is clean, consistent and readily available for analysis.

Scalability and Performance Bottlenecks:

As popular games generate millions of data events, the analytics system must be designed to scale effectively to handle this growing volume. Without a scalable architecture, performance bottlenecks can emerge, potentially impacting data processing speed and reliability. Additionally, scaling up the infrastructure to meet demand can lead to significant increases in operational costs.

Tooling Suggestions:

- **GameAnalytics**: Widely used in mobile and F2P titles

- **Amplitude**: Premium behavioural analytics

- **Unity Analytics/PlayFab**: Cross-platform compatibility for PC/console teams looking to upgrade

Soft Launches and Staged Rollouts

As mentioned earlier in the chapter, mobile teams often release in a single country or to a specific platform before expanding. This lets them test progression, server stability and economy tuning in controlled environments.

PC and console teams often launch globally and absorb all risk at once. Some Steam early access and platform-specific betas are now following mobile's lead, but the practice is not yet mainstream.

Lesson: Staggered exposure reduces launch trauma.

Design-Test-Refactor Loops

In mobile, feedback loops are fast: Test this week, tune next week. PC/console tends to front-load design and delay testing until QA are invited or during alpha/beta. That means changes are harder, slower and riskier.

Lesson: Learning earlier reduces waste. Mobile proves that.

CROSS-PLATFORM TAKEAWAY

The mobile sector shows us that testing is not just about polish, but also product discovery. PC and console teams would benefit from adopting:

- Live telemetry visibility

- Weekly test cadences

- Player segmentation during testing

- Controlled rollouts and regional launches

- Data-informed cuts, not just creative gut checks

My conclusion to this chapter may seem pithy, but it is important: Your QA culture does not have to be mobile, but it should be modern.

REFERENCES

Amplitude. (2024, April). *Multi-armed bandits vs. A/B testing: Choosing the right approach.* Retrieved from: https://amplitude.com/blog/multi-armed-bandit-vs-ab-testing

Bungie. (2015). *Destiny beta postmortem.* GDC Vault. Retrieved from: https://www.gdcvault.com

Capcom. (2023). *Player testing and QA labs in Japan.* Capcom IR Reports. Retrieved from: https://www.capcom.co.jp/ir/english/

De Bernardi, H. (2025). *How game studios quietly out-test the competition* [Conference presentation]. Game Developers Conference 2025. Retrieved from: https://www.youtube.com/watch?v=6ArUVXlzOUc

DZone. (2024, June). *Beyond A/B testing: How multi-armed bandits can scale complex experimentation.* Retrieved from: https://dzone.com/articles/beyond-ab-testing-multi-armed-bandits

EA. (2023). *EA playtesting overview.* Retrieved from: https://playtesting.ea.com

Eppo Labs. (2023). *Bandit vs experiment testing: Which is right for you?* https://www.geteppo.com/blog/bandit-or-experiment

Eurogamer. (2014). DF-9 and the perils of early access. Retrieved from: https://www.eurogamer.net

Keywords Studios. (2024). QA and certification testing services. Retrieved from: https://www.keywordsstudios.com/en/services/globalize/qa-testing/

Keywords Studios. (2024). Case study: Supercell. Retrieved from: https://www.keywordsstudios.com/en/case-studies/keywords-studios-and-supercell-total-integration-for-global-success/

Keywords Studios. (2024). Case study: Back 4 blood collaboration. Retrieved from: https://www.keywordsstudios.com/en/case-studies/success-through-collaboration-on-back-4-blood/

Medium. (2024, October). *Accelerating decision-making in mobile gaming: A/B testing meets machine learning.* Retrieved from: https://medium.com/operations-research-bit/accelerating-decision-making-in-mobile-gaming-a-b-testing-meets-machine-learning-a3d5eb958fd0

miHoYo. (2023). *The feedback loop behind Genshin impact*. Developer Q&A Panel. Retrieved from: https://www.hoyoverse.com

NetEase Games. (2024). *Live Ops and UX in the China market*. NetEase Developer Summit (translated summary). Retrieved from: https://game.163.com

Nexon. (2023). *Game insight and live operations pipeline*. Nexon Developers Conference. Retrieved from: https://ndc.nexon.com/

O'Hagan, M., & Mangiron, C. (2013). *Game localization: Translating for the global digital entertainment industry*. John Benjamins Publishing.

Polygon. (2018). The fall of Telltale games: Crunch and collapse. Retrieved from: https://www.polygon.com

Riot Games. (2023). *Player insights and research careers*. Retrieved from: https://www.riotgames.com/en/work-with-us/jobs/team/player-insights

Runge, J. (2025, January). *Experimentation in gaming: An adoption guide*. SSRN. Retrieved from: https://www.researchgate.net/publication/389280256_Experimentation_in_Gaming_an_Adoption_Guide

Tencent. (2023). *Tencent games careers – UX research*. Retrieved from: https://careers.tencent.com/en-us/position

Ubisoft. (2023). *Inside Ubisoft's user research lab*. Ubisoft News. Retrieved from: https://news.ubisoft.com/en-us/article/7Lw3B8KqHi4oOHB8g3jKwe/inside-ubisofts-user-research-lab

VWO. (2025, May). *What is multi-armed bandit testing?* https://vwo.com/blog/multi-armed-bandit-algorithm/

Wired. (2024). Test, test, test: Inside Wooga's design-driven A/B testing culture. Retrieved from: https://www.wired.com

Xbox Research. (2024). *Xbox insider program and playtesting guidelines*. Retrieved from: https://insider.xbox.com

Zagal, J. P., & Tomuro, N. (2013). *Are there cultural differences in how we play? Examining social network game data*. Proceedings of the Digital Games Research Association Conference (DiGRA). Retrieved from: https://www.digra.org

CHAPTER 38

Player Community and Social Media Risks

INTRODUCTION

In today's gaming landscape, community dynamics have evolved into a central production risk. Platforms like Reddit, Discord, Twitch and Twitter/X are not just channels for engagement but are volatile ecosystems where a single post or leak can derail months of development and marketing efforts. Understanding and managing these dynamics is crucial for the success and longevity of any game.

COMMON RISK TRIGGERS

- **Inadequate Moderation**: Lack of effective moderation on platforms like Discord and Reddit can lead to toxic environments, misinformation spread and harassment.

- **Misinformation Amplification**: Influencers or streamers sharing unverified information can rapidly spread misinformation, affecting public perception.

- **Out-of-Context Developer Comments**: Developer statements taken out of context on social media can lead to misinterpretations and backlash.

- **Harassment of Team Members**: Developers and community managers may face personal attacks due to unpopular content decisions or representation choices.

- **Review Bombing**: External controversies can lead to coordinated negative reviews on platforms like Steam, impacting game ratings.

- **Uncontrolled Leaks**: Unauthorised disclosures of unannounced content can disrupt marketing plans and player expectations.

DOI: 10.1201/9781003646082-43

- **Miscommunication of Updates**: Poorly communicated delays or patches can be misinterpreted, leading to community frustration.

- **Fan Entitlement and Backlash**: Changes in monetisation or lore can trigger strong negative reactions from dedicated fanbases.

MITIGATION STRATEGIES

- **Comprehensive Community Risk Assessment**: Conduct thorough evaluations of potential community risks during the pre-launch phase.

- **Empowered Moderation Teams**: Establish well-trained moderation teams with clear guidelines and escalation procedures to manage community interactions effectively.

- **Proactive Influencer Engagement**: Build and maintain relationships with key creators and community advocates to foster positive discourse.

- **Real-Time Sentiment Monitoring**: Implement dashboards to track community sentiment and flag potential issues promptly.

- **Developer Communication Training**: Provide training for developers on effective communication strategies to prevent misinterpretations.

- **Integrated Crisis Protocols**: Develop cross-functional protocols involving communications, legal and production teams to respond swiftly to crises.

- **Community Ambassador** Programmes: Engage with community members through ambassador programmes to gather early feedback and identify potential issues.

MITIGATION CHECKLIST

- Conduct community sentiment forecasting and influencer mapping

- Run pre-launch risk assessments on platform and audience reactions

- Create clear moderation escalation paths and train trusted community managers

- Establish a rapid response protocol for misinformation and leaks

- Align trailers, influencer demos and marketing promises with final deliverables

- Maintain live dashboards for real-time sentiment and streamer activity alerts

REAL-WORLD EXAMPLES

Case Study: *Hogwarts Legacy* and the Streamer Boycott

In 2023, Hogwarts Legacy became a lightning rod for controversy due to its association with J.K. Rowling and her public stance on trans rights. Although Rowling had no direct involvement in the game, the backlash spread across Twitch, Reddit and Twitter. Calls for a boycott were prominent, with popular streamers like Will Overgard and Nikatine publicly refusing to play or facing criticism if they did. Despite this, the game achieved record-breaking Twitch viewership, illustrating the complex relationship between online moral debates and player behaviour. Studios must prepare for such divergences between sentiment and sales.

Case Study: *No Man's Sky* – Redemption Through Transparency

As referenced previously, No Man's Sky launched in 2016 amid immense hype, only to face near-instantaneous backlash for lacking many of the features promised pre-release. Review bombing on Steam and harsh Reddit threads dominated the early discourse. Rather than retreat, developer Hello Games adopted a silent but steady strategy of free content updates, culminating in the "Atlas Rises" update and subsequent re-engagement campaigns. By 2023, the game was widely celebrated for its transformation and hailed in the Financial Times as a rare redemption arc through persistence and community re-engagement.

Case Study: *The Day Before* – Collapse of Trust

Marketed as an ambitious open-world survival MMO, *The Day Before* drew considerable attention with cinematic trailers and viral buzz. However, a pattern of delayed updates, missed milestones and developer silence led to escalating scepticism. The final straw came when the game launched with widespread reports of technical issues and features that did not match expectations. Community backlash intensified across YouTube and Reddit, with prominent influencers and community voices labelling it a scam. Steam later removed the game following disputes over its legitimacy. The absence of a transparent engagement plan and functional moderation channels contributed significantly to the reputational collapse.

Case Study: *Baldur's Gate 3* – The Power of Community Alignment

Larian Studios earned praise not only for the quality of *Baldur's Gate 3* but also for its transparent development process. During Early Access, the team released detailed patch notes, acknowledged feedback publicly and frequently engaged with the community on platforms like Reddit and Discord. Influencers were treated as strategic partners, not just marketers – a model that helped align player expectations with development goals. When balancing issues or bugs arose, the studio's rapid and transparent response reinforced trust. This strategy, widely covered in games press, set a gold standard for community-driven development.

Case Study: *Warframe* – Community Management as a Core Competency

Digital Extremes has built a reputation for Warframe's exceptional community engagement. Livestreams like *Devstreams* and *TennoCon* create transparency, while community managers actively moderate Discord and Reddit to de-escalate issues. The result is a loyal player base that often defends the studio from external criticism. As noted in interviews and coverage by outlets such as Eggplante, the studio emphasises honest, two-way communication as foundational to trust. Warframe demonstrates how institutionalising community engagement can serve as a buffer against volatile backlash.

KEY RISK PATTERNS

1. Streamer Spiral

- **Definition**: Negative influencer reactions cause mass sentiment collapse.
- **Trigger**: A controversial feature or association is amplified by streamers.
- **Outcome**: Online boycotts, community splits and media narratives spiral.

2. Moderation Failure Cascade

- **Definition**: Inadequate moderation allows toxicity to fester and dominate discourse.
- **Trigger**: Understaffed or passive community management on Reddit, Discord, or forums.
- **Outcome**: Developer harassment, player churn and media scandals.

3. Misinformation Wildfire

- **Definition**: False or misleading claims spread virally before studio response.
- **Trigger**: Unverified leaks, out-of-context dev comments, or fake trailers.
- **Outcome**: Distrust, patch panic and fractured player loyalty.

4. Expectation Backlash Loop

- **Definition**: Hype cycles built on selective previews cause disconnect with actual product.
- **Trigger**: Influencer previews, cinematic trailers, or early access builds.
- **Outcome**: Review bombing, refund surges, long-term perception damage.

SIDEBAR: STREAMERS AS STAKEHOLDERS. WHY INFLUENCERS ARE NOW PART OF YOUR RISK MODEL

Influencers can make or break the perception of your game in real time. Treat them as stakeholders: brief them before announcements, give them early access under embargo and monitor their feedback like you would press or QA. Many community flashpoints today begin with or are amplified by a creator's reaction. Your influencer strategy is now part of your risk strategy.

SIDEBAR: MODERATION AS OPERATIONAL RISK CONTROL

Moderation is not just a community issue for us – we can plug it into operational risk control. Inadequate moderation can lead to brand damage, developer harassment, legal violations (e.g. hate speech) and negative press cycles. Ensure clear roles, escalation chains and tooling support. Evaluate third-party moderation vendors for larger communities or consider AI-assisted tools only if humans remain in the loop.

   See the downloadable *Player Community Risk Toolkit* for the full audit template, escalation tracker, influencer risk log and sentiment radar.

COMMUNITY CHAOS IS HERE TO STAY

Designing games now requires anticipating and integrating community reactions. Features, pacing and monetisation strategies must consider real-time feedback loops. Effective risk management involves recognising the community as both a co-creator and a potential disruptor, necessitating proactive engagement and transparent communication.

REFERENCES

Eggplante. (2013). *Warframe, free-to-play and community: My day with digital extremes.* Link.
Financial Times. (2022). *How hello games turned no man's sky around.* Link.
Forbes. (2023). *Hogwarts legacy video game controversy: Boycotts and JK Rowling's comments on transgender community.* Link.
PC Gamer. (2023). *The day before has been delisted from steam and devs are offering refunds after a disastrous launch.* Link.
Rock Paper Shotgun. (2023). *Baldur's Gate 3 devs are proving early access can work if you talk to your players.* Link.
The Atlantic. (2023). *What the Hogwarts legacy boycott tells us about gaming culture.* Link.
Wired. (2017). *No man's sky one year later: Hello games' road to redemption.* Link.

CHAPTER 39

Security and Data Privacy in Games

ADDRESSING SECURITY VULNERABILITIES IN GAMES

Games face diverse security threats across PC, console and mobile. On the client side, attackers exploit reverse-engineering, mods and infected game builds to cheat or steal data. For example, *Fortnite* was found to have account takeover bugs allowing attackers to hijack players and even make unauthorised V-buck purchases (Check Point Research, 2019). Mobile titles often see patched APKs or "lucky patcher" hacks that bypass in-app purchase checks. Rooted or jailbroken devices make cheating even easier (bypassing app integrity checks), and asset manipulation hacks (e.g. modified textures or memory editors) reveal hidden game information or automate play. Malware injection is also common: Fraudulent cheat apps may harbour trojans that steal credentials or crypto-miners that abuse player machines.

Security in games is often treated as an infrastructure issue. However, it is also a reputational risk, a trust risk and a live operations risk. A single exploit or exposed API can trigger platform takedowns, negative press and player churn, far beyond the scope of technical repair.

On the server side, unsecured backends and APIs can leak or corrupt data. For example, poor network security in Sony's infrastructure led to the infamous 2011 PlayStation Network breach, which exposed personal data for ~77 million accounts (Reuters, 2011). Inadequate validation of purchases or game commands on the server can enable payment tampering and fraud (e.g. forging purchase receipts to grant free items). Other server risks include SQL/API injection, misconfigured cloud servers, distributed denial-of-service (DDoS) attacks against game servers and insider threats (compromised developer credentials). Together, these client- and server-side flaws can undermine both game integrity and user trust.

DOI: 10.1201/9781003646082-44

SECURITY INCIDENTS ARE PLAYER TRUST INCIDENTS

Most security issues do not damage games because of what happened technically; they damage them because of how players feel afterwards. Whether it is a breached account, stolen data or DDoS outage, the lasting impact is almost always a loss of player confidence. Technical fix does not equal trust restored. Players have feelings and you probably just hurt them.

Vulnerability	Platform Scope	Impact/Example
Authentication flaws	All (especially online)	Account hijacking (e.g. Fortnite account takeover)
Payment tampering	Mobile/PC	Forged in-app purchases or free items via hacked clients
Malware injection	All	Trojanized cheat software, DDoS bots
Rooted/Jailbroken devices	Mobile/Console	Unchecked cheat mods run with full privileges
Asset manipulation	PC/Console	Texture or map hacks (wallhacks, aimbots)
Server-side vulnerabilities	All	Data breaches (e.g. PSN 2011 breach of 77M accounts)

The table above shows the breadth of risks, but each has a data privacy component as well. As games become more service-oriented, the amount of personal, device and behavioural data collected has grown. That has triggered not only regulatory scrutiny but also growing concern from players themselves.

DATA PRIVACY CONCERNS: IN-APP PURCHASES AND USER DATA

Modern games collect extensive personal and transactional data, raising serious privacy concerns. User behaviour tracking is pervasive: Games log playtime, session length, item use, device IDs, location and even audio (for voice chat) to optimise engagement and monetisation. For example, free-to-play titles like *Clash of Clans* and *Fortnite* rely on deep analytics and ad targeting. Such tracking is now constrained by privacy regulations and platform policies – notably Apple's App Tracking Transparency (ATT) in 2021 reshaped the industry by requiring opt-in user consent.

Beyond tracking, in-app purchases (IAPs) generate sensitive data (payment tokens, account emails, purchase history). Game backends and cloud services (AWS, PlayFab, Firebase, etc.) must handle this securely. Developers should use strong encryption and tokenisation (e.g. PCI DSS compliance for payment data) and avoid storing raw credit-card info. Cloud platforms typically offer encryption-at-rest and in-transit by default. For instance, AWS's GameLift service explicitly requires TLS 1.2+ for all communications and recommends multi-factor authentication for developer access (Amazon GameLift Documentation, n.d.). However, compliance is only as good as implementation.

CHECKLIST: WHAT GAME DATA AM I COLLECTING?

Before a single player logs in, your SDKs, ad networks, analytics and platform services may already be collecting:

- Device ID and model
- IP address and rough location
- Session data and item usage
- Ad viewability, clickstream and spending behaviour
- Voice chat or friend interactions (if enabled)

Ask yourself: Are you collecting anything you are not actively using? If so, why?

KEY ASPECTS OF DATA COMPLIANCE

Data Protection Management System:

We need to have in place a data protection management system (DPMS) for continuous monitoring and improvement of our data protection management system. The DPMS ensures that all aspects of data protection are managed systematically. The DPMS includes policies, procedures and guidelines that govern data protection practices, with regular audits to ensure compliance.

Data Protection by Design and Default:

This ensures that data protection principles are integrated into the design and operation of all systems and processes. All organisations must adhere to the principles of Data Protection by Design and Default, integrating data protection into the development and operation of all products and services. This involves: Designing for Privacy, Default Settings and Ongoing Assessments.

Encryption:

Collecting Personally Identifiable Information (PII) requires consent and secure handling under laws like GDPR (EU/UK), CCPA (California) or PDPA (Singapore).

All sensitive data, including should be encrypted both in transit and at rest, in compliance with GDPR requirements (Art. 32 (1) (a) of the GDPR) in EU/UK.

EXAMPLES OF PERSONALLY IDENTIFIABLE INFORMATION
- Full name
- Email address
- Home address
- Phone number
- Date of birth
- National Insurance number or other government-issued ID numbers
- IP address (in some jurisdictions)
- Login credentials

- Biometric data (e.g. fingerprints, facial scans)
- Payment or financial account details

Authorisation Control:
Role-based access controls ensure that employees only access data necessary for their duties.

Input Control:
Logging mechanisms are in place to record data input activities, ensuring accountability and traceability.

Resilience Control:
Systems are designed to withstand and recover from failures, ensuring minimal disruption to data processing activities.

Data Breach Policy:
Organisations need to establish a comprehensive Data Breach Policy to ensure the security of personal data and to comply with GDPR requirements. This policy includes procedures for detecting, reporting and responding to data breaches. Automated monitoring tools, regular audits and employee training are employed to detect potential breaches, while an Incident Response Team (IRT) is tasked with managing any incidents that occur.

In the event of a breach, organisations must be committed to promptly notifying the relevant supervisory authority within 72 hours and informing affected data subjects if their rights are at high risk. The policy also emphasises immediate containment, thorough risk assessment and effective mitigation measures to minimise the breach's impact.

The Data Breach Policy also requires detailed documentation of each incident, including the breach summary, response actions, notifications made and lessons learned. Regular reviews and testing of the policy are conducted to ensure it remains effective and up to date. Employee training is an essential component, with all staff educated in breach awareness and the importance of swift reporting. Through these measures, studios aim to protect personal data, maintain trust with stakeholders and ensure regulatory compliance.

Privacy Laws:
Finally, games must obey privacy laws in all operating regions. In the EU, GDPR mandates user consent for data collection, data minimisation and rights to access or delete personal data. For example, enforcement actions such as the Grindr GDPR fine in Norway highlight the growing scrutiny of data practices (Reuters, 2021). In the US, COPPA protects users under 13 (requiring parental consent and limiting data on children) and CCPA/CPRA grants California users rights over their data.

Regulation	Applies to	Key Requirements
GDPR (EU)	EU residents' data (worldwide)	Explicit consent for data use; rights to view/erase user data; strict breach notification
COPPA (USA)	Children under 13	Parental consent for child data collection; limit on personal info storage
CCPA/CPRA (CA)	California residents	Right to opt-out of data sales; rights to access/delete personal data

PROPOSING SOLUTIONS TO COMMON SECURITY RISKS

Security is not just the job of one team. Secure coding, access control, infrastructure resilience and fraud protection must be part of your regular production planning. Every game will face exploits. The question is whether your controls are ready and whether your team knows what to do when they fail.

- **Secure Coding and Architecture**: Follow OWASP/mobile security guidelines and secure SDLC principles. Validate all inputs on both client and server. Use code obfuscation and tamper-detection. Isolate trust on the server side wherever possible.

- **Encryption (TLS/SSL)**: Encrypt all client-server traffic. Require TLS 1.2+. Encrypt sensitive data at rest. Use managed encryption services by default.

- **API Security**: Use authentication (OAuth tokens/API keys), rate limiting and avoid hard-coded secrets. Use API gateways/WAFs. Monitor for anomalies.

- **Database Encryption**: Encrypt PII and financial data. Enforce least-privilege access to databases. Avoid exposing PII in free-form fields.

- **Data Obfuscation**: Where possible, organisations must employ pseudonymisation techniques to protect personal data, minimising the risk of identification of data subjects (Art. 32 (1) (a) of the GDPR; Art. 25 (1) of the GDPR).

- **Two-Factor/Multi-Factor Authentication (2FA/MFA)**: Require MFA on accounts. Epic Games promoted 2FA in Fortnite with in-game rewards, improving adoption significantly (TechCrunch, 2018).

IMPLEMENTING BEST PRACTICES

- **Security Audits and Testing**: Code reviews, third-party audits, SAST/DAST tools. Integrate into the secure SDLC.

- **Bug Bounty Programs**: Run programs via HackerOne or Bugcrowd. Reward ethical disclosure.

- **Employee Training**: Educate teams on secure coding, phishing risks and incident response (Cyber Management Alliance, 2024).

- **Secure SDLC Integration**: Scan new code, maintain security checklists and keep dependencies patched.

- **Backend Tooling**: Use secure, cross-platform systems (PlayFab, AWS GameLift, Firebase) with RBAC and monitoring dashboards.

- **User Education**: Use in-game prompts or help centres to educate users about strong passwords, scams and security options.

SECURITY AND PRIVACY ARE NOW CORE GAME SYSTEMS

Security risks often seem to be a big surprise when they suddenly switch to a real issue. A single breach or badly handled privacy issue can collapse a game's momentum and brand value. In a world of livestreams, TikTok leaks and platform suspensions, your security incidents are not private for long.

The best security posture is to be technically competent, but also encouraging of team-wide awareness, proactive planning, layered defences and rapid communication. Games only as resilient as their weakest layer.

REFERENCES

Amazon GameLift documentation. (n.d.). *Data protection in Amazon GameLift Servers.* Retrieved from: https://docs.aws.amazon.com/gamelift/latest/developerguide/security-data-protection .html

Check Point Research. (2019). *Hacking Fortnite accounts.* Retrieved from: https://research.check-point.com/2019/fortnite-vulnerability/

Cyber Management Alliance. (2024). *Phishing scams in the gaming community.* Retrieved from: https://www.cm-alliance.com/cybersecurity-blog/phishing-scams-in-the-gaming -community

Reuters. (2011). *Sony PlayStation suffers massive data breach.* Retrieved from: https://www.reuters .com/article/us-sony-idUSTRE73P6WB20110426

Reuters. (2021). *Grindr faces GDPR fine.* Retrieved from: https://www.reuters.com/article/us-nor-way-privacy-grindr-idUSKBN29Z0KT

TechCrunch. (2018). *Epic Games just gave a perk for folks to turn on 2FA.* Retrieved from: https:// techcrunch.com/2018/08/23/epic-games-just-gave-a-perk-for-folks-to-turn-on-2fa/

CHAPTER 40

Risk Realities Across Studio Models

INTRODUCTION

The world of game development is incredibly diverse and so too are the risks faced by teams of different sizes and structures. Whether a studio is an early-stage indie, a mid-sized independent developer or part of a vast multi-studio organisation, the way they approach risk – and the risks they are exposed to – can differ significantly. This chapter explores those differences, providing insight into how scale, funding and team structure influence exposure to risk and the strategies available to mitigate it.

Most emphasis is placed in this chapter on the Indie, as it faces unique and critical risks in the current external landscape.

While we went into detail on Risk Trends in the Overview, it is worth revisiting a few of these now, as they are directly relevant to the challenges different types of studios are facing (Polygon, 2025a).

TRENDS REVISITED: WHAT THEY MEAN BY STUDIO TYPE

While Chapter 4 introduced the industry-wide risk trends shaping the current environment, it is worth revisiting the most impactful here – this time through the lens of how they affect studios differently depending on their size, structure and funding model.

Publisher Consolidation and Studio Mergers

The consolidation wave, epitomised by Embracer's divestments, Tencent's Western investments and Square Enix's strategic retreat (GameSpot, 2022), has had cascading effects across the ecosystem (Polygon, 2023).

DOI: 10.1201/9781003646082-45

- **For Indie Studios**, these shifts narrow the pool of viable publishing partners and raise the bar for creative autonomy. Many small teams must now contend with fewer potential allies, each wielding more leverage and demanding more polish up front.

- **For Independent-Funded Studios**, the risk lies in volatility. Publisher advances may dry up mid-cycle or shift in priority overnight, as seen in Riot Forge's abrupt closure (Wikipedia, 2024). These teams often face milestone-based funding tied to external strategy pivots.

- **For Multi-Studio Organisations**, consolidation leads to internal competition and prioritisation battles. Even flagship projects may be delayed or shelved due to boardroom recalibration. Political risk increases – your studio may be compliant, but if a sister studio underperforms, the whole portfolio may be restructured.

Financial Strain and Investment Drought

The steep drop in gaming investments – from $14.6 billion in 2022 to $4.1 billion in 2023 – has reshaped survival strategies across the board (Wired, 2024) (Wikipedia, 2025a).

- **Indie Studios** now face an even harsher funding climate. Investors want late-stage, near-finished products, often leaving early-stage indies to bootstrap or fundraise through high-effort channels like Patreon or conference demos.

- **Independent-Funded Studios** must fight for runway. Funding milestones become inflexible chokepoints. A single delay in production or a rejected build may threaten the entire studio's financial stability.

- **Multi-Studios**, while better capitalised, are under pressure to justify burn rates. Budgets are scrutinised, redundancies made visible and cross-project ROI becomes a metric for survival. Studios like BioWare and Visceral have seen how top-down reprioritisation can override years of work (GameSpot, 2024).

Platform Shifts and Discovery Dynamics

From the rise of PC parity to the volatility of live service games and the influence of streamers, platform dynamics are now both fragmented and fast-moving (Polygon, 2025b).

- **For Indies**, the stakes are highest. A streamer spike can make or break a launch window. Without marketing support or real-time response capability, discovery risk is critical.

- **Independent Studios** face a double bind: Required to commit to multiplatform from the start, but often without the resources to scale QA, patching or cross-platform parity effectively.

- **Multi-Studio Teams** must coordinate global launches across time zones, platforms and player bases. Integration pipelines, liveops and regional compliance can all derail a polished delivery if platform shifts (or PSN policy backlashes) are not tracked early.

Live Service Pressure and Post-Launch Complexity

The dream of evergreen engagement continues to challenge studios of all sizes (Wikipedia, 2025b).

- **Indies** often lack the infrastructure or team size to deliver regular content drops, respond to player churn or run 24/7 ops. Even a modest live service ambition can result in burnout or collapse.

- **Independent-Funded Studios** must walk the tightrope: Live service execution must be "good enough" to avoid churn, but must also fit within publisher-imposed budget and cadence constraints.

- **Multi-Studio Organisations**, while better equipped, face slower response cycles due to layered approvals and shared resources. A surge in players may be good news – until your infrastructure team is ten time zones away and prioritised for another title.

This trend backdrop defines the constraints within which risk must be managed.

TABLE: STUDIO TYPE DEFINITIONS

Studio Type	Typical Size	Funding Model	Characteristics
Indie (Modern)	5–35	Self-funded, crowdfunded or small publisher	Flat structure, overlapping roles, self-promotion required, limited runway
Independent-Funded	30–150	Publisher advances or private funding	Departmental structure, milestone-driven, reliant on publisher relationships
Multi-Studio/AAA	100+ (multi-site)	Internal funding, franchise backing	Complex hierarchy, multiple locations, formal governance and oversight

THE UNIQUE CHALLENGE FOR INDIES

Evolving Definition of Indie Studios

Indie studios may be self-funded, crowdfunded or receive publisher advances, and they often operate with overlapping roles and flat hierarchies. The line between indie and AA studios is increasingly blurred, especially as some indie studios collaborate with major publishers or leverage well-known IPs to boost visibility. Single-person Indies still exist and still make hit games, but most disappear into Discovery oblivion.

(Source: VG Insights 2024 Indie Games Market Report)

The traditional assumption that indie studios are micro-teams of five or fewer developers no longer holds. Many indie studios now consist of up to 35 individuals, some with dedicated roles across production, design, art and QA. What distinguishes them is not size but independence – financial, creative and structural.

Funding Challenges

Securing funding has become increasingly difficult for indie developers. Many investors and publishers are hesitant to fund projects that are not near completion. For instance, Heart Machine, known for "Hyper Light Drifter", turned to Patreon as a supplementary revenue source amid financial struggles, highlighting the broader funding challenges in the industry (The Verge, 2024). The overall downturn in the video game industry has led to widespread layoffs and studio closures, further exacerbating funding difficulties (Lanata, 2023).

Marketing and Publisher Risks

Marketing remains a significant hurdle for indie developers. A lack of effective pre-launch marketing strategies can lead to poor visibility and sales, regardless of a game's quality. Common pitfalls include insufficient advertising, misunderstanding player expectations and rushing into early access without adequate preparation (CloutBoost, 2023). Partnerships with publishers can be a double-edged sword. While they can provide resources and exposure, misaligned visions and inadequate marketing support from publishers can hinder a game's success. The closure of Riot Forge, despite its critical successes, underscores the risks associated with publisher relationships.

> It's actually incredibly challenging to find marketing reports outside of Steam for indies. If you are a mobile, VR or niche developer, be prepared to take large-scale studies and apply them to your current situation, if you can find any studies at all!
>
> Pre-launch marketing strategies are essential for indie devs, but marketing always presents itself as an opportunity cost. If you are marketing, you are not developing. Consider partnering with a marketing expert to organise community events and compile feedback while getting your game out to the public.
>
> Crowdfunding has changed from a grassroots fundraising method to a marketing machine. Building a community ready to support your game is crucial for crowdfunding, and one should not rely on platform discovery to reach their goal. In some cases, people will lower their goal in relation to actual expenses needed so that they can be "funded in 24-72 hours and make the most of that momentum through journalists and owned media. It's par for the course, but has questioned the integrity of crowdfunding as it stands today. Do not test concepts on crowdfunding sites and consider growing a social media community first.

> As a virtual reality indie studio, it often feels like the odds are stacked against us. With less than expected VR growth and a dynamic target audience, VR developers are struggling with a lack of dedicated market insights, increased challenges in promoting, and consistent user experience mishaps such as motion sickness, limited playing space, and player expectation misalignment. Virtual reality games have the power to stand out in the games industry, but they should also be treated as an alternative to PC/Console gaming. In some cases, VR can learn a thing or two from mobile gaming! I encourage folks in the VR space to cast a smaller net and expect a lack of publisher funding for the next couple of years.
> – MICHAEL GALLEGOS, INDIE FOUNDER & MARKETING CONSULTANT

Risks of Self-Promotion and Conference Attendance

Attending conferences is a common strategy for indie developers seeking funding and exposure. However, this approach carries its own set of risks, including significant financial costs for travel and accommodation and the potential for burnout. While conferences can offer networking opportunities, they do not guarantee funding or success, making them a high-risk investment for resource-constrained indie studios.

Due Diligence Requirements for Funding and Marketing

Due diligence is a critical process where investors or publishers assess a studio's readiness, competence and alignment before funding. While the ideal game pitch might include a nearly finished product built by a proven team with prior commercial success, reality often demands a rigorous evaluation to manage risk.

Due Diligence – Key Areas of Focus

Development Capability

- Knowledge of the game engine and toolchain

- Experience in the genre and platform being developed for

- Current state of the build and clarity on what remains

- Key staff named and committed

Operational Viability

- Technical infrastructure, equipment, backups

- Financial stability and competitive salary structures

- Studio's communication culture and delivery track record

Production and Delivery

- Senior management and production experience

- Openness to production oversight and support

- Evidence of risk tracking and prior delivery performance

- Willingness to engage in feedback and change

Strategic Fit and Intangibles

- Long-term partnership potential

- Expected response when challenged or pushed by the publisher

- External references and industry reputation

- ROI potential from a marketing and distribution standpoint

Joakim Achrén, an industry investor and adviser, reinforces that studios should prepare a structured data room covering all of the above categories. Transparency is valued above polish. A solid risk matrix often impresses more than a flashy deck.

SIDEBAR: WHAT IS A DATA ROOM?

A data room is a secure, organised repository of essential documentation that investors or publishing partners use to evaluate a studio during due diligence. Its purpose is to centralise all relevant information, enabling efficient, transparent review.
   What Should Be Included:

- **Corporate Documentation**: Legal incorporation, shareholder structure, board minutes
- **Financials**: Recent statements, budget forecasts, cash runway, cap table
- **Game Build Assets**: Screenshots, gameplay videos, build access, version roadmap
- **Intellectual Property**: Ownership verification, licences, registered trademarks
- **Team Overview**: Key staff bios, org chart, hiring plan
- **Development Pipeline**: Milestones, timelines, delivery risks
- **Legal Agreements**: NDAs, contractor agreements, publishing contracts
- **Risk registers**: Known issues, mitigation plans, contingency frameworks

   Why It Matters:
   According to Joakim Achrén and other game investors, polish is less important than completeness and clarity. A well-prepared data room reflects a studio's maturity, readiness and openness. It can make the difference between investor confidence and hesitation.

SIDEBAR: WHAT IDEAL GAME SUBMISSIONS LOOK LIKE (AND WHY THEY RARELY EXIST)

We know that an ideal game submission probably looks something like this:

- A nearly finished game (not a concept or design doc)
- Created by an experienced team whose last game sold well
- A technical and graphical marvel
- Highly addictive and satisfying in terms of gameplay
- Highly watchable and viewer-friendly
- Low development risk
- High production values
- The "cool factor" – there is something about the game that makes it unique, cool and different
- Fun. Buyers play and replay, telling their friends to buy it too!

However, we do not live in a perfect world, which is why we have to accept that there are many risks when investing in a developer partner and a lot to consider.

Case Study: Red Hook Studios – *Darkest Dungeon*

Studio Type: Indie

Primary Risks: Crowdfunding expectations, burnout, post-launch support

What Happened: Red Hook Studios turned to Kickstarter in 2014 and raised over $300,000. While the funding enabled development, it also created strong backer expectations. The small team encountered development delays, crunch periods and public pressure. They were also responsible for sustaining visibility post-launch with a limited marketing budget.

Mitigation Strategy: The team maintained transparency through updates and community engagement, launched into early access to involve players and invested heavily in post-launch support. These efforts built a strong community and long-term trust.

Lesson: Crowdfunded indie teams must plan for expectation management, marketing momentum and sustainable development pacing.

KEY RISK THEMES BY STUDIO TYPE

Indie-Specific Risks

- **Funding Drought (2023–2025)**: Most investors and publishers now only fund near-complete projects, creating a severe cash flow challenge.

- **Publisher Dependency**: Poor marketing execution, mismatched audience targeting or miscommunication with publishers can derail success.

- **Self-Promotion Risk**: Attending global conferences to secure funding is essential but expensive. The return on investment is uncertain.

- **Due Diligence Pressures**: External producers scrutinise legal structure, IP ownership and financial preparedness.

- **Burnout and Opportunity Cost**: Studio heads often juggle creative work, business development and travel.

Single Studio Risks

- Funding milestones create financial stress.

- Directional shifts from publishers can destabilise plans.

- Departmental silos reduce visibility and collaboration.

Multi-Studio Risks

- Cross-location communication breakdowns.

- Delays from time zone misalignment.

- Conflicts from shared codebase or tools.

- Inconsistent quality and cultural mismatches across studios.

MULTI-STUDIO DEVELOPMENT: NAVIGATING THE COMPLEXITIES OF COLLABORATIVE GAME PRODUCTION

The landscape of AAA game development has evolved to encompass intricate networks of internal and external studios collaborating across various regions. This model, while offering scalability and diverse expertise, introduces a multitude of risks that can jeopardise project timelines, quality and team cohesion.

Key Risks in Multi-Studio Development

1. Integration Challenges

Coordinating the integration of assets and features developed by disparate teams can lead to significant delays. For instance, Ubisoft's *Assassin's Creed: Unity* involved ten teams across six countries, presenting substantial logistical hurdles in synchronising development efforts.

2. Communication Barriers

Time zone differences and cultural disparities can impede effective communication. Ubisoft's global operations have faced such challenges, necessitating robust communication protocols to maintain alignment across teams.

3. Resource Allocation Conflicts

Studios may be reassigned to assist struggling teams, disrupting their original workflows. In the development of *Dune: Awakening*, co-developed by Funcom and Yager, the collaboration required meticulous coordination to manage shared responsibilities effectively (Yager, 2024) (VentureBeat, 2020).

4. Tool and Workflow Discrepancies

Divergent development tools and workflows among studios can lead to compatibility issues, affecting the seamless integration of game components.

5. Political and Strategic Misalignments

Parent companies may impose strategic decisions that override studio preferences, leading to friction. Tencent's acquisition of Funcom and subsequent involvement in projects like the aforementioned *Dune: Awakening* illustrate the complexities introduced by such corporate dynamics.

Case Study: Ubisoft's Multi-Studio Approach

Studio Type: Multi-Studio (Ubisoft Montreal lead; approximately ten global studios contributed) (Fast Company, 2014)

Primary Risks: Integration breakdown, QA inconsistencies, fragmented testing pipelines across teams (Signiant, 2023).

What Happened:

Ubisoft tasked over ten development studios – including Montreal, Toronto, Singapore, Bucharest and others – with building *Unity*'s massive Paris environment, character systems and co-op gameplay. At release in November 2014, the game was plagued by widespread technical issues: severe frame-rate drops, graphical glitches (notably missing or distorted faces), recurring crashes, dysfunctional co-op sessions and broken mission triggers.

Mitigation Strategy (Post-Release):

Ubisoft issued a string of major patches (over 300 bug fixes) targeting performance, stability, matchmaking and graphics (Screen Rant, 2020). The publisher also provided free DLC (*Dead Kings*) (Wired, 2014) and halted sales of the season pass, apologising publicly via CEO Yannis Mallat, who said the game's "overall quality … was diminished by bugs and unexpected technical issues" (Polygon, 2014).

Lesson:

Even with scale and resources, multi-studio pipelines require strict toolchain standardisation, unified QA protocols and early integration milestones. *Unity* serves as a cautionary example of how decentralised development can fracture final delivery without governance and end-to-end testing baked into the workflow, rather than delayed until the end.

Mitigation Strategies

To address these risks, studios can implement the following measures:

- **Establish Clear Communication Channels**: Regular meetings and updates can ensure all teams are aligned.

- **Standardise Tools and Workflows**: Adopting common development tools can minimise compatibility issues.

- **Define Roles and Responsibilities**: Clearly delineating tasks can prevent overlaps and confusion.

- **Implement Integration Calendars**: Scheduling integration points can help manage dependencies effectively.

- **Foster a Collaborative Culture**: Encouraging mutual respect and understanding among teams can enhance cooperation.

PUBLISHER PARTNERSHIP RISKS

Publisher relationships can help indies survive, but they also introduce serious strategic and operational risk. The dream is partnership. The reality is often pressure, misalignment and loss of creative control.

Key Risk Patterns:

- **Creative Pigeonholing**: Publishers may attempt to reshape the game to match their portfolio, diluting the original vision.

- **Misunderstood Audience**: Marketing efforts may target the wrong player base, wasting budget and weakening launch impact.

- **Delayed Decision-Making**: Publisher approval cycles can stall updates, trailers, localisation efforts or liveops responses.

- **Lack of Prioritisation**: If multiple games are being published simultaneously, your project may not get the needed attention or budget.

- **Inflexible Milestones**: Milestone-based funding may force teams to ship incomplete features just to receive the next payment.

Real-World Parallels:

- Several developers under Riot Forge and similar initiatives were unable to grow their brand or maintain creative autonomy.

- Indie teams with breakout potential were sidelined by slow publisher response during key opportunities (e.g. influencer trends, emerging platforms).

Best Practice:
Studios must vet publishers as carefully as publishers vet them. Due diligence should go both ways: ask how many other titles they are publishing concurrently, who controls final marketing and what happens if your creative vision diverges.

A bad partnership can cost you more than just money. It can cost momentum, reputation and morale.

Comparative Guide: Notable Game Publishers and What They Mean for You

Publisher	Known For	Relevance to Indie	Relevance to Independent-Funded	Relevance to Multi-Studio/ AAA	Risk Notes
Devolver Digital	Offbeat, stylish indies; strong brand identity	Friendly to bold, artistic projects with strong identity	Can provide marketing boost, but may be hands-off on production	Rarely relevant	Good for visibility, but not a fit for studios needing operational support

Publisher	Known For	Relevance to Indie	Relevance to Independent-Funded	Relevance to Multi-Studio/ AAA	Risk Notes
Annapurna Interactive	Narrative-driven, auteur-led games	Supports creative control, prestige platforming	Suitable for established indies with proven track record	Unlikely partner	Highly curated – hard to get in, but low publisher interference
Private Division (Take-Two)	AA+ and high-end indies; longer cycle projects	Less accessible for first-time teams	Fits mature indies scaling up; offers funding and production guidance	May be stepping stone into Take-Two's larger ecosystem	Stricter on milestones and scope; brand protection focus
Raw Fury	Developer-first philosophy; supportive stance	Accessible to early-stage indies	May be too lightweight for larger needs	Not relevant	Small team = inconsistent capacity; pick carefully
Team17	Publishing and co-dev with varied indies	Strong across indie and mid-tier co-dev	Provides QA, localisation, marketing	Not used for AAA	Mixed feedback from devs on support and terms – research is key
Epic Games Publishing	High budget, developer-friendly terms (e.g. Remedy's Alan Wake 2)	Unlikely for small indies	Strong fit for studios with proven IP or tech	Relevant for high-profile, multi-studio games	Attractive revenue split, but competitive entry
505 Games	Global reach, varied portfolio including AA	Moderate entry bar for indies	Reasonable fit for independent studios	Scales into multi-site support (e.g. Control)	Some developer complaints about inconsistent marketing
Focus Entertainment	European publisher with AA focus (e.g. Plague Tale)	Too high-tier for early indies	Strong match for structured, mid-size devs	AAA-adjacent support possible	Production expectations are high; longer greenlight times
Kowloon Nights	Investment fund model with no publishing interference	Ideal for experienced indies with a vision	Provides funding, not operational support	Not relevant	Good autonomy, but needs clear plan and credibility upfront

Publisher	Known For	Relevance to Indie	Relevance to Independent-Funded	Relevance to Multi-Studio/ AAA	Risk Notes
Thunderful Publishing	Mix of internal and third-party projects; often with Nordic roots	Mid-sized indie support; some debut teams	Good production and localisation backing	Rarely relevant for AAA	Better suited to culturally aligned teams or EU-based studios
Microsoft/Xbox Game Studios	Platform support, funding, distribution	Game Pass visibility possible for standout indies	Requires strong pitch and alignment with Xbox strategy	Key partner for AAA co-devs	Milestone and QA scrutiny is high; platform policy risk exists
Sony Interactive Entertainment	Prestige curation; co-devs and exclusives	Some funding via PlayStation Indies	Requires proven quality and alignment with platform interests	Major player for multi-studio titles	PSN policies, platform timelines and marketing control are risks

How to Use This Table

- **Indie studios** should look for brand-aligned, hands-off publishers who enhance discoverability and offer manageable oversight.

- **Independent-funded teams** need to balance funding and visibility with realistic support expectations and milestone scrutiny.

- **Multi-studio/AAA studios** typically partner at a platform or portfolio level, where political risk and integration control become dominant.

Top Tip: Always request details about concurrent projects, QA ownership, milestone definitions and marketing rights before signing.

Case Study: Romero Games – Publisher Withdrawal and Strategic Fallout
Studio Type: Indie (Established, narrative-focused developer)
Primary Risks: Strategic funding withdrawal, publisher dependency, external decision override

What Happened:

In July 2025, Irish studio Romero Games (co-founded by Brenda and John Romero) announced layoffs (GamesIndustry.biz, 2025) following the sudden cancellation of a project they were developing under an undisclosed publisher (Game Developer, 2025). According to a statement on Bluesky, the cancellation "was the result of a strategic decision made at a high level within the publisher, well above our visibility or control" (Bluesky, 2025).

Although the project was progressing as expected from Romero's side, the decision reportedly followed Microsoft's sweeping cuts to Xbox Game Studios and related project portfolios, suggesting that the funding publisher may have been indirectly affected or reassessing its own risk exposure. This left Romero Games abruptly without financial runway for the in-progress title.

I met John Romero at a Develop Brighton games conference a few years ago and was struck by his incredible knowledge and passion for games. He is one of many veterans who set up a studio with heart and soul, but recently has fallen victim to a ruthless financial sky raining down from above.

Mitigation Strategy (Partial):

The studio issued a public statement to clarify the situation and protect its brand. It also worked to retain core leadership and evaluate future publishing or funding options. However, the team confirmed layoffs of key developers and did not specify a new active project.

Lesson:

Even indie studios with experienced leadership and credible publishers can be blindsided by portfolio-level decisions made above the operational layer. This case reinforces the need to:

- Conduct due diligence on your publisher's financial and strategic exposure.

- Include clear exit clauses, IP reversion rights and fallback plans in contracts.

- Diversify revenue sources or maintain contingency runway wherever possible.

Comparative Guide to Notable Investors and VCs in Games

Investor/VC	Known For	Relevance to Indie	Relevance to Independent-Funded	Relevance to Multi-Studio/AAA	Risk Notes
Kowloon Nights	Developer-first, hands-off funding	Strong match if you have a strong concept and team	Offers autonomy and fast decisions	Not applicable	No marketing or operational help – only money
Lupa Systems/ Hiro Capital	Portfolio of games, fitness and media startups	Limited indie relevance	Good for Series A/growth-stage indies	Sometimes part of larger funding rounds	More structured than angel investors – want growth metrics
London Venture Partners (LVP)	Gaming-only VC; early-stage specialists	One of the few open to first-time founders	Ideal for 10–50 person studios with a prototype	Less active with large multi-site teams	Expect deep industry DD; pitch must show sharp market fit
Makers Fund	Global games and adjacent tech focus	Rarely backs very early indies	Very strong for AA-scale live service or platform plays	Relevant at scale or expansion stage	Tends to favour growth trajectories and cross-platform reach
Bitkraft Ventures	Big-name VC with broad global portfolio	Occasionally backs indies with disruptive concepts	Great fit for multiplayer, metaverse or live-ops studios	Often leads large Series A/B rounds	Data-driven, expects scaling strategy; not passive
Play Ventures	Gaming VC focused on mobile, Asia and infrastructure	Accessible for mobile-first indies	Good match for middleware and service-side studios	Not focused on AAA game content	SaaS thinking dominates; expect pitch deck rigour
The Games Fund	Europe/Eastern Europe focused, game-only fund	Strong fit for EMEA indies and mid-size teams	Provides mentorship as well as capital	May co-invest in AAA platforms or tooling	Can be hands-on; clearer pathway to follow-on rounds
Andreessen Horowitz (a16z Games)	Massive fund with Web3, platform, infra focus	Unlikely unless you're building something with tech edge	Strong for platform plays, engines, tooling or community-led products	Relevant to future-of-gaming innovation layers	Media coverage and pressure follow – choose carefully
Angels (e.g. Joakim Achrén, ex-Supercell)	Niche, founder-friendly checks with fast feedback	Great for early teams who need runway + advice	May co-invest with publishers or funds	Not used by large studios	Relationship driven – less structured, but higher variance

Target Wisely: Indie teams should focus on gaming-specialist VCs or experienced angels who understand risk tolerance, team burn and production realities. Generalist funds may push for metrics (e.g. MAUs, CAC, LTV) that do not apply pre-launch.

Strategic Superpowers in the Games Industry

Entity	Known For	Influence on Indie	Influence on Independent-Funded	Influence on Multi-Studio/AAA	Risk Themes
Tencent	World's largest gaming company by revenue; stakes in Riot, Epic, Ubisoft	Indirect – may acquire platforms or publishers relied on	Strategic risk if partner is Tencent-funded	Direct – strategic redirection of studios, regional compliance	Regulatory pressure, IP control, governance conflicts
Microsoft	Xbox, Game Pass, cloud infra (Azure), multiple studio acquisitions	Game Pass exposure; ID@Xbox support for some indies	Attractive for mid-tier devs with Game Pass potential	Owns major AAA portfolios (Bethesda, Activision Blizzard)	Platform dependency, service cannibalisation, PSN-equivalent risk
Sony	PlayStation Studios, platform exclusives, prestige brand curation	Strong marketing for a few select indies via PlayStation Indies	Can offer dev kits and funding to aligned mid-size studios	Major AAA partner or platform gatekeeper	Policy reversals (e.g. PSN/ Helldivers II), certification bottlenecks
Meta	VR ecosystem (Quest), heavy XR investment, Horizon platform	Critical if developing for Quest or pitching immersive content	Grants and funding support for AR/VR indies	Less relevant unless doing metaverse or social platform integration	Volatility of focus, fragmentation risk, closed ecosystem dependencies
Amazon	Twitch, AWS infra, Luna cloud gaming, in-house studios	Twitch is essential to discoverability; AWS infra relevant to multiplayer	AWS credits and GameLift use in mid-tier ops; Luna partnerships	Owns key channels, infra and liveops tooling	Discoverability reliance, infra costs, unclear publishing roadmap
Google	Android, Play Store, YouTube, failed Stadia	Platform governance for mobile indies; YouTube for marketing	Play Store policy and UA (user acquisition) costs shape mobile strategy	Less directly involved in AAA game funding	Platform cuts, algorithm volatility, ad model opacity
Apple	iOS App Store, hardware + distribution control	Essential for mobile indies; limits creative monetisation	High UA cost and monetisation restrictions affect viability	Rarely directly involved	App store tax, IDFA/privacy restrictions, ecosystem rigidity
NetEase	Major China-based publisher; owns/partners with global studios	Increasingly investing in indie-style titles with global ambitions	Mid-tier acquisitions and global studio growth (e.g. Quantic Dream)	Co-developing AAA titles across regions	IP control, liveops expectations, state influence and licensing risk

Risk Insight: These companies do not just influence the games market but in many cases they define the rules, particularly if you want to get onto their platforms. From app store taxes to subscription splits and platform exclusivity, their decisions reshape how developers survive. Risk professionals must consider ecosystem dependency, platform volatility and governance asymmetry when planning multi-year roadmaps.

Xbox Job Cuts: A Cautionary Tale

On July 2, 2025, Microsoft announced the largest round of global layoffs in over two years – 9,000 jobs across the company (News.com.au, 2025), including significant cuts within Xbox Game Studios and subsidiary teams like King, Turn 10, ZeniMax, Rare, The Initiative and more.

- Project and Studio Chaos

Some high-profile projects were abruptly cancelled – notably *Perfect Dark* (led by The Initiative) and *Everwild* from Rare – with studios shut down or dramatically downsized in the wake (AS.com / MeriStation, 2025).

- Internal and External Backlash

Employee groups like the CWA union denounced the layoffs despite Microsoft's strong financial results, including $245B in revenue and the $70B acquisition of Activision Blizzard (PC Gamer, 2025a).

Xbox leadership framed the cuts as strategic moves to "improve agility and focus on AI-driven and cloud-first initiatives".

- Aftermath of Sudden Cuts

Reports describe layoffs affecting ~50% of Turn 10's workforce, along with job losses at King, ZeniMax's marketing teams and frontline ops (Windows Central, 2025). Xbox executive messages even suggested displaced employees "use AI for emotional clarity", triggering online controversy (80.lv, 2025).

Strategic Takeaways

1. **Even the most resource-rich parents cut at the margin**

Microsoft's Game Pass-led strategy prioritised infrastructure over traditional studio-led AAA titles, illustrating how larger corporate imperatives can override even major creative projects.

2. **Peripheral teams bear the brunt**

Subsidiary studios (e.g. The Initiative, Rare, King) can be the first to be downsized or closed when the parent reshapes its priorities.

3. **Creative leaders do not shield you from risk**

Even experienced teams and legacy IPs aren't immune when global strategy shifts; independent studios must prepare for sudden funding reroutes.

4. Reputation risk is real

Sudden announcements and insensitive internal messaging hurt morale, brand perception and future recruitment. Our risk response must include human and cultural considerations.

Risk Comparison Table

Risk Factor	Indie	Single Studio	Multi-Studio/AAA
Risk Appetite	High	Moderate	Low
Funding Stability	Unstable, often crowdfunded	Publisher-tied, milestone-based	Internal funding, strategic portfolios
Marketing Capability	Self-driven, conference-heavy	Publisher-supported	Centralised, often global campaigns
Response Agility	High (fast pivoting)	Moderate	Low (layered approvals, stakeholder alignment)
Communication Complexity	Low	Moderate	High (time zones, studio politics, layered chains)
Integration Overhead	Minimal	Moderate	High (engine/versioning/tools vary by studio)
Strategic Autonomy	Total, but with high survival pressure	Medium (within publisher expectations)	Low (top-down directives, limited pushback options)
LiveOps Readiness	Often unscalable	Varies	Strong infrastructure, but harder to react quickly
Political Risk	Low external pressure	Moderate internal conflicts	High (parent company influence, turf wars, executive shifts)
Burnout and Key Person Risk	Very High	High	Moderate (but harder to track across locations)

THE RISKS OF MULTI-STUDIO DEVELOPMENT DURING PRODUCTION PHASE

More AAA games today involve multiple studios working on different features. Multi-studio development introduces coordination risk at a different scale. Communication, delivery timings and integration pipelines all become more complex. Even if each team delivers on time, it may not mean the project is progressing smoothly.

While this approach can accelerate development, it also introduces significant risks:

- **Feature Integration Issues**: When different teams work on separate game components, merging them into a cohesive final product can be challenging.

- **Communication Breakdowns**: Time zone differences, studio cultures and remote collaboration create misalignment risks.

- **Last-Minute Studio Support**: Studios are often told to "go help" another team that is struggling, leading to production slowdowns and shifting priorities. If it takes three to six months to fully bring a new mid-level developer up to speed when they join a new studio, how long does it take to bring entire studios?

- **Dependency Risks**: If Studio A needs a feature from Studio B, but Studio B is behind schedule, the entire production pipeline can be delayed.

There are many examples of games where outsourcing partners delivered assets late or where a core gameplay system developed by one studio failed to integrate smoothly into the final product, causing costly reworks late in development.

Tip: Consider a shared "integration calendar" across studios, so dependencies are tracked and owned. I would consider this a critical artefact, pulled together at programme level.

Case Studies

Case Study: Tango Gameworks – Hi-Fi Rush

Studio Type: Single Studio (Publisher-Owned)

Primary Risks: Creative divergence, secrecy, minimal external testing

What Happened: Known for horror titles, Tango Gameworks secretly developed *Hi-Fi Rush* – a colourful rhythm-action game. The project was developed quietly, without traditional marketing buildup and launched with minimal testing.

Mitigation Strategy: The studio used internal resources, avoided pre-launch pressure by bypassing traditional hype cycles and surprise-launched the game on Xbox Game Pass. This reduced marketing risk and gave them platform support.

Lesson: Smaller studios under a larger umbrella can mitigate creative risks by managing visibility, using publisher support selectively and launching with distribution flexibility.

Case Study: BioWare – Mass Effect: Andromeda

Studio Type: Multi-Studio

Primary Risks: Coordination failure, fractured vision, engine misfit

What Happened: *Andromeda* was developed across BioWare's Montreal and Edmonton studios using EA's Frostbite engine, which was poorly suited for RPG development. The split in responsibilities, unclear ownership and incompatible workflows led to delays, performance issues and public criticism.

Mitigation Strategy (Partial): EA and BioWare responded with post-launch patches and leadership changes. However, misaligned planning and lack of shared tooling early in development meant key issues were not addressed in time.

Lesson: Multi-studio teams must invest in alignment tools, shared workflows and early technical feasibility reviews. Organisational complexity multiplies risk unless proactively addressed.

Case Study: Electronic Arts (EA) – Project Ragtag

Studio Type: Multi-Studio (Internal + Shared Resources)

Primary Risks: Distributed development, engine incompatibility, executive misalignment

What Happened: In the early 2010s, EA began developing *Project Ragtag*, a narrative-driven Star Wars game under Visceral Games. EA brought in support from Motive Studios and other internal resources, attempting to co-develop across multiple teams. The project was built on Frostbite, an engine poorly suited for third-person action games.

Challenges:

- The Frostbite engine created major development barriers, particularly for non-FPS gameplay.
- Teams across time zones experienced coordination breakdowns.
- There were conflicting creative visions between Visceral and EA leadership.

Outcome: After several years and major investment, EA cancelled the game in 2017. The failure highlighted the organisational and technical risks of multi-studio projects without a unified vision.

Lesson: Cross-studio collaboration must include shared creative alignment, engine feasibility and well-structured communication hierarchies from the start.

Case Study: NetEase – Knives Out

Studio Type: Multi-Studio (Internal Teams Across Regions)

Primary Risks: Infrastructure scale, liveops coordination, high concurrency maintenance

What Happened: NetEase developed *Knives Out* with regional teams managing ongoing operations, marketing and technical performance. Rapid user growth – especially in Japan – forced NetEase to manage high peak traffic across time zones, requiring seamless coordination across multiple teams.

Mitigation Strategy:

- NetEase adopted Amazon Web Services (AWS) infrastructure to support real-time scaling (Amazon Web Services, 2023).
- They achieved 40% cost savings using EC2 instance optimisation.

- Strong cross-functional coordination was enforced through a centralised DevOps and analytics backbone.

Outcome: The game scaled effectively, became a top-grossing title in multiple regions and demonstrated how infrastructure cohesion can neutralise the chaos of multi-team operation.

Lesson: Multi-studio coordination does not only require production alignment, but strong architectural foresight and platform readiness.

RISK MANAGEMENT IN A POLARISED INDUSTRY

What this chapter reveals is not just a difference in risk profiles, but a growing divide in how studios exist and survive.

On one end, massive parent-owned studio networks are now expected to deliver blockbusters through distributed, politically complex development chains. Production risk becomes a negotiation between cultures, workflows and corporate directives. Games are not just "made" anymore in your garage or across a couple of floors in a studio – they are assembled from parts, under pressure, across borders. Jeux sans frontieres?

On the other end, independent studios face an environment where funding is withheld until the finish line is in sight. Expectations are rising, budgets are falling and risk sits squarely on the shoulders of small, overstretched teams. I know the actual humans within many such teams and many are struggling to survive under the pressures.

For both ends of the spectrum, traditional risk management is no longer sufficient. It must adapt – strategically, structurally and culturally – to the new power dynamics shaping how games are made. I hope that you will adopt risk management in your place of creation to at least give the teams the chance they deserve to wrestle order from chaos.

REFERENCES

80.lv. (2025, July). *Xbox producer offers laid-off devs to use AI for emotional clarity*. Retrieved from: https://80.lv/articles/xbox-producer-offers-laid-off-devs-to-use-ai-for-emotional-clarity-confidence

Amazon Web Services. (2023). *NetEase Games achieves cost savings with EC2 for Knives Out.* Retrieved from: https://aws.amazon.com

AS.com / MeriStation. (2025, July 2). *Xbox cancels Perfect Dark, closes The Initiative amid mass layoffs*. Retrieved from: https://as.com/meristation/noticias/adios-a-joanna-dark-xbox-cancela-perfect-dark-en-plena-oleada-de-despidos-masiva-en-microsoft-n

Bluesky Post by Romero Games. (2025, July 1). Quoted via industry summaries. (Cited in coverage by Game Developer and GI.biz)

CloutBoost. (2023, July). *Top 10 mistakes indie game publishers make - and how to avoid them.* Retrieved from: https://www.cloutboost.com/blog/top-10-mistakes-indie-game-publishers-make-and-how-to-avoid-them

Fast Company. (2014, November). *How a massive international effort built Ubisoft's Assassin's Creed: Unity.* Retrieved from: https://www.fastcompany.com/3038416/how-a-massive-international-effort-built-ubisofts-assassins-creed-unity

Game Developer. (2025, July 2). Report: Romero Games makes layoffs after publisher cancels project funding. Retrieved from: https://www.gamedeveloper.com/business/report-romero-games-makes-layoffs-after-microsoft-cancels-project-funding

GameSpot. (2022, May). *Why Square Enix sold its Western studios.* Retrieved from: https://www.gamespot.com/articles/why-square-enix-sold-its-western-studios/1100-6503122

GameSpot. (2024, February). *Video game industry layoffs are worse than ever - How did we get here?* Retrieved from: https://www.gamespot.com/articles/video-game-industry-layoffs-are-worse-than-ever-how-did-we-get-here/1100-6521799

GamesIndustry.biz. (2025, July 2). Romero Games hit by layoffs following project cancellation. Retrieved from: https://www.gamesindustry.biz/romero-games-hit-by-layoffs-following-project-cancellation

Lanata, A. (2023, August). *Why indie game developers succeed - and some fail. Medium.* Retrieved from: https://medium.com/@alberto.lanata

News.com.au. (2025, July). *Microsoft announces 9,000 job cuts amid restructuring.* Retrieved from: https://www.news.com.au/finance/work/at-work/microsoft-announces-9k-job-cuts-across-global-workforce-in-second-round-of-redundancies/news-story/14fb68c830f0639ddb7929d27e4d0a90

PC Gamer. (2025, July 3). *CWA union derides Microsoft layoffs despite record profits.* Retrieved from: https://www.pcgamer.com/gaming-industry/cwa-union-derides-microsoft-layoffs-when-the-company-is-prospering-we-are-living-through-a-moment-of-profound-corporate-consolidation-and-disruption

Polygon. (2014, December). Assassin's creed unity patch 4 delayed. Retrieved from: https://www.polygon.com/2014/12/15/7395995/assassins-creed-unity-patch-4-delayed

Polygon. (2023, September). *Tencent increases investment in Ubisoft's key franchises.* Retrieved from: https://www.polygon.com/news/548281/ubisoft-tencent-investment-assassins-creed-far-cry-rainbow-six

Polygon. (2025a, January). *The video game industry's 2025 turning point.* Retrieved from: https://www.polygon.com/gaming/512115/2025-video-games-big-events-releases

Polygon. (2025b, January). *PC gaming has gone mainstream - Here's what that means for consoles.* Retrieved from: https://www.polygon.com/gaming/500266/pc-gaming-mainstream-console-comparison-2025

Screen Rant. (2020, November). Assassin's creed unity is actually good now. Retrieved from: https://screenrant.com/assassins-creed-unity-good-bugs-fixed-stealth-parkour

Signiant. (2023, October). *Creator of worlds: How Signiant helps power Ubisoft's global game development.* Retrieved from: https://www.signiant.com/resources/customer-stories/creator-of-worlds-how-signiant-helps-power-ubisofts-global-game-development

The Verge. (2024, March). *Heart Machine turns to Patreon.* Retrieved from: https://www.theverge.com

VentureBeat. (2020, January). *Tencent makes $148 million offer to acquire Funcom.* Retrieved from: https://venturebeat.com/business/tencent-makes-148-million-offer-to-acquire-all-shares-of-dune-developer-funcom

VG Insights. (2024). *Global indie games market report.* Retrieved from: https://vginsights.com/assets/reports/VGI_Global_Indie_Games_Market_Report_2024.pdf

Wikipedia contributors. (2024, December). *Riot Forge. Wikipedia.* Retrieved from: https://en.wikipedia.org/wiki/Riot_Forge

Wikipedia contributors. (2025a, March). *2022 - 2025 video game industry layoffs. Wikipedia.* Retrieved from: https://en.wikipedia.org/wiki/2022%E2%80%932025_video_game_industry_layoffs

Wikipedia contributors. (2025b, April). *Live service game. Wikipedia.* Retrieved from: https://en.wikipedia.org/wiki/Live_service_game

Windows Central. (2025, July). Microsoft Xbox layoffs include Turn 10, King, Rare, ZeniMax. Retrieved from: https://www.windowscentral.com/gaming/xbox/microsoft-xbox-layoffs-july-2025

Wired. (2014, November). Ubisoft offers free games to apologize for unity debacle. Retrieved from: https://www.wired.com/2014/11/assassins-apology

Wired. (2024, April). *The year the bottom fell out of the games industry.* Retrieved from: https://www.wired.com/story/2024-was-the-year-the-bottom-fell-out-of-the-games-industry

Yager. (2024, January 24). *Yager supports Funcom with Dune Awakening.* Retrieved from: https://yager.de/2024/01/24/yager-supports-funcom-with-the-co-development-of-dune-awakening

PART VI

Tools and Resources

CHAPTER 41

Evidence-Based Tools for Risk Management in Games

While many risk management practices in the games industry are passed down informally through experience, this appendix takes a different approach: it grounds its guidance in empirical, peer-reviewed research, drawing on foundational frameworks such as the *Digital Game Maturity Model (DGMM)* proposed by Aleem, Capretz and Ahmed (2016). The five tools included here are not arbitrary – they were distilled from a rigorous review of more than 20 academic papers examining real-world game development projects, postmortems, team behaviours, technical failures and production patterns.

Each tool emerged from a specific study that uncovered repeatable patterns or tested mitigation approaches. For example, the **Premortem Workshop Kit** is based on a 2023 study by Roose et al., where student game teams used premortems to uncover an average of 17.8 distinct project risks, most of which were not previously documented.

The **Anti-Pattern Risk Deck** reflects an extensive analysis by Politowski and Ullmann of over 400 game project failures, revealing that the vast majority fell into a defined set of recurring pitfalls.

The **Kill-Gate Funnel** draws from both Schmalz's interviews with AAA producers and Tschang's foundational work on creative chaos in games, highlighting how structured prototyping gates can prevent sunk-cost spirals.

Similarly, the **LiveOps Exit Tree** was built from Dubois and Chalk's multi-case study on why major live games shut down, providing a model for teams to assess reputational and strategic risks before pulling the plug.

Finally, the **Technical Debt Tracker** is based on survey and interview data from Borowa et al., which showed that while studios acknowledge debt, few systematically manage it, leading to predictable breakdowns near release.

Together, these tools represent a bridge between academic insight and studio action. They are plug-and-play templates, but each is grounded in data about what actually causes game projects to fail or succeed. For producers, leads and executives, they offer not only

DOI: 10.1201/9781003646082-47

tactics but reassurance: These are field-tested practices shown to reduce risk and improve outcomes.

PREMORTEM WORKSHOP KIT

Purpose: Surface latent project-killer risks before they derail progress.
When to Use: Early pre-production and before each major milestone.

Implementation:

- Schedule a 60-minute session with the team.
- Prompt: "Imagine the project has failed catastrophically. What went wrong?"
- Each person silently lists failure causes.
- Round-robin sharing and clustering of common issues.
- Identify the top 5 risks and convert them into mitigation tasks with owners and deadlines.

Real-World Signal: In a study of student game teams, premortems uncovered an average of 17.8 unique risks and 16.7 mitigations per session, many of which were previously unacknowledged.
Primary Citation: Roose et al. (2023) – *HFES Proceedings*
Pitfall: These sessions fail when dominated by senior voices. Use silent brainstorming and clustering to ensure inclusive input.

ANTI-PATTERN RISK CARD DECK

Purpose: Identify and act on recurring project pitfalls during retrospectives.
When to Use: Every sprint retrospective.

Implementation:

- Import the card deck into your tracking tool or print them out
- At each retro, ask: "Did we trigger any of these anti-patterns?"
- Rate each on probability and impact.
- Log a mitigation task or change for any repeated pattern.

Real-World Signal: Mapping over 400 postmortem issues showed that most failures align with a known anti-pattern, supporting proactive detection.
Primary Citations: Ullmann et al. (2022); Politowski et al. (2021)
Role Takeaway:

- *Producer*: Use this as a routine retro prompt.

- *Artist*: Flag when tool delays or unclear briefs appear.

- *Tech Lead*: Highlight technical bottlenecks or under-scoped work.

PROTOTYPE KILL-GATE FUNNEL

Purpose: Avoid high-cost development on unviable concepts.
When to Use: During prototyping and early production planning.

Implementation:

- **Gate 0**: Paper or digital prototype must pass a fun factor test (e.g. 70% positive feedback from ten external testers).

- **Gate 1**: Vertical slice must meet performance, visual and budget thresholds (e.g. under X cost/week).

- Fail at any gate → pivot or kill.

Real-World Signal: AA and AAA producers cited this process as the most effective method to avoid sunk-cost disasters.
Primary Citations: Schmalz et al. (2014); Tschang (2005)
Metric: Track how many projects pass Gate 1 with minimal rework needed downstream.

LIVEOPS EXIT TREE

Purpose: Manage the reputational and financial risk of withdrawing features or games.
When to Use: Before sunsetting any live feature or game.

Implementation: Build a decision tree with these branches:

- *Attend to Company*: Is ROI below strategic threshold?

- *Attend to Players*: Are toxicity levels high or DAU in sharp decline?

- *Attend to Core Product*: Is this mode damaging the main experience?

- Map each "yes" to: Retain, Refactor or Retire.

- Each path includes a comms script, comp offer and PR timeline.

Real-World Signal: Studios with predefined exit plans saw lower backlash during service withdrawal.

Primary Citation: Dubois and Chalk (2024) – *Convergence*

Role Takeaway

- *Exec:* Evaluate brand impact and investor optics.

- *Community Manager:* Prepare scripts and timing.

TECHNICAL DEBT TRACKER

Purpose: Reduce the risk of late-stage instability by treating code debt proactively.
When to Use: Throughout production; especially useful in maintenance and porting phases.

Implementation:

- Maintain a Technical Debt (TD) ledger with source, impact and fix effort.

- Reserve every 4th sprint as a TD Paydown Sprint.

- Track TD hours burned vs accrued on a visible dashboard.

Real-World Signal: Studios using TD sprints reported fewer late-cycle delays and smoother post-launch patches.
Primary Citation: Borowa et al. (2021) – *IEEE Software*
Pitfall: Do not treat this as optional or "nice to have". Link it to delivery risk explicitly.

CLOSING NOTE

These five tools represent evidence-backed practice across key risk areas: Project planning, sprint execution, prototyping, technical health and live service transitions. By adopting them, studios can reduce reliance on gut feeling and systematically surface, track and respond to the risks that derail projects.

For downloadable versions of these templates, visit game-production.com/riskbook/.

Each toolkit introduced in this book's main chapters complements these evidence-based practices. Together, they offer a complete, real-world-ready system for managing uncertainty in game development.

REFERENCES

Aleem, S., Capretz, L. F., & Ahmed, F. (2016). A digital game maturity model (DGMM). *Entertainment Computing, 17*, 1–13. Retrieved from: https://doi.org/10.1016/j.entcom.2016.04.001

Borowa, K., Zalewski, A., & Saczko, A. (2021). Living with technical debt - A perspective from the video game industry. *IEEE Software, 38*(6), 52–59. Retrieved from: https://doi.org/10.1109/MS.2021.3099616

Dubois, L.-E., & Chalk, A. (2024). Service withdrawal: The uncertain future of the games-as-a-service model. *Convergence: The International Journal of Research into New Media Technologies, 30*(1), 223–242.

Politowski, C., Petrillo, F., Ullmann, G., & Guéhéneuc, Y.-G. (2021). Game industry problems: An extensive analysis of the gray literature. *Information and Software Technology, 134*, 106542. Retrieved from: https://doi.org/10.1016/j.infsof.2021.106542

Roose, K. M., Lehman, B. R., & Veinott, E. S. (2023). Premortems in game development teams: Impact and potential. *Proceedings of the Human Factors and Ergonomics Society Annual Meeting, 67*(9), 600–604. Retrieved from: https://doi.org/10.1177/2169-5067/2316709

Schmalz, M., Finn, A., & Taylor, H. (2014). Risk management in video game development projects. In *Proceedings of the 47th Hawaii International Conference on System Sciences (HICSS)*, 4325–4334. Retrieved from: https://doi.org/10.1109/HICSS.2014.531

Tschang, F. T. (2005). Videogames as interactive experiential products and their manner of development. *International Journal of Innovation Management, 9*(1), 103–131. Retrieved from: https://doi.org/10.1142/S1363919605001184

Ullmann, G., Politowski, C., Petrillo, F., & Guéhéneuc, Y.-G. (2022). Video-game project-management anti-patterns: An empirical study. *Empirical Software Engineering, 27*(3), 1–31. Retrieved from: https://doi.org/10.1007/s10664-022-10114-3

CHAPTER 42

Premortem Workshop Kit – Risk Management Template

Based on Roose et al. (2023), adapted for game development projects

PURPOSE

To surface hidden risks early in a project by imagining a catastrophic failure and working backward to identify causes. This tool helps uncover threats not yet formalised in risk registers or project plans.

WHEN TO USE

- Project kick-off (pre-production)
- Start of major milestones (e.g. Alpha, Beta)
- Before large feature development or outsourcing engagement

PARTICIPANTS

- Full development team (cross-disciplinary)
- Ideally 5–12 people
- Optional: Include stakeholders (e.g. publisher rep, liveops lead)

MATERIALS REQUIRED

- Sticky notes or digital equivalent
- Premortem Worksheet (see the section below)
- Timer (for silent brainstorming phase)

DOI: 10.1201/9781003646082-48

- Whiteboard or clustering board for risk grouping

AGENDA (60 MINUTES TOTAL)

Time	Activity
0–5 min	*Setup*: Explain the premise and psychological safety norms.
5–15 min	*Silent Brainstorm*: Everyone individually lists reasons why the project failed.
15–30 min	*Round-Robin Sharing*: Read out each idea; facilitator clusters similar risks.
30–45 min	*Theming and Prioritisation*: Name clusters, vote on most severe or likely.
45–55 min	*Mitigation Planning*: For the top 3–5 risks, define actions, owners and deadlines.
55–60 min	*Wrap-Up*: Capture all outputs; assign someone to digitise or integrate into Jira.

FACILITATOR TIPS

- Frame with empathy: "You're not predicting doom, you're preventing it".

- Enforce equal voice: Use silent brainstorming and ensure junior team members contribute.

- Encourage brutal honesty – it is better to surface uncomfortable truths now.

- Prioritise impact × likelihood when shortlisting top risks.

PREMORTEM PROMPT EXAMPLES

- "The game launched to terrible reviews – why?"

- "We missed our console certification by 6 weeks – what happened?"

- "The team burned out and half resigned – what led to that?"

- "Multiplayer never worked properly – where did it go wrong?"

PREMORTEM WORKSHEET

Project: [Title]

Date: [dd/mm/yyyy]

Facilitator: [Name]

Participants: [List names or roles]

Imagined Failure: *Write a 1–2 sentence summary (e.g. "The project failed to deliver on time and was panned for poor quality".)*

Individual Risk Brainstorm

List up to ten possible reasons why this failure occurred.

1.
2.
3.
4.
5.
6.
7.
8.
9.
10.

Group Risk Clusters

Clustered risk themes and key insights from team discussion:

- Theme 1: [e.g. Unrealistic Scope]

- Theme 2: [e.g. Toolchain instability]

- Theme 3: [e.g. Poor communication across teams]

Top Risks + Mitigation Plan

Risk Theme	Mitigation Action	Owner	Deadline
[Theme]	[Action]	[Person/Role]	[dd/mm/yyyy]
[Theme]	[Action]	[Person/Role]	[dd/mm/yyyy]
[Theme]	[Action]	[Person/Role]	[dd/mm/yyyy]

FOLLOW-UP ACTIONS

- Transcribe final outputs to risk register or Jira.

- Assign follow-ups and review status in next standup or sprint planning.

- Schedule the next premortem at the next major phase change.

This template is based on peer-reviewed research and validated in game project environments. It is especially powerful in surfacing people-related, scope and vision risks that may be missed in traditional planning.

REFERENCE

Roose, K. M., Lehman, B. R., & Veinott, E. S. (2023). Premortems in game development teams: Impact and potential. *Proceedings of the Human Factors and Ergonomics Society Annual Meeting, 67*(9), 600–604.

CHAPTER 43

Anti-Pattern Risk Deck

Based on Politowski et al. (2021) and Ullmann et al. (2022), adapted for game development retrospectives.

1. PURPOSE

To identify and act on recurring risk patterns in team behaviours, workflows and planning decisions. By referencing known anti-patterns during retrospectives or project reviews, teams can spot warning signs early and make pre-emptive adjustments.

It is worth noting that this book has included dozens of additional anti-patterns not identified in the research. This is due to the lens through which this book was created. You may wish to take Key Risk Patterns from specific chapters and follow the same process below for them.

2. WHEN TO USE

- Every sprint retrospective

- Monthly delivery reviews

- End-of-milestone postmortems

- Onboarding for new producers or QA leads

3. PARTICIPANTS

- Scrum teams or pods

- QA leads and producers

- Project and discipline leads

DOI: 10.1201/9781003646082-49

4. MATERIALS REQUIRED

- Anti-pattern deck (physical or digital import into project management tool)
- Optional: Print-out checklist for group walkthrough
- Whiteboard or shared notes tool for logging mitigation actions

5. IMPLEMENTATION FLOW (15–30 MINUTES)

Time	Activity
0–5 min	Pick 5–10 cards to scan through as a group. Start with those most recently triggered.
5–15 min	Ask: "Did we trigger this anti-pattern last sprint?" For any 'yes' or 'maybe', note symptoms.
15–25 min	For repeated patterns, discuss root cause and assign mitigation tasks.
25–30 min	Log mitigations to Jira or task board. Schedule a review next retro.

6. EXAMPLE OUTPUT

Anti-Pattern	Root Cause	Mitigation	Owner
Missing Metrics	Rushed planning	Define KPIs for Alpha	Producer
Tool Overload	Team-level tool choice	Standardise art pipeline tools	Tech Lead

7. ROLE TAKEAWAYS

- **Producer**: Use deck to structure retros and track repeat issues across sprints.
- **QA Lead**: Raise technical or test bottlenecks that emerge as recurring patterns.
- **Artist/Designer**: Flag unclear briefs, misalignment with tech or rework drivers.
- **Tech Lead**: Identify process or tooling patterns that create long-term drag.

8. REAL-WORLD SIGNAL

In a review of 429 postmortems, Ullmann et al. (2022) found that the vast majority of root causes mapped to a small number of behavioural and planning anti-patterns. Using structured prompts helped teams catch and address them earlier in the lifecycle.

9. ANTI-PATTERN CARDS INDEX

Each of the 29 cards follows this format:

- Title
- Description

- Typical Triggers
- Example Symptoms
- Suggested Mitigation

1. Feature Creep

   Category: Planning

   Description: The uncontrolled addition of features beyond initial scope.

   Triggers: Lack of clear scope boundaries; stakeholder pressure; creative overreach.

   Symptoms: Delays, burnout, inconsistent game vision.

   Mitigation: Implement change control; enforce MVP criteria; visualise impact of added features.

2. Incomplete Requirements

   Category: Planning

   Description: Core features or tech needs are not fully defined.

   Triggers: Rushed pre-production; weak tech/design sync.

   Symptoms: Rework, tool rebuilds, shifting goals.

   Mitigation: Formalise discovery; use checklists in early planning.

3. Late Tooling

   Category: Technology

   Description: Toolchains built too late, slowing development.

   Triggers: Prioritising features over pipelines.

   Symptoms: Manual processes, long iteration times.

   Mitigation: Schedule tooling as a core deliverable in early sprints.

4. Missing Metrics

   Category: Planning

   Description: No clear KPIs to track progress or quality.

   Triggers: Focus on vision over measurement.

   Symptoms: No way to assess success; gut-feel decisions.

   Mitigation: Define success criteria per milestone; track KPIs early.

5. Unrealistic Timelines

Category: Planning

Description: Schedule does not reflect true complexity.

Triggers: Wishful thinking; top-down planning.

Symptoms: Crunch, missed milestones, morale collapse.

Mitigation: Use bottom-up estimates; sanity-check with similar projects.

6. Over-Polishing Early

Category: Process

Description: Excessive time spent perfecting early assets or features.

Triggers: Art-first culture; perfectionism.

Symptoms: Progress stalls; rework wasted.

Mitigation: Use blockmesh + placeholders early; focus on integration first.

7. Under-tested Code

Category: Technology

Description: Features are delivered without robust testing.

Triggers: Pressure to show progress; no dedicated QA.

Symptoms: Hidden regressions; bugs emerge late.

Mitigation: Automate tests; embed QA from day one.

8. Tool Overload

Category: Technology

Description: Too many overlapping tools without integration.

Triggers: No tech ownership; every team chooses its own stack.

Symptoms: Sync errors, duplicate work.

Mitigation: Standardise tech stack; assign integration ownership.

9. Absent Product Owner

Category: Leadership and Ownership

Description: No one available to clarify vision or make trade-offs.

Triggers: Role unfilled or overloaded.

Symptoms: Drift, confusion, blocked decisions.

Mitigation: Appoint clear decision-maker; clarify escalation paths.

10. Communication Breakdown

Category: Communication

Description: Teams or disciplines are not sharing key updates.

Triggers: Remote work; siloed roles; unclear rituals.

Symptoms: Mismatched assumptions; redundant effort.

Mitigation: Mandate standups + cross-team demos.

11. Art-Design Mismatch

Category: Design Alignment

Description: Visual style does not align with gameplay.

Triggers: Parallel pipelines without sync.

Symptoms: Rework in polish; player confusion.

Mitigation: Joint reviews; use annotated prototypes.

12. Tech-Design Mismatch

Category: Design Alignment

Description: Engine limits or system design blocks creative goals.

Triggers: Unvalidated tech assumptions; poor feasibility checks.

Symptoms: "Looks great on paper but cannot ship".

Mitigation: Require tech feasibility sign-off in greenlight process.

13. Burnout Risk

Category: Culture and People

Description: Sustained overwork reduces performance and morale.

Triggers: Unrealistic planning; poor load balancing.

Symptoms: Staff attrition; low creativity.

Mitigation: Cap sprint hours; promote "work-life visible" leadership.

14. Gold Plating

   Category: Process

   Description: Teams over-deliver far beyond what is needed.

   Triggers: Perfectionism; undefined success bar.

   Symptoms: Scope bloat; effort misallocation.

   Mitigation: Define "done"; reward delivery not polish.

15. Crunch Acceptance

   Category: Culture and People

   Description: Team culture accepts late-stage crunch as inevitable.

   Triggers: Prior history; hero culture.

   Symptoms: Fatigue; repeat crisis cycles.

   Mitigation: Plan buffers; name crunch as a failure.

16. Feedback Bottlenecks

   Category: Communication

   Description: Too few people authorised to give feedback.

   Triggers: Centralised leadership; unavailable leads.

   Symptoms: Slow reviews; blocked iterations.

   Mitigation: Delegate feedback powers; timebox responses.

17. Overlapping Roles

   Category: Leadership and Ownership

   Description: Multiple people unclear about ownership.

   Triggers: Flat hierarchy; fast scaling.

   Symptoms: Double-work; accountability gaps.

   Mitigation: Define RACI; make ownership visible.

18. Invisible Work

   Category: Process

   Description: Significant effort is not tracked or visible to leads.

Triggers: Side tasks; mentoring; internal tools.

Symptoms: Burnout; unfair performance reviews.

Mitigation: Log all effort types; include in planning.

19. Stale Backlog

Category: Process

Description: Stories are old, vague or no longer relevant.

Triggers: No grooming ritual; backlog as dumping ground.

Symptoms: Confusion during planning; wasted effort.

Mitigation: Clean backlog monthly; delete irrelevant items.

20. No Definition of Done

Category: Process

Description: Teams disagree on what completion means.

Triggers: Lack of documentation; informal process.

Symptoms: Reopened tickets; blame culture.

Mitigation: Define and display "Done" per discipline.

21. "Just a Quick Fix" Culture

Category: Technology

Description: Pressure to hotfix instead of solving root causes.

Triggers: Liveops fires; fear of delays.

Symptoms: Compounding bugs; spaghetti systems.

Mitigation: Log root causes; enforce fix-allotment policy.

22. Stakeholder Overreach

Category: Leadership and Ownership

Description: External stakeholders micromanage dev details.

Triggers: Weak gatekeeping; unclear boundaries.

Symptoms: Distracted teams; de-scoped priorities.

Mitigation: Define stakeholder roles; hold vision alignment sessions.

23. No Exit Criteria

Category: Planning

Description: Teams do not know when to pivot or kill a feature.

Triggers: Fear of sunk costs; attachment.

Symptoms: Endless iteration; resource drain.

Mitigation: Define kill-gates upfront with metrics.

24. "Launch Is the End" Mentality

Category: Planning

Description: No planning for post-launch support or failure.

Triggers: Waterfall mindset; no LiveOps lead.

Symptoms: Unpreparedness for feedback or scale issues.

Mitigation: Treat launch as midpoint; build post-launch roadmap.

25. No Shared Vision

Category: Communication

Description: Teams interpret goals differently.

Triggers: Weak kickoff; lack of alignment sessions.

Symptoms: Mismatched outputs; friction.

Mitigation: Create project vision doc; repeat it often.

26. Premature Optimisation

Category: Technology

Description: Teams over-engineer before validating design.

Triggers: Engineer-driven architecture; unclear priorities.

Symptoms: Time waste; inflexible systems.

Mitigation: Focus on working first, optimised later.

27. Feedback Ignored

Category: Communication

Description: Player or team feedback is gathered but not acted upon.

Triggers: No review system; bias or ego.

Symptoms: Trust erosion; repeated issues.

Mitigation: Log and respond visibly to feedback.

28. Unclear Priorities

Category: Planning

Description: Teams lack clarity on what matters most.

Triggers: Poor roadmap; reactive leadership.

Symptoms: Whiplash; wasted effort.

Mitigation: Revisit priorities weekly; define top 3 objectives.

29. Siloed Ownership

Category: Communication

Description: Teams work in isolation without collaboration.

Triggers: Discipline-led planning; no cross-functional rituals.

Symptoms: Integration problems; duplicated logic.

Mitigation: Use feature teams; embed cross-team reviews.

CHAPTER 44

Prototype Kill-Gate Funnel – Risk Management Template

Based on Schmalz et al. (2014) and Tschang (2005), adapted for game development pipelines.

PURPOSE

To prevent high-cost investment into games that have not yet demonstrated core viability – either in fun factor, strategic alignment, or technical feasibility. This tool provides structured decision gates that determine whether to pivot, kill, or proceed into full production.

WHEN TO USE

- End of pre-production
- After early prototyping
- Prior to greenlighting full production or major funding
- Whenever you have doubts

GATE STRUCTURE OVERVIEW

Gate	Evaluation Focus	Decision Options
Gate 0	Player experience and potential	Kill/Iterate/Proceed to Gate 1
Gate 1	Technical, cost and strategic alignment	Kill/Greenlight for production

DOI: 10.1201/9781003646082-50

GATE 0 – "IS IT FUN ENOUGH?"

Input: Playable prototype or experience slice (paper or digital)

KPIs:

- ≥ 70% of test players report "positive engagement" or enjoyment
- Core mechanics are teachable within five minutes
- Key differentiator is evident (what makes this game stand out?)

Evaluation Steps:

- Conduct structured playtests (internal or external)
- Collect feedback using a consistent template
- Score against the KPIs above

Example Outcomes:

- Positive feedback but key mechanic too confusing → Iterate
- Majority found it repetitive or boring → Kill
- Players finished prototype and wanted more → Proceed to Gate 1

GATE 1 – "CAN WE ACTUALLY BUILD THIS?"

Input: Vertical slice or early MVP build

KPIs:

- Achieves minimum frame rate and resolution targets (platform-specific)
- Weekly burn rate within budget (< £X/week)
- Team alignment on scope, platform, genre and timeline
- No red flags from tech, art, QA, or production leads

Evaluation Steps:

- Internal review across all discipline leads
- Review team capability, engine/tool readiness and asset pipelines
- Estimate schedule and cost against current resourcing

Example Outcomes:

- Tech can deliver core experience but art pipeline is underdeveloped → Pause or Iterate

- Build fails perf targets and cannot scale → Kill

- All teams sign off with confidence → Greenlight

TEMPLATE – KILL-GATE EVALUATION SHEET

Project Title: [Insert Name]

Gate: [0 or 1]

Date: [dd/mm/yyyy]

Facilitator: [Name or Role]

Summary of Build or Prototype

- Description:

- Current status:

- Platforms targeted:

KPI Scoring Table

KPI	Achieved?	Notes
[e.g. 70% player engagement]	Yes/No	[Insert feedback summary]
[Burn rate < target]	Yes/No	[Insert finance review]
[Tech readiness confirmed]	Yes/No	[Comments from Tech Lead]

Go/No-Go Recommendation

Option	Tick	Justification
Kill	☐	[Reasons]
Iterate	☐	[Key fix areas and timeline]
Proceed/Greenlight	☐	[Evidence of readiness]

FOLLOW-UP ACTIONS

- Share gate results with leadership

- Archive evaluation document and versioned build

- Update risk register and roadmap

- If iterating: schedule next gate review (include timeline + success definition)

This structured funnel supports the idea that "fail fast" is not just a lovely Agile slogan, but is a protective filter that preserves resources, morale and product quality. Designed to protect against sunk-cost bias and passion-driven overcommitment.

REFERENCES

Schmalz, M., Finn, A., & Taylor, H. (2014). Risk management in video game development projects. *Proceedings of the 47th Hawaii International Conference on System Sciences (HICSS)* pp. 4325–4334). IEEE Computer Society. https://doi.org/10.1109/HICSS.2014.531.

Tschang, F. T. (2005). Videogames as interactive experiential products and their manner of development. *International Journal of Innovation Management, 9*(1), 103–131.

CHAPTER 45

LiveOps Exit Tree – Risk Management Template

Based on Dubois & Chalk (2024), adapted for game studios managing live features or services.

PURPOSE

To support structured, reputationally safe decision-making when retiring live game features or entire services. This tool helps teams evaluate continuation versus withdrawal based on business metrics, player sentiment and product alignment.

WHEN TO USE

- Before removing any major game feature (e.g. PvP mode, currency system)
- When considering sunset of a live title
- During post-launch portfolio reassessment or downsizing

EXIT TREE DECISION NODES

Node	Question	Decision Routes
Node 1	ROI below strategic threshold?	Retire/Refactor/Retain
Node 2	Player engagement or sentiment in decline?	Retire/Refactor/Retain
Node 3	Does this feature dilute or damage core experience?	Retire/Refactor/Retain

DOI: 10.1201/9781003646082-51

Route Definitions:

- **Retire**: Plan complete removal and compensation; communicate publicly

- **Refactor**: Redesign or rebalance feature; announce changes with timeline

- **Retain**: Keep unchanged; monitor and revisit after next milestone

KPI SIGNALS BY NODE

Node 1: Company

- Monthly ROI < cost of feature upkeep

- Developer time cost exceeds value delivered

- Feature performance lags vs competitors

Node 2: Players

- Toxicity reports rising (moderation load ↑)

- DAU/MAU metrics falling sharply

- NPS scores or reviews flag specific frustrations

Node 3: Core Product

- Feature consistently breaks balance, immersion or onboarding

- Content pipeline distorted by maintaining legacy feature

- Player feedback or test data shows confusion/frustration

COMMS AND COMPENSATION PLANNING

Element	Description
Public Statement	Tone: Transparent, player-focused. Format: Blog, social media, in-game news
Transition Period	Allow players to use remaining assets/time (e.g. 30-day wind-down)
Compensation Plan	Refunds, bonus currency or loyalty bundles for active users
Internal Briefing	Support teams with FAQ, refund scripts and escalation path

LIVEOPS EXIT EVALUATION TEMPLATE

Project/Feature: [Insert Name]

Evaluators: [List roles]

Date: [dd/mm/yyyy]

Version/Build: [Optional]

Decision Path Review

Node	Answer (Y/N)	Rationale	Data Used
Node 1 – ROI < Threshold?	Y/N	[Insert reason]	[e.g. internal KPI dashboard]
Node 2 – Engagement Declining?	Y/N	[Insert reason]	[e.g. DAU trends, reviews]
Node 3 – Product Misaligned?	Y/N	[Insert reason]	[e.g. design feedback]

Recommendation Summary

Option	Tick	Justification
Retire	☐	[Reasons to sunset]
Refactor	☐	[Proposed changes + timeframe]
Retain	☐	[Why it should continue]

Communications Checklist

- Statement drafted and approved

- FAQ and support team briefing complete

- Player compensation items defined and tested

FOLLOW-UP ACTIONS

- Lock PR and CS rollout dates

- Update patch notes, store listings and community roadmap

- Schedule a retrospective after player response window closes

- Feed learning into future feature planning and roadmap reviews

By applying this framework, studios can de-risk player backlash, avoid rushed decisions and handle live feature exits with clarity and care. This reinforces long-term brand trust while protecting operational resources.

REFERENCE

Dubois, L.-E., & Chalk, A. (2024). Service withdrawal: The uncertain future of the games-as-a-service model. *Convergence: The International Journal of Research into New Media Technologies*, *30*(1), 223–242.

CHAPTER 46

Technical Debt Tracker – Risk Management Template

Based on Borowa et al. (2021), adapted for game development pipelines.

PURPOSE

To make technical debt (TD) visible, trackable and manageable as a planned part of production. This tool helps reduce surprise instability late in development by proactively identifying and addressing TD across systems.

WHEN TO USE

- Throughout production and post-launch support
- Especially during mid-to-late stage sprints, porting or DLC builds
- Following a major refactor or platform expansion

KEY CONCEPTS

- **Technical Debt (TD):** Any temporary, suboptimal technical decision made to gain short-term speed at the cost of future effort.
- **Debt Ledger:** Central record of known technical debt instances.
- **TD Sprint:** A regularly scheduled sprint focused on repaying high-risk debt.
- **Debt Burn Rate:** How many hours per sprint are spent addressing TD.

DOI: 10.1201/9781003646082-52

TD LEDGER FORMAT

Use a shared Notion board, spreadsheet or Jira dashboard.

ID	System/Area	Description of Debt	Risk Impact	Estimated Fix Time (hrs)	Owner	Status
TD-001	Save System	Legacy file format blocks cloud sync	High	8	Tech Lead	Backlog
TD-002	AI NavMesh	Manual update required for every new level	Medium	6	Gameplay Engineer	In Progress
TD-003	UI Tooling	No preview in editor – slows iteration	Low	4	UI Lead	Done

SPRINT PLANNING GUIDANCE

- **Frequency:** Reserve every fourth sprint as a "TD Paydown Sprint"
- **Budget:** Allocate ~15–25% of dev time per quarter to TD fixes
- **Criteria:** Prioritise by risk impact × cost to fix
- **Visibility:** Display TD burn rate alongside velocity metrics on team dashboards

TD EVALUATION SHEET (SPRINT-LEVEL)

Sprint: [Sprint # or Date Range]

Lead: [Engineering or Tech Owner]

Debt Items Reviewed: [Insert total number or IDs]

TD Activity Summary

Metric	Value
TD Hours Planned	[e.g. 32]
TD Hours Completed	[e.g. 28]
TD Items Fully Resolved	[e.g. 4]
TD Burn Rate	[e.g. 87.5%]

Lessons Learned

- E.g. "Underestimated effort for ShaderGraph fix – need cross-team estimate review".

- E.g. "Fixed deprecated logging system – stability improved in live QA".

FOLLOW-UP ACTIONS

- Integrate top TD items into product roadmap and backlog grooming

- Review TD burn trend quarterly

- Present highlights to production and exec leadership for visibility

Proactively managing tech debt avoids the all-too-common risk of build collapse late in development. Been there, done that, do not want to repeat. Teams that schedule TD pay-down sprints and maintain a transparent ledger report smoother delivery, better morale and faster post-launch iteration.

REFERENCE

Borowa, K., Zalewski, A., & Saczko, A. (2021). Living with technical debt – A perspective from the video game industry. *IEEE Software, 38*(6), 52–59.

CHAPTER 47

Wrapping Up the Risk Management Journey

THANK YOU FOR GETTING this far. If you have reached this point in the book, I want to acknowledge how much ground you have covered. It has been a comprehensive journey, and I hope you found the content practical, grounded and (most importantly) usable in your real world.

THE RISK COMPETENCY SET

Across the chapters, you have picked up tools, frameworks and habits that can now be adapted to your own context. You should now be able to:

- **Identify and prioritise risks** using structured categories and team inputs.

- **Build risk registers, RAID logs and heat maps** with meaningful action paths.

- **Lead risk meetings** that clarify ownership and maintain momentum.

- Spot **recurring anti-patterns** in team behaviour and workflow structure.

- **Navigate** live service pressure, regulatory change and strategic ambiguity.

- **Coordinate** risk across project, program and portfolio levels.

- **Apply crisis readiness practices** such as scenario walkthroughs and tabletop simulations.

None of this is theoretical. If it stayed theoretical, this book would have failed.

DOI: 10.1201/9781003646082-53

REAL-WORLD APPLICATION

Everything here is ready to be used. If you are handling a mobile launch, managing a feature pipeline, reworking monetisation or simply trying to survive a delivery crunch, I truly hope something in this book will help you.

Return to the case studies. Glance again at the tools. Use them as scaffolding. They are not rigid frameworks. They are here to help you notice earlier, act more clearly and keep yourself and your team a little less exposed to unnecessary risk.

What Comes Next

Game development continues to shift. Roles change. Tools change. What you are measured against may not be what you were trained to do. Risk practice must adapt with it.

If you want to keep sharpening your judgement and learning from others:

- Revisit this material.

- Try out a new tool.

- Join our Discord community to exchange notes and postmortems.https://discord.gg /69nAY46A47

- Watch the walkthroughs and examples on the YouTube channel for practical usage.

- Share what you build. I will post better versions if you send them in.

Completion Tools and Ongoing Support

All templates, risk trackers and examples are downloadable at:
https://www.game-production.com/riskbook
What's there:

- Risk register and RAID templates

- Retrospective and anti-pattern decks

- All accompanying chapter toolkits

They are free to use, adapt or quietly ignore.

A Note on Style and Substance

In the companion course, I described risk as something that's often treated as "boring" and a leftover from corporate project management. I still agree with that view, to a point, whenever risk is abstracted too far from the work. As I said in my course:

> When you make a game of any kind, you're exploring. You're out there trying to discover: can we find the fun? Is it viable? And what will it take to release it properly?

Now, risks aren't interruptions to that – they're *signals*. They're the things that tell you where not to go blindly. If you listen to them early enough, they help you steer. That's what risk management really is.

That was the point of this book: To show you how to listen earlier, respond more deliberately and reduce the noise.

Final Words

You now have what you need to shape your own approach to risk management. It does not need to be complicated. Use the templates if they help or build your own. Whether you use a spreadsheet, Jira, Miro or a whiteboard, just start. Use it, adapt it, share it.

If you've got something worth passing on – a better version of a tool, a note on what worked, a short case study – please send it over. Post it on the Discord, or just get in touch. I would rather improve this work with input from people who are actually doing the job.

And if the material has helped you, please encourage others to buy a copy and spread the word.

Thanks for reading. Let me know what you do with it.

Liam Wickham
game-production.com
https://discord.gg/69nAY46A47

Index

For Product Safety Concerns and Information please contact our EU
representative GPSR@taylorandfrancis.com
Taylor & Francis Verlag GmbH, Kaufingerstraße 24, 80331 München, Germany

www.ingramcontent.com/pod-product-compliance
Lightning Source LLC
Chambersburg PA
CBHW080656220326
41598CB00033B/5225